W9-BLM-069

## ALSO BY LAURA INGRAHAM

*Power to the People*

*Shut Up and Sing*

*The Hillary Trap*

# LAURA INGRAHAM

# THE OBAMA DIARIES

**THRESHOLD EDITIONS**

NEW YORK LONDON TORONTO SYDNEY

BOCA RATON PUBLIC LIBRARY
BOCA RATON, FLORIDA

Threshold Editions
A Division of Simon & Schuster, Inc.
1230 Avenue of the Americas
New York, NY 10020

Copyright © 2010 by Laura Ingraham

All rights reserved, including the right to reproduce this book or portions thereof in any form whatsoever. For information address Threshold Editions Subsidiary Rights Department, 1230 Avenue of the Americas, New York, NY 10020.

First Threshold Editions hardcover edition July 2010

THRESHOLD EDITIONS and colophon are trademarks of Simon & Schuster, Inc.

For information about special discounts for bulk purchases, please contact Simon & Schuster Special Sales at 1-866-506-1949 or business@simonandschuster.com.

The Simon & Schuster Speakers Bureau can bring authors to your live event. For more information or to book an event contact the Simon & Schuster Speakers Bureau at 1-866-248-3049 or visit our website at www.simonspeakers.com.

Designed by Ruth Lee Mui

Manufactured in the United States of America

10   9   8   7   6   5   4   3   2   1

Library of Congress Cataloging-in-Publication Data

Ingraham, Laura.
   The Obama diaries / by Laura Ingraham. — 1st Threshold hardcover ed.
      p. cm.
1. Obama, Barack—Humor.   I. Title.
E908.3.I54   2010
973.932020'7—dc22                                    2010019945

ISBN: 978-1-4391-9751-6
ISBN: 978-1-4391-9844-5 (ebook)

BOCA RATON PUBLIC LIBRARY
BOCA RATON, FLORIDA

*For Maria and Dmitri*

# CONTENTS

# INTRODUCTION

You might call what follows the drama behind Obama.

I didn't go looking for what you are about to read; rather in the grand designs of destiny, it found me. On May 20, 2010, I did what I do every Thursday—I treated myself to a pedicure. It was forty-five minutes of sheer uninterrupted bliss, and I left the salon at the Watergate complex feeling relaxed and carefree. The elevator to the underground parking garage was under repair, so I walked the four floors down to retrieve my car. As I pressed the remote to unlock the car door, my eye caught a thick manila envelope lying on the hood of the car. The words "Property of the American People" were scrawled in black Magic Marker on the front. As I cautiously lifted the package, a deep baritone voice called out from the nearby stairwell. "Just read it," he said. "You'll know what to do." Except for his high-top sneakers, his identity was obscured by the shadows.

"Who are you? What is this?!" I shouted back. The mystery man stood silent for a few seconds and then vanished faster than Obama's high approval ratings. Shaking, I threw the envelope in my car, unsure of what I should do next, or where I should go. Being alone did not seem like a good idea, nor did going straight home. So I drove over to the W hotel, maybe a hundred yards from the White House, where the rooftop bar was humming. I ordered a drink, found a little nook, plopped down, and ripped open the envelope. What I found inside took my breath away—literally. For almost two hours, I sat there—oblivious to the loud dance beat booming over the speakers—leafing through the papers, totally transfixed.

In my possession were copies of excerpts from what appeared to be many of President Barack Obama's handwritten "diaries," as well as those of Michelle Obama; her mother, Marian Robinson; Vice President Joe Biden; Rahm Emanuel; David Axelrod, and others. Here was a firsthand account of the Obama presidency, as it happened, in the words of those who shaped it.

One "diary" was more fascinating and more revealing than the next. The intrigue, the emotion, the struggles, the sheer arrogance of these people jumped off the pages. When I finished reading the last entry in the packet, I found myself aching for more. Each installment told us something new and revealing about the personalities in the Obama White House.

As I began to think about what to do with this treasure trove of information, I looked through the bar's floor-to-ceiling windows at the Washington Monument framed in an ethereal orange trim. Just then, I heard Marine One, the president's helicopter, as it rose off the South Lawn of the White House. Inside might have been Barack Obama jaunting off somewhere for the weekend—was he aware that some of his "diaries" had been copied? Was the FBI already on the case? My heart began pounding at the thought of what lay ahead, as I knew these writings would send shock waves through Washington, the country, and the world.

It was then that I decided not to keep the "diaries" for my own personal amusement, but to release them to the public, to share them with others for the good of the country and the world.

I tried to call Bob Woodward, but he wouldn't take my call. Then I attempted to send an e-mail to Matt Drudge, but my air card couldn't find a signal. *Maybe these are signs that I should release the "diaries" myself*, I thought.

Of course, the problem with diaries is that you can never be sure if the author, particularly a public figure, is telling the whole truth or shading it for posterity. Rather than commenting on the "diaries" or vouching for their veracity, I have elected simply to place them in historical context. The "diary" entries are arranged by topic and framed by relevant facts and quotes from the parties involved. I am very free with my opinions about

the public record of Team Obama, but thought it best to withhold judgment on the explosive material in the "diaries" and let the authors speak
for themselves. Discerning fact from fiction in these "journals" will be up to
you. Ultimately, I feel this approach will permit readers to come to their own
conclusions about Obama, his intimates, and their designs.

While working on this book and reading these "diaries," I must admit
that I had previously overlooked something about the Obamas—they are
flippin' hilarious!

It is hard to think of a more self-important president than Barack
Obama, and harder to imagine a press corps more willing to prop up his
outsize ego. They have created a mythic image of Obama as redeemer—a
secular savior virtually beyond reproach. The Obama mythos has been
shaped by the repetition of the various superlatives used to describe him:
brilliant . . . a phenomenal listener . . . calm under pressure . . . a master
communicator . . . empathetic . . . a uniter, not a divider . . . works tirelessly
for the American people. They have exalted him above all others.

This deification of the president is one of the biggest con jobs in American political history.

Beneath that elevated chin and that purposely furrowed brow is a man
who I believe is truly worthy—worthy of satire, that is. Such arrogance and
pomposity screams out for ridicule.

The satiric diaries bring the Obama reality show into clear and frighten-
ing focus: the titanic egos . . . the devious plans . . . the stunning incompe-
tence.

As we suffer under the rule of Obama, it's easy to get depressed and
discouraged. But before you reach for the Paxil, I want to suggest another
path. Take the time to see this president and his administration for what
they are: buffoons. Whatever your political bent, put your feet up, and allow
our president to fulfill his campaign promise to bring us together: together
in hysterical laughter!

I wrote this book because I believe we are at the crossroads of history.
In my other books, I warned about the liberal elites who are amassing more
and more power over the American people. With the rise of the Obama
administration, I fear that we have reached what may be a tipping point, and

that we risk a future in which average Americans have less power over their lives than their parents had. Since Obama was sworn into office, Americans have been mobilizing to fight his agenda. With so much at stake, it is important to see all the issues in context, so we can truly appreciate the unprecedented power grab that is taking place.

If you really want to roll back the Obama agenda, you must understand who Obama truly is and the motives behind his ruinous policies. Oh, and by all means, feel free to have a laugh at his expense. After all, you've paid for it.

# DRAMATIS PERSONAE

**BARACK HUSSEIN OBAMA**      President of the United States, Community-Organizer-in-Chief, aka "Smokey," Ego Maximus

**MICHELLE ROBINSON OBAMA**      First Lady of the United States, Fashion Plate, Gardener-in-Chief, Food Czarina, aka "Miche," Ego Magnus

**MARIAN ROBINSON**      First Grandmother of the United States, mother of Michelle Obama, aka "Mother Robinson," Chief White House babysitter

**JOE BIDEN**      Vice President of the United States, Master of the Malaprop, Amtrak Guest Rewards Select Plus Member

**DESIREE GLAPION ROGERS**      White House Social Secretary (February 2009–March 2010), Razzle-Dazzler-in-Chief, Fashionista Extraordinaire, Professional White House dinner guest, former Obama pal

VALERIE JARRETT — Senior Advisor and Assistant to the President, arguably the most influential person in the White House, current Obama pal

REGGIE LOVE — Special Assistant and Personal Aide to the President, Obama's "Body Man," sports and traveling companion

DAVID AXELROD — Senior Advisor to the President, Obama's in-house political strategist, honorary member of D.C.-area Weight Watchers, aka "Axe"

RAHM EMANUEL — White House Chief of Staff, former ballet dancer, Master of the Expletive, House Gym shower habitué

HILLARY RODHAM CLINTON — United States Secretary of State, former First Lady, former Senator, Would-Be President

NANCY PELOSI — Speaker of the United States House of Representatives, California Democratic Congresswoman, self-described "ardent practicing Catholic," Botox cover girl

HARRY REID — Senate Majority Leader, Nevada Democratic Senator, racial healer, often mistaken for elderly mountain woman

TIMOTHY GEITHNER — United States Secretary of the Treasury, TurboTaxEvader

LARRY SUMMERS

Director of the White House National
Economic Council, former Secretary of
Treasury and Chief Economist of the World
Bank

PETER ORSZAG

Director of Office of Management and
Budget, aka "Nerdy-Sexy," part-time
spokesman for Hair Club for Men, full-time
Munchkin voice double

JON FAVREAU

Director of Speechwriting for the White
House, former speechwriter for John Kerry,
dating Quincy Jones' daughter

ROBERT GIBBS

White House Press Secretary, inveterate
babbler, aka "Giblet," "Gibbopotamus,"
"Gibbotron"

DAVID PLOUFFE

Political consultant and presidential
strategist on House and Senate Races,
former campaign manager for Obama's
2008 presidential run

# THE
# OBAMA
# DIARIES

The Diary of President Barack Hussein Obama

# CHAPTER 1

# *WHAT IS AMERICA TO ME?*

There is an inspiring World War II song, "The House I Live In," that asks:

> *What is America to me?*
> *A name, a map, or a flag I see;*
> *A certain word, democracy.*
> *What is America to me?*

It's a question we don't consider often enough, if at all. But today, a kind of soul searching is needed. Our understanding of America will profoundly shape our actions—and those actions will leave their mark on America and the rest of the world. How we see our country and our role as citizens will either lead us to protect, defend, and nurture her—or sit idly by as our precious heritage slips away.

At this moment in our history, when we face so many challenges at home and abroad, we need to consider anew this crucial question.

What is America to me?

Who are we as Americans? Who do we want to be? What traditions and principles do we need to preserve as we move forward? What of our

American experience is worth fighting for? (And just because you might not wear a military uniform, don't think you are exempt from answering that last question.) These are queries that should be pondered by all Americans and all those who wish to be.

To me, America will always be a land of unbridled opportunity, unrivaled beauty, and unlimited possibility. It is a place where each of us has a shot to reach our potential. Rooted in truth, decency, and timeless values, America is ever forward looking; constantly innovating while inspiring the rest of the world. Echoing John Winthrop (and the Bible), Ronald Reagan captured it best when he described America as "the shining city on a hill." In his farewell address, he unpacked this vision and explained what we are, and must be, in this new millennium:

> In my mind, it was a tall, proud city built on rocks stronger than oceans, wind-swept, God-blessed, and teeming with people of all kinds living in harmony and peace; a city with free ports that hummed with commerce and creativity, and if there had to be city walls, the walls had doors and the doors were open to anyone with the will and the heart to get here. That's how I saw it, and see it still . . . after two hundred years, two centuries, she still stands strong and true on the granite ridge, and her glow has held steady no matter what storm. And she's still a beacon, still a magnet for all who must have freedom, for all the pilgrims from all the lost places who are hurtling through the darkness, toward home.

Just reading the words puts a lump in my throat. Which isn't an isolated occurrence. I also happen to get choked up at ball games. Not by the game itself, but by the National Anthem. Every time I hear it sung or see a stadium full of people with their hands over their hearts, I feel a little tingle. Whenever I spot a veteran standing at attention before a passing flag in a Memorial Day parade, tears inevitably well up in my eyes. It's not sentimentality, but an emotional reaction to this truth: many have sacrificed for what those stars and stripes represent, and the sacrifice continues. How can one help but be moved and humbled by the long trail of blood and sweat that established our "city on a hill" and defended her promise around the world?

Our challenge now, as engaged citizens, is to translate our emotions into clear principles, practices, and habits that rise above the political or cultural winds of the moment. What can we do, personally, to expand the greatness of our country? What steps can we take to extend the sacrifice of those who paid the ultimate price for our freedom to make choices?

I believe that our work needs to begin deep within ourselves. We the people must refine ourselves, as individuals, before we can refine our community and our nation. No one else will do it for us. Not the government, not the media, and certainly not the "international community." We are the ones who will either stand up and defend what we know to be true, or permit others to twist and destroy the last, best hope of mankind. What is at stake is our way of life, our ideals, and our very future.

> *The house I live in,*
> *A plot of earth, a street,*
> *The grocer and the butcher,*
> *Or the people that I meet;*
> *The children in the playground,*
> *The faces that I see,*
> *All races and religions,*
> *That's America to me.*

Like the first settlers in this land, people continue to come to our shores seeking freedom. They embrace and celebrate our ideals in ways that shame native-born Americans. The English writer G. K. Chesterton, in his work *What I Saw in America,* put in this way: "[T]he great American experiment . . . a democracy of diverse races . . . has been compared to a melting-pot. But even that metaphor implies that the pot itself is of a certain shape and a certain substance; a pretty solid substance. The melting-pot must not melt. The original shape was traced on the lines of Jeffersonian democracy; and it will remain in that shape until it becomes shapeless. America invites all men to become citizens; but it implies the dogma that there is such a thing as citizenship."

What gives our country her "shape" is our shared, common belief in what America is. Chesterton observed that we are the only nation founded on a creed. That creed is found in the Declaration of Independence, where Jefferson wrote: "We hold these truths to be self-evident, that all men are created equal" and "that they are endowed by their Creator with certain unalienable Rights, that among these are Life, Liberty and the pursuit of Happiness." Embracing and advancing this vision is at the heart of what it means to be an American. We are not observers in this country, but participants. Citizenship requires that we struggle to protect these ideals of Life, Liberty, and the Pursuit of Happiness. We must all do our part. But the troubling question we face is: Do we all really believe in the American creed?

---

## THE DIARY OF PRESIDENT BARACK OBAMA

### INAUGURATION NIGHT

January 20, 2009

. . . Hell, yes, it's the first time we're proud to be Americans! I can't believe these people actually voted for me! What a place this country is! A measly stint in the Illinois legislature and a breath or two in the Senate, add a few groovy iconic posters and some "Hope & Change" and . . . bingo! I am the f---ing president! They actually bought it when I said I wanted to "form a more perfect union." I think Aretha was crying beneath that Easter basket hat of hers when I said that line . . . hey, I <u>am</u> the perfect union! Good looks, big brains, and a damn fine jump shot at my age.

You should have seen the way Beyoncé looked at me at that ball tonight. Damn! I played it cool though. I didn't even look back at her. I grabbed Michelle's hand, did a few twirls with her in that toilet paper dress, and made my way offstage like a cool cat. They were yelling for me to come back, but I just gave them a wave over the shoulder. I like to leave 'em fired up and ready to go.

Pastor Jeremiah was right; to hell with "America the Beautiful." It's the era of Barack the Beautiful. Long may I reign.

---

Unfortunately for Americans, the leader of the United States and his intimates have a deeply distorted view of America. Throw in unhealthy doses of class warfare, envy, and narcissism, and the long-cherished vision of America becomes almost unrecognizable—like Nancy Pelosi after a long Botox session.

Leaders from George Washington to Teddy Roosevelt to Ronald Reagan celebrated this country apart from themselves; praising her virtues, her ideals. President Obama takes a different tack. To understand where he is coming from and where he means to take us, it helps to look back.

In March 2008, while on the campaign trail, then-senator Obama offered this touching salute to America: ". . . for as long as I live, I will never forget that in no other country on earth is *my story* even possible."

No matter the topic, no matter the occasion, whenever Barack Obama is talking, rest assured that the oration will somehow relate back to *him*! His personal narrative is always in evidence. Like Rome, all roads lead to Barry. Even America and her long, noble history must bend to accommodate the "story" of Barack Obama. But at least he is consistent. He always sings in the same key: Me, Me, Me, Me, Me . . .

Michelle and Barack Obama have a truly lamentable track record when it comes to celebrating America as the greatest country on the face of the earth. Probably because they don't believe it's true. Now, for those who think I am being petty—with apologies to the president—let me be clear: I've been around politics long enough to know, if you want to understand what a person really thinks and feels, don't listen to the scripted speech. Listen when they speak off the cuff. Listen for what they don't say. The truth is far more likely to come tumbling out when the teleprompter is off. And it has tumbled out.

On February 18, 2008, at a campaign rally in Madison, Wisconsin, Michelle Obama uttered the now-infamous proclamation about America: "For the first time in my adult lifetime, I am really proud of my country—and not just because Barack has done well, but because I think people are hungry for change. And I have been desperate to see our country moving in that direction and not just feeling so alone in my frustration and disappointment."

"For the first time in my adult lifetime, I am really proud of my country . . ."

Can you imagine reaching the age of forty-four and never having been proud of your country? Michelle Obama couldn't find one American virtue or laudable quality that stirred pride in her heart in all those years? Worse, she added that she was frustrated and disappointed in the country. Like her husband, the First Lady saw no objective goodness in America until they arrived on the scene.

During the 2008 campaign, Lauren Collins profiled Michelle Obama for the *New Yorker*. She wrote: "[Michelle] Obama begins with a broad assessment of life in America in 2008, and life is not good: we're a divided country, we're a country that is 'just downright mean,' we are 'guided by fear,' we're a nation of cynics, sloths, and complacents."

I have often tried to figure out why it is that liberals—especially Ivy League–educated liberals—have such a hard time loving America unconditionally. Whether it is a multimillionaire actor like Sean Penn or a business tycoon émigré like George Soros, our country's most privileged liberal elites seem genetically predisposed to think the worst about the country that helped them achieve their wealth and celebrity. Why is this? What other country on the planet is better, freer, more beautiful than ours? (Both would probably scoff at the previous sentence for its "mindless flag-waving sentimentality.")

Surely, as individuals, we can be critical of our political leadership—Lord knows I am—yet at the same time love our country and be grateful for the sacrifices of our forefathers. While I can certainly understand one having a dim view of certain political figures or events, I cannot understand the overall negative, cynical view shared by so many Obama boosters. You know the mind-set—the type who reflexively feel the need to remind the world that America has screwed up royally.

For them, America is better now only because it has embraced the Obamas. But by any measure, America is a great country. She was magnificent and set apart before the Obamas came along and will continue to be "the shining city on the hill" long after they are gone.

---

## The Diary of First Lady Michelle Obama

### The White House

*January 21, 2009*

*I've got to tell you, making history is exhausting. After the parade and the balls and the Jonas Brothers' drop-by, I am now stuck in this drafty, white mausoleum of a house, arranging bedrooms! I'd like to see Barack get five people situated in a new house overnight.*

This morning, I'm sitting with Mama at the breakfast table in my robe, just worn out, and Barack walks in all spiffed up, giving me that "The First Lady have big plans today?" jazz. I threw my newspaper down, looked him straight in the eye, and said, "Listen, buddy, you go arrange the girls' bedrooms and I'll go meet with the national security team, okay? Believe me, that's easier. And I probably know more about national security than you!"

He didn't say a word. When he tried to quietly slink away, Mama gave him the evil eye and said, real loud, "This First Lady's got bigger plans than you'll _ever_ have, string bean!" Even the servants were laughing.

I begged those Bushes to let us stay at Blair House, the White House guest residence, after the election and bring our things in slowly. But noooo! They had "dignitaries to accommodate." So we were cooped up like refugees over at the Hay-Adams. (Do you know they didn't even have conditioner in the bathroom?) The Bushes should have gotten the hell out of this house in November after the election and let us move in. We're historic! Mrs. Literacy and Mr. Illiterate should have gone to a hotel. Didn't they already have their eight years?

After I unpack Sasha's room, I've got to get dressed and go to some damn military thing. Just what I need today. All that flag-waving, hillbilly music, hand-on-the-heart crap. To think that for the next four years I have to ooh and aah over the "sacrifice" of people who never graduated college . . . You want to know what sacrifice is? Giving up a cushy, six-figure, hospital board salary to play second fiddle to a man who still leaves his dirty socks in the middle of the bedroom floor.

But Desiree says, as First Lady, I've got to distance myself from the "first time I'm proud of my country" comments. So here I go: hugging and saluting and singing "Yankee Doodle Dandy"—again! Desiree picked out a blue sheath dress with a stars-and-stripes bow on the front. And I've got to say, my arms look fine in it. If I play my cards right, I might get an <u>American Legion</u> magazine cover out of this thing.

---

*The place I work in,*
*The worker by my side,*
*The little town or city*
*Where my people lived and died.*
*The howdy and the handshake,*
*The air and feeling free,*
*And the right to speak my mind out,*
*That's America to me.*

How we speak of our country, how we treat the symbols of our freedom, the gratitude we show to our military and veterans—all of this defines who we are as Americans. Words and gestures, even the things we wear, express in a concrete way what's in our hearts. A big part of patriotism is showing everyone we meet that we believe in the American creed—that we are proud of this country and her history, regardless of her shortcomings. President Obama has disparaged such displays. As a senator and presidential candidate, he made a point of removing his flag lapel pin in 2007.

"The truth is that right after 9/11, I had a pin. Shortly after 9/11, particularly because as we're talking about the Iraq War, that became a substitute for, I think, true patriotism, which is speaking out on issues that are of importance to our national security," Obama said in Cedar Rapids, Iowa, that year. "I decided I won't wear that pin on my chest. Instead I'm going to try to tell the American people what I believe, what will make this country great, and hopefully, that will be a testimony to my patriotism."

So Obama is going to tell the American people "what will make this country great." You'd swear he was a coach positioning himself to save a losing team—as if the country isn't great now, but after it adopts *his* agenda, it will be spectacular. No wonder he would later attempt to, in his words, "fundamentally transform the United States of America."

Obama is simply wrong. Our patriotism, our devotion to country, should never be swayed by the passing policies of the government. I agree with Mark Twain, who wrote, "Patriotism is supporting your country all the time, and your government when it deserves it." I would argue that the lapel pin and displays like it are an outgrowth of our patriotism, tangible signs of faith in America.

Obama's lapel-pin comments drew a firestorm of criticism, prompting him to further dismiss the importance of such displays in (ironically) Independence, Iowa: "After a while, you start noticing people wearing a lapel pin, but not acting very patriotic. Not voting to provide veterans with resources that they need. Not voting to make sure that disability payments are coming out on time. My attitude is that I'm less concerned about what you're wearing on your lapel than what's in your heart."

Who knew that among Obama's many gifts was the reading of hearts? To defuse the controversy, Obama began wearing the flag pin throughout the campaign and continues wearing it today. What, then, does the pin on his lapel actually mean, given his admitted feelings?

Barack Obama's flawed thinking about America and how to present her to the world has now bled into his presidency, with disastrous results.

## WHY WE'RE GREAT

Born of our revolutionary spirit and belief in the Almighty, America has long seen itself as exceptional—a people and a land set apart. Alexis de Tocqueville was the first to call America "exceptional." But the principle has been enlarged and confirmed by our astounding growth and leadership in the world for more than two centuries.

The *Encyclopedia of American Foreign Policy* describes American exceptionalism as "a term used to describe the belief that the United States is an extraordinary nation with a special role to play in human history; a nation that is not only unique but also superior." Our national pride and confidence come from this notion of American exceptionalism. It gives America the strength to seek out those things that are in her best interests and in the best interests of those in other lands.

If you have traveled outside the country for any length of time, you know there is nothing like coming home to the United States. That doesn't mean there aren't problems (like going through customs), but when one returns from a trip abroad, the marks of our exceptionalism are more apparent than ever by contrast. In the power of our industry. In the self-reliant, independent spirit of our people. The generosity of Americans. Their concern for their fellow man and the common good. These are the qualities that define us. (Just look at the outpouring of support for the people of Haiti during their recent tragedies—in the midst of a recession, I might add.) The proof of America's exceptionalism is in evidence for anyone with eyes to see it.

> *The things I see about me,*
> *The big things and the small,*
> *The little corner newsstand,*
> *And the house a mile tall;*
> *The wedding and the churchyard,*
> *The laughter and the tears,*
> *And the dream that's been a growing*
> *For more than two hundred years.*

It is obvious from our founding documents that the Framers considered America exceptional as well. They saw us as a people led by Providence, rooted in the ideals of equality under the law and freedom for all. Somewhere along the way, President Obama must have missed that lesson in history class. When asked about American exceptionalism at the NATO conference in April 2009, the leader of the free world said:

> I believe in American exceptionalism, just as I suspect that the Brits believe in British exceptionalism and the Greeks believe in Greek exceptionalism. . . . Now, the fact that I am very proud of my country and I think that we've got a whole lot to offer the world does not lessen my interest in recognizing the value and wonderful qualities of other countries, or recognizing that we're not always going to be right, or that other people may have good ideas, or that in order for us to work collectively, all parties have to compromise and that includes us.

Inspiring, isn't it?

Just one day before, at the G-20 summit on April 2, 2009, in London, the president offered this nugget: "I do not buy into the notion that America can't lead in the world, but it is very important for us to be able to forge partnerships as opposed to dictating solutions."

Notice the language: in Obama's worldview, before he came on the scene America was a dictator, a bully—"downright mean." This perspective serves only to dilute the moral authority and influence of the United States and embolden the world's true dictators. Obama thinks he's being the sophisticated anti-Bush by offering foreign nations greater opportunities for "dialogue and understanding." But, of course, the result is the diminishment of America's leverage and strength in the world. No wonder they all think they can roll us now.

Throughout the NATO and the G-20 summits of 2009, Europe set the ground rules and led the way. Which was hardly a surprise. It was exactly what the president desired. When he first arrived at the G-20, he told British prime minister Gordon Brown that he had come "to listen, not to lecture." At a press conference with German chancellor Angela Merkel at the start of the NATO summit, Obama announced: "I don't come bearing grand designs . . . *I'm here to listen, to share ideas, and to jointly, as one of many NATO allies, help shape our vision for the future.*"

This practical repudiation of American exceptionalism was the capper of what might be called the Obama Contrition Tour. If the president's feet are on foreign soil, chances are that at some point during the trip, he will apologize for America. When he speaks of the United States, he speaks as if he is somehow above America. He is the detached Messiah analyzing but unmarred by this deeply flawed country. He is in America, but not quite of it. Victor Davis Hanson has dubbed Obama the first postnational global citizen. Which sounds about right when you hear him speak overseas.

At a town hall meeting in Strasbourg, France, on April 3, 2009, he remarked: "In dealing with terrorism, we can't lose sight of our values and who we are. That's why I closed Guantanamo. That's why I made very clear that we will not engage in certain interrogation practices. I don't believe that there is a contradiction between our security and our values. And when you start sacrificing your values, when you lose yourself, then over the long term that will make you less secure."

Mea culpa, mea culpa, mea maxima culpa . . .

In Trinidad and Tobago, on April 17, 2009: "I know that promises of partnership have gone unfulfilled in the past, and that trust has to be earned over time. While the United States has done much to promote peace and prosperity in the hemisphere, *we have at times been disengaged, and at times we sought to dictate our terms.*"

Given his confessional posture in foreign lands, the president and Michelle might ask their dressers to select some new fashion accessories next time they travel abroad: sackcloth and ashes.

His recitation of America's purported sins creates an equivalency between the United States and nations that do not begin to approach our economic, military, or cultural strength. This idle chatter to win the affections of the aggrieved in the end diminishes America. As described by the president, the United States seems like just another defective member of the League of Nations.

In an interview with Fox News in December 2009, former vice president Dick Cheney could barely disguise his disgust with Obama's international confessions as well as the president's habit of bowing to foreign princes:

> I think most of us believe, and most presidents believe, and talk about the truly exceptional nature of America: Our history, where we come from, our belief in our constitutional values and principles, our advocacy for freedom and democracy. . . . There's never been a nation like the United States of America in world history.
>
> And yet when you have a president who goes around and bows to his host and then proceeds to apologize profusely for the United States, I find that deeply disturbing. That says to me, this is a guy who doesn't fully understand or share that view of American exceptionalism that I think most of us believe in.

President Obama's words and example have led Americans down a path of self-loathing and have taught the world to disrespect our nation and our history. When then–Prime Minister Gordon Brown, following a series of meetings with the president of the United States, announces, "The old Washington consensus is over; I think a new world order is emerging with the foundation of a new progressive era of international cooperation," it's time to start worrying. The tragedy is, America was not overwhelmed by other nations but was in fact cut down by her own leader and served up on a platter.

## The Diary of President Barack Obama

### The Oval Office

April 21, 2009

8:30 a.m. Just finished reading <u>Open Veins of Latin America: Five Centuries of the Pillage of a Continent,</u> the book that Hugo Chavez handed me at the Americas Summit last week. President Chavez inscribed it: "For Obama with affection." Where's the president of the United States part? Or "the most honorable"? And all he's got for me is affection? Couldn't he have spared a "with love" or "in adoration" or "in humble homage to . . ."? Affection. That's cold.

But I've got to say, his manners and diversity of shirt color aside, the man can select a good read. It is criminal how the United States and all of Western Europe raped and plundered Latin America. (I just told Jon [Favreau] to work some of this material into my next apology when I'm down in South America.) Reading the way the U.S. abused the continent, it's easy to understand why Hugo and Fidel go off at times. And Hugo particularly gets a bad rap. He has instituted some sweeping reforms in Venezuela that make a lot of sense. His initiatives to nationalize energy and take control of his country's broadcast entities are sound policies. If only I could get Roger Ailes to embrace this approach.

Hell, if Bill O'Reilly worked for the FCC I'd go on the <u>Factor</u>

every night. Maybe even broadcast an <u>Obama Factor</u> from the Oval Office—no guests, just me telling the American people what's wrong with this country and laying out my solutions.

That's another thing Hugo does right. He's got his own TV show, and since he controls the stations, he talks as long as he likes. When you're president, there's nothing more important than connecting with your followers. No one should obstruct that communication. What we really need is an Obama Network. I'll show them what the most trusted name in news looks like. Move over, Anderson Cooper. I'm going to get Gibbs working on that right away.

---

Part of this president's reluctance to celebrate America can likely be traced to his background. Barack Obama was the son of an African father he barely knew. Raised by a free-spirited mother who carted him off to Indonesia for a number of years, Barry Obama never really fit in. He was a biracial American in the Far East who attended a Catholic school while being raised as a Muslim. The circumstances no doubt confused the boy about the world and his place in it. At ten, he returned to Hawaii, where he lived with his grandparents. This journey would disorient anyone—never mind a child whose friends claim he had abandonment issues and struggled with racial intolerance. If you want to know what the man thinks of his country, find out what the child was taught. This doesn't only apply to President Obama, but to all of us.

## RESHAPING AMERICA IN THE CLASSROOM AND THE CULTURE

Our perceptions of America are not only shaped by our family but also by what we learn in the classroom and in our culture. Increasingly, the views of young Americans are being shaped by teachers and textbooks packing an agenda.

*The words of old Abe Lincoln,*
*Of Jefferson and Paine,*
*Of Washington and Jackson*
*And the tasks that still remain;*
*The little bridge at Concord,*
*Where Freedom's fight began,*
*Our Gettysburg and Midway*
*And the story of Bataan.*

If you asked most Americans to cite the importance of any of the battles recalled in that lyric, you would likely get blank stares. A good deal of the blame rests on the American history textbooks forced upon the young. There was a time when graduates were familiar with figures like John Adams, Alexander Hamilton, Frederick Douglass, and Eli Whitney. But imparting the stories of great American lives and celebrating the spirit of this land was not enough for some academics. In time, a revisionist taint seeped into textbooks. And politically correct agendas came to the fore.

Textbooks began to feature the full litany of American sins. Suddenly slavery and the harsh treatment of Native Americans became the centerpiece of U.S. history. The glories of our country's past—the daring battles, the idealists who fought for their dreams—were soon edged out entirely. Dr. Diane Ravitch described the twisted history created within American public schools as "an adversary culture that emphasized the nation's warts and diminished its genuine accomplishments." This is a long-term tragedy—because not only does it perpetuate historical stupidity; it also undermines America herself.

These highly prejudiced textbooks lay waste to our common stories and make America out to be the bad guy. As I mentioned earlier, Americans are not held together by race or blood, but by a shared belief in the founding principles of the republic. By focusing on the grievances of isolated racial or social groups, these books don't draw us together as Americans, but drive us apart.

Frances Fitzgerald, in her book *America Revised*, writes: "The message of the texts would be that Americans have no common history, no common culture, and no common values, and that membership in a racial or cultural group constitutes the most fundamental experience of each individual." They also teach young people that it's perfectly acceptable to loathe America while taking advantage of all the benefits of living here.

Subversive pop historians are only too happy to add to the confusion. James Loewen, author of the bestselling *Lies My Teacher Told Me: Everything Your American History Textbook Got Wrong*, has managed to convince millions of Americans that what they know about their country is probably wrong. He has made a career of spotlighting how European settlers imported nothing but disease to the New World, and how Americans in the South got their kicks holding community lynchings on weekends. In 2009, he launched a new curriculum for K–12 teachers called *Teaching What Really Happened: How to Avoid the Tyranny of Textbooks and Get Students Excited About Doing History*. It could have been called: *Teaching What I Think Happened: How to Ditch History and Get Students to Hate Their Country*. It should be noted that Loewen does, however, feature American exceptionalism in his curriculum. He encourages educators to ask their students to identify "two ways the U.S. is exceptional—one positive, one negative." He then goes on to offer his own examples:

> The U.S. wound up with the smallest proportion of Native people in the Americas (except possibly Uruguay).
> The U.S. is the only nation to have fought a Civil War over slavery.
> The U.S. remains the only nation ever to have used nuclear weapons on another nation.

These facts, Loewen says, will help students grasp that "exceptional need not always be good." More deep thoughts from academe.

One of Loewen's biggest promoters was himself a master of distorting America's past: Howard Zinn. The Marxist author of *A People's History of the United States,* Zinn sought to recast America in deep shades of red. His book became an instant sensation and a must-read for America-haters everywhere.

This is how Zinn describes the founding of the United States of America in his book: "Around 1776, certain important people in the English colonies made a discovery that would prove enormously useful for the next two hundred years. They found that by creating a nation, a symbol, a legal unity called the United States, they could take over land, profits, and political power from the favorites of the British Empire."

In Zinn's eyes, all of U.S. history can be reduced to greedy capitalists grabbing money and power from native peoples or the poor. For those seeking America's finest moments, don't bother. The D-day invasion is totally ignored, as is George Washington's farewell address. Though there is a delightful recounting of the My Lai massacre for all you sadists out there.

Shortly before his death in early 2010, Zinn announced a new initiative to corrupt young Americans. He too now had a K–12 curriculum to teach kiddies the number of presidents who owned slaves and the many ways capitalism fuels oppression.

Predictably, it is the millionaire Hollywood set that has embraced Zinn's catechism of hatred. Matt Damon, Bruce Springsteen, Josh Brolin, Benjamin Bratt, and others (capitalists all) lent their voices to a History Channel documentary based on Zinn's ramblings called *The People Speak.* It was narrated by Zinn himself and used the power of celebrity to bring his admittedly "biased account" of American history to the masses. I don't know about you, but Jasmine Guy reading a commencement address by Marian Wright Edelman is not exactly my idea of bringing American history to life!

And don't think that the Hollywood elites have ended their march on America there. They clearly delight in creating movies and documentaries to propagate their socialist dogma. (Meanwhile, where is the film about Chairman Mao and his systematic extermination of seventy million people? Or the exposé of Joseph Stalin, who is responsible for deaths of at least thirty million?) The cinematic flop *Green Zone* is a perfect example. In this Matt Damon thriller, Zinn's little prodigy plays a soldier determined to learn the truth about weapons of mass destruction. Hard as he tries, little Mattie just can't find those WMDs. As expected, everything is blamed on the Bush administration. The movie conveniently ignores the fact that scads of Democrats supported the war (before they began blaming Bush for everything) and that the intelligence agencies of other governments indicated that WMDs were present in Iraq. Forget reality—like a Zinn history come to life, *Green Zone* casts America as the aggressor and, believe it or not, actually goes out of its way to portray an Iraqi general in a compassionate light. No such kindness is shown to American military leaders, but there sure are lots of explosions.

And, apparently, stupid is as stupid does. While flogging his HBO miniseries *The Pacific*, Tom Hanks made comments about America that reveal why he should have retired after *Splash*. Despite his work on behalf of World War II vets, Hanks told *Time* magazine: "Back in World War II, we viewed the Japanese as 'yellow, slant-eyed dogs' that believed in different gods. They were out to kill us because our way of living was different. We, in turn, wanted to annihilate them because they were different. Does that sound familiar, by any chance, to what's going on today?"

On MSNBC, Hanks described the Pacific war as a campaign of "racism and terror." To think that the historian Doug Brinkley had the gall to crown Hanks "American history's highest-ranking professor." Funny, I always think of him as the guy in the dress on *Bosom Buddies*! Dr. Hanks will be exploring the JFK assassination next. God help us.

—⁓—

## THE DIARY OF VICE PRESIDENT JOE BIDEN

WASHINGTON, D.C.

January 27, 2010

Man, I am beat. It is exhausting posing behind POTUS during the State of the Union. What a pressure cooker! I thought Justice Lido [sic] was going to jump out of his seat when POTUS took a swipe at SCOTUS (POTUS . . . SCOTUS . . . It rhymes!). Anyway, I have to admit, I started zoning out when Barack went on about "the threat of nuclear weapons." That old saw?! (I personally do whatever I can to avoid having to pronounce the word proliferation. My trick is that I break it down to pro-lifer and then add the ation part. But then it sounds like an abortion thing. Oh well.) Then just as Barack was prattling on about some Afghan schoolgirl example (z-z-z-z-z-z), an e-mail bulletin from Variety landed in my B-Berry. (This "vibrator" function is amazing!) Anyway, Hollywood is abuzz about the magical new program on the big screen—it's called Atavan, or something. Looks like it was hijacked by the Blue Man Group. It has apparently overtaken Titanic as the most profitable film ever made. Very cool!

That James Cameron fellow knows his stuff. Gotta get him on

the blower this week—why couldn't the Joe Biden Saga end up on the big screen? Since Cameron seems to like one-word movie titles, we could simply call it Amtrak. I lived the equivalent of three lifetimes on that wondrous Acela going between Wilmington and D.C. The stories I could tell about late nights in the Café Car . . . We live in a great f----ing country. Where else could a movie about a train company make more money than the company made in its entire history?

---

The top-grossing film of all time, *Avatar*, was itself a subversive and, might I add, blue Trojan horse that lacerated America. In this digitized 3-D cartoon, vindictive military conquerors (the United States) will stop at nothing to obtain a natural energy resource on the planet Pandora. To get it, they intend to lay waste to the peace-loving, kindhearted (overgrown Smurf) natives of the planet, the Na'vi. In the end, the military imperialists get their comeuppance and the liberal, sci-fi revenge flick draws to a merciful conclusion. Howard Zinn really should have gotten at least a co-writer credit on this monstrosity.

Director James Cameron admitted that his masterpiece was a "comment about the colonial period in North America and South America." What a surprise. This is from the same James Cameron who suggested in a documentary a few years ago that Jesus's resurrection never happened and that the Messiah was a married family man whose bones had been discovered in a Middle Eastern tomb. I liked it better when Cameron made movies that clearly telegraphed his core message—remember *True Lies*?

Oliver Stone, who can always be relied on to bash America, is working on a ten-part documentary series for Showtime called *Oliver Stone's Secret History of America*. The man who brought us the kinder, gentler side of Hugo Chavez has now found subjects truly worthy of his talent. Stone's objective: to rehabilitate the most despicable characters of the twentieth century at the expense of America. The director shared his plan with the Television Critics Association during preproduction. He said, "Stalin, Hitler, Mao . . . these people have been vilified pretty thoroughly by history . . . I've been able to walk in Stalin's shoes and Hitler's shoes to understand their point of view. We're going to educate our minds and liberalize them and broaden them. We want to move beyond opinions. . . . Go into the funding of the Nazi party. How many American corporations were involved, from GM through IBM." Only in Stone's twisted mind can the country that liberated and rebuilt Europe be responsible for the rise of the Third Reich!

Like his fellow comrades, Stone has a method to his madness. He told the television critics that he intends to send his *Secret History* documentaries to schools so students can consider another take on their history. "It would be a very different counterweight to what they're learning," Stone maintains. But after flipping through a few history textbooks, I think it would be a reiteration of what they are already learning.

Each of these destructive revisionists has one goal in mind: to reprogram Americans, young and old. They want to weaken confidence in the historical foundations of the country and wean us off this ideal of America the beautiful.

—◦◦◦—

## THE DIARY OF PRESIDENT BARACK OBAMA

### THE PRIVATE RESIDENCE

March 11, 2010

10:35 p.m. Tom Hanks and Steve Spielberg just left the screening room. They wanted to show me their new miniseries, The Pacific. Personally, I would have liked to finish watching Che with Reggie. (That Benicio del Toro looks just like the great man! If Desiree were still around I'd have del Toro in for a night of revolutionary poetry reading. But Axe says we have to cool it with the showy events, at least until the midterm elections are over.)

Anyway, Hanks and Steve originally wanted to show us four hours of this epic. I wouldn't sit through four hours of a documentary about me much less some HBO thing about old white guys shooting up my brothers and sisters in the Pacific! So they edited together a preview reel for us. One hour and we were out of there. For appearances, we had to invite all the military brass and some WWII vets. I always get a little squeamish being at the movies with those people. It's like sitting in the dark with Ted Bundy or Scott Peterson—no telling what they might do, especially if they see something that brings on a flashback.

The highlight of the screening was when Hanks got up for his preamble and said he was amazed at what America did to the Japanese people. He said that he and Steve wanted to dramatically show the true expressions of racism and terrorism unleashed by our soldiers at this moment in our history. I tried not to laugh when I saw the expression on the war vets' faces. The VFW people and some of the Joint Chiefs looked like they had just been sprayed with napalm.

When it was over, Miche and I were clapping and cheering. The brass didn't budge. Neither did the vets. So I stood up like Lincoln and thanked Tom and Steve for being "true patriots, unafraid to confront history with honesty and clarity." Like Miche said as we went upstairs, "If those vets don't like the truth, let 'em go rent a John Wayne movie."

---

## A LOVE WORTH FIGHTING FOR

It is not enough to think well of America: we must learn to love her again. When we hear the phrase "love of country," does it mean to us what it meant to past generations? It should. America was founded through great struggle and bloodshed in order that our citizenry could live in freedom, to pursue our own destinies. Our Founding Fathers did not believe that our national pride and patriotism should depend on how much the government is doing for *us*. Our system of government was ingeniously devised by men who gave us the opportunity to set the course for the nation. We are supposed to be steering the boat, not just acting like anxious passengers waiting on board to be told what our orders are. Where we end up as a nation depends on whether the American people are willing to continue the battle for liberty. It is not written on some tablet somewhere that America will last forever—she will only endure so long as we are committed to protecting our founding principles.

Our loyalty to our country should be everlasting and immovable. This is not "blind loyalty," as leftists would aver. In fact, this loyalty and love actually lead us at times to criticize the course our nation is taking. We love our parents and our children unconditionally, but that does not mean that they are beyond reproach regardless of what they do or how they behave. True love means being committed despite the shortcomings of the one we adore. While offering honest, constructive criticism, we train ourselves to focus on the good in the other person. And with America, we should never lose sight of the astounding accomplishments and advances, the rich, noble history, and the many gifts America continues to give the world.

We fight and risk our lives only for those things that we truly love—which is why the epidemic trashing of America is so destructive. It weakens our resolve and our commitment. America remains the world's best hope and she is worth our sacrifice. This is the deep devotion and love that we must kindle once more in ourselves and in our children.

*The house I live in,*
*The goodness everywhere,*
*A land of wealth and beauty,*
*With enough for all to share;*
*A house that we call Freedom,*
*A home of Liberty,*
*And it belongs to fighting people*
*That's America to me.*

My mother and father taught me to love my country, and I am so grateful to them for instilling that sentiment in me. I think we all learn love of country from our families. Sadly, today there are many who tell the next generation that America is fundamentally flawed—a place where only the rich and privileged succeed. This thinking, like it or not, will affect not only the future of those who accept it, but also our collective future. We have to correct these false ideas right and redouble our commitment to America's creed.

My father is a proud World War II veteran and my mother had a fierce loyalty about all things American. I remember one evening with my parents as a child in the early 1970s, watching radicals burning flags on the evening news. My mother turned to me, serious as General Patton, and said, "Don't you ever do that." I've never forgotten her words.

Developing a personal love of this country and coming to a deeper appreciation of what America is remains a civic responsibility—our patriotic duty. We cannot allow America to forget herself. In his farewell address, Ronald Reagan issued this caution: "If we forget what we did, we won't know who we are. I'm warning of an eradication of the American memory that could result, ultimately, in an erosion of the American spirit."

That spirit is a fighting spirit—a faithful spirit, a hopeful spirit, a spirit capable of overcoming any obstacle or setback. We need that fighting spirit again. To summon it, we have to recall honestly, free of distortions, what America did and how she did it.

A few years ago, friends of mine took their young sons to a Veterans Day celebration in Washington, D.C. At first the boys seemed uninterested, but as they watched generations of warriors march by, it touched something within them. For the first time these children considered the sacrifices that allowed them to live free. They spoke to a wheelchair-bound Korean War vet seated next to them. To remember the moment, my friends took a picture of the boys and the veteran, and that framed photo sits on the boys' dresser in their bedroom to this day. Over the years it has become a touchstone of American sacrifice for them. They revere this man for his contribution to the country and for the example that inspired them to investigate the Korean War for themselves. They now make an effort to thank all members of the military for their service. Americans should all take the time to be this curious about our history and this grateful for those who paid the price to shape it. Now it is our turn.

Our forefathers and mothers battled a repressive Crown bent on stifling their liberty. Today we face an equally repressive government bureaucracy that is slowly sapping our freedom and mortgaging our future. We are lulled into complacency by a pop culture that is as deadening as it is corrosive. This is the moment to take a stand—to say, "No more." This is a time for patriots, a time to revive our American spirit and fight for the principles upon which our country was founded.

Samuel Adams spoke the truth when he said, "If ever a time should come, when vain and aspiring men shall possess the highest seats in Government, our country will stand in need of its experienced patriots to prevent its ruin." To answer that call, we must be "experienced" and ready for the challenge. And that only comes from doing the intellectual, interior work needed to be a fully engaged citizen.

I am elated to see elections all over the country where citizens, not professional politicians, are willing to step forward and seek public office. We are returning to the example of the founders. From Washington to Jefferson to Hamilton, these men lent their expertise to the service of the nation for a time, before returning to the private sector. Public service was not a retirement destination, but a temporary contribution for the benefit of the country. I hope the rise of the citizen legislators that we are witnessing now will follow that historical model. We need farmers, lawyers, doctors, teachers, mothers, and small business owners who willingly offer their talents to their fellow Americans for a time, and know when to go back to their private lives.

If we put America above our own self interest, perhaps that spirit of generous public service will return. The people are watching, especially the young.

The fight for freedom never ends; it just changes form. In the Revolutionary War, our citizens took up muskets against the British. In the civil rights struggle, Rosa Parks refused to sit in the back of the bus. Today we use new technology to organize and petition our political leaders and find new candidates to run.

## THE WINNING WAY

There are concrete things each of us can do to help revive our love of America. The following books will help give you an accurate appreciation of our spirit, a sense of the amazing people who shaped the country, and remind you what America truly means:

*1776,* **David McCullough.** America's favorite historian offers a brilliant snapshot of our country's most important year. It reveals the difficulties faced by this ragtag band of patriots and proves that the battle for liberty is never easy.

***George Washington: The Indispensable Man,*** James T. Flexner. This is the one-volume distillation of Flexner's Pulitzer Prize–winning, four-volume biography of Washington. In it you will find the story of this "great and good man" told with honesty and panache.

***America: The Last Best Hope,*** Bill Bennett. This two-volume set is a fantastic general history of the United States that candidly confronts the highs and lows of America's past. But the final effect, and Bennett's intention, is to inspire love of country—and boy does he succeed.

***A History of the American People,*** Paul Johnson. For an overview of the whole American experience this is a great place to start. Any book that begins, "The Creation of the United States of America is the greatest of all human adventures," and concludes that America is "still the first, best hope for the human race" is a must-read.

***The Federalist Papers,*** Alexander Hamilton, James Madison, John Jay. If you want the Founding Fathers' take on the Constitution and our government, this is it. These eighty-five articles explain and defend our republican form of government like no other single volume. And though parts of it can be a rough slog, it should not be overlooked by any true patriot.

***The Adventures of Huckleberry Finn,*** Mark Twain. The image of Huck and Jim floating down the mighty Mississippi still captures our American thirst for freedom and liberty. It is one of those indispensable American reads filled with Twain's trademark wit and perfect dialogue.

***The Rise of Theodore Roosevelt/Theodore Rex,*** Edmund Morris. The first two volumes of Morris's trilogy is a thrilling exploration of the events and people that formed one of America's great presidents. He didn't win the Pulitzer for nothing.

## Other Resources

To prepare young patriots for the inheritance that is theirs, the two-volume Bill Bennett book *America: The Last Best Hope* has now been transformed into a curriculum. It is called *The Roadmap to America: The Last Best Hope* and can be found at www.roadmaptolastbesthope.com.

I also came across a wonderful resource for families making travel plans. Why not turn your vacation into a patriotic pilgrimage? This National Park Service site identifies historic places in every state that can be used to teach some part of American history to all citizens. These are trips worth taking that connect us to the past in a visceral way. Visit www.nps.gov/history/nr/twhp/standards.htm for a full list of locations.

And we cannot forget the music of America that is a brilliant reflection of her soul. Our songbook is chock full of neglected treasures. We should take time to reacquaint ourselves with the American masters who shared the sound of freedom with the world (and I don't mean Lady Gaga). Give a listen to the music of these American musical giants:

John Philip Sousa

Scott Joplin

George Gershwin

Aaron Copland

Harry Warren

Richard Rodgers and Oscar Hammerstein

Irving Berlin

Duke Ellington

Stephen Sondheim

# CHAPTER 2

# "DON'T EVER TAKE SIDES . . . AGAINST THE FAMILY"

It has now reached the point where simply approaching the supermarket checkout aisle fills me with dread. This is because invariably, while I'm placing the applesauce and gallon of milk on the conveyor belt, I see a member of the Obama family staring back at me from the magazine rack. There is no escaping them.

Over the last two years the Obamas have stalked all of us from the covers of *Vogue, Essence, US Weekly, People, Men's Fitness, Golf Digest, Glamour, O Magazine, Vanity Fair, GQ, Life & Style, Condé Nast Traveler, Ladies' Home Journal, Prevention, Vibe, Time, Black Enterprise, Newsweek, Rolling Stone,* and *Farm Home Journal* (just kidding). President Obama appeared on *Time* magazine's cover a staggering twenty-four times during his first year in office. For comparison's sake, George W. Bush landed on *Time's* cover only thirty-one times during his entire eight-year presidency.

For access to this "bright," "young," "fashionable" "most elegant" family, the magazines have to give up only one precious commodity: their objectivity. As a result, the fawning coverage of the Obamas is usually stuffed with spoon-fed ephemera that has now become mythic. From the swing set to the dog to the date nights to the burger and ice-cream runs, everything this family does is exalted and treated as if it were being done for the first time in human history. Like the Osbournes before them, the Obamas have transformed their family life into a type of reality show—but with a political twist. As an NBC reporter recently observed with a straight face, "The Obamas are like the new Brangelina." It's a good thing Huntley and Brinkley are dead, because watching news coverage like this would surely have killed them both.

The highly manipulated media portrait of the Obama family carries with it many negatives (which I will delve into in the coming pages), but there is an important positive that should not be missed. The fact that the media spends so much time celebrating this young, intact, African-American family living in the White House underscores an essential truth, namely, that there is a family ideal in this country. One man and one woman, bound by marriage and raising their children is something worth celebrating and preserving. Three cheers for the Obamas for putting this vision of family first.

---

## THE DIARY OF VICE PRESIDENT JOE BIDEN

WASHINGTON, D.C.

April 10, 2010

Okay, I have just about had it. Here we are, fifteen months in, and the Biden family has yet to be featured on the cover of Time, Newsweek, or People magazine once! We can't even score a sidebar feature in US Weekly! Meanwhile, the Obamas go get ice cream and the entire world has to read about it. Don't get me wrong, the girls are adorable and all, but please! My son Beau is a freaking war veteran! And have they not seen my drop-dead-gorgeous wife? She's pushing sixty but doesn't look a day over fifty-eight! But where are the profiles of her? (I have to get my communications director Jay Carney on this pronto. He used to work for Time magazine, so he knows how to generate fluff!) And I'm not talking about the Bidens on the cover of AARP magazine either—I'm talking something really big like OK! or inTouch Weekly! You know, a publication with some heft. We deserve it. I look at Jill every day and I think . . . man, is she the luckiest woman on the face of the planet, or what?

---

Family is the basic building block of our society, and stable families are a crucial part of ensuring our future. A healthy American democracy depends on a moral people to guide it. Families are where the morals and virtues that touch all aspects of public life are first taught and best learned. Families lay the interior foundation that will propel the next generation on to greatness or into oblivion. That future is being directed each day at the dinner tables and in the dens of America—and instinctively, the people know it.

Without the media fully appreciating it, their gratuitous coverage of the Obamas reinforces the message that parental involvement in the lives of our children is important and that strong marriages are critical to our nation's survival. Being a single mother, I realize that families come in all shapes and sizes. And though we may not always reach the ideal, owing to circumstances or events beyond our control, there is no doubt that the traditional family is the best environment for raising a child and incubating America's future. For that reason, above all others, we must defend and reinforce this foundational institution in American life—even when the Obamas fail to do so beyond the photo op.

————————————— ∽∾∾— —————————————

## The Diary of First Grandmother Marian Robinson

### The White House

January 14, 2010

Miche made a big scene in the dining room tonight about me feeding the girls snacks "between meals." She hit the roof when she noticed that Sasha had chocolate around her mouth when she sat down for dinner. I don't see how two little girls sharing a couple of Peppermint Patties and a bag of bar-b-que chips with their grandmother is a national crisis. Since she dug that vegetable garden, you'd think Miche never touched a dessert in her life. I know better! I've seen the panels they added to the back of that state-dinner dress.

"Mama, next month I'm launching my anti-obesity movement and what message does it send if my own daughter starts to look like Meghan McCain?" Miche harrumphed at me during dinner, "If Sasha's Body Mass Index goes up as much as five points, I'm blaming you!" For the record, Miche, not my granddaughters, had seconds.

After supper, Miche, Sasha, Malia, Barack, and I went to Sidwell Friends for "Back to School Night." It was the first time Barack had been to the school in months. Usually Miche and I have to go alone. With this earthquake in Haiti and the health-care bill, Barack was grousing about having to go. But I told him that he missed Malia's poetry night—the least he could do was show up at her recital. The girls were so excited to have him with us.

Our motorcade shut down traffic on Wisconsin Ave. (poor rush hour commuters—ha!) so we got to the school in no time. But still the ride coming and going seemed like an eternity with Miche carrying on about me "making the girls fat" and Barack needing to get up to Massachusetts for some senator's race. Barack and I just looked out the window and let her rant. I felt like telling her, "If you don't like the way I raise your daughters, raise them yourself. And if getting up to Massachusetts is so important to the nation, you go." But I decided it would be better to hold my tongue and keep my peace. Which I did.

---

## THE DIARY OF PRESIDENT BARACK OBAMA

### THE WHITE HOUSE

January 14, 2010

Malia plays the flute like James Galway—amazing! She must get that from my side of the family. I think one of my half brothers is a pianist and, of course, if I had not been so dedicated to organizing for the community, I could easily be opening at Carnegie Hall tonight. I would have preferred to hear Malia play here at the House and not at that uppity Sidwell Friends School. After all I've done for that place you would think they'd treat me with a little more respect. Michelle and I sent them autographed pictures of our magazine covers to auction off last year and everything. What more do these people want from us?

Most of the parents were appropriately in awe of my presence, but this one flabby, typical white man comes over and says: "If the Republican takes Ted Kennedy's seat, that could be big trouble for your health-care plan, huh?" Who died and made him George Will! As if that's going to happen. The Kennedy name is the gold standard up there.

The good news is, I was in and out of there quickly. Reggie requested that the Secret Service close off all the streets. Then just as we were about to leave, they tell me they're concerned about it being rush hour. I told the Secret Service, "I'm the president of the damn United States. The commuters can sacrifice an hour for their president and his family. This is important to my daughter."

Mother Robinson was amazed at how fast we breezed over to the school. I just kind of smiled and told her we must have hit a good traffic pattern. Michelle wanted me to stay for the whole event, but I put my foot down. I told her, "One hour only!" I needed to get back in time to see The Mentalist—that's the only time I really get to relax on Thursdays. With Haiti, all these special elections, and Joe Biden, I've got a lot of disasters weighing on me.

Sasha came in during the show and wanted me to review some essay on George Washington. If her mother wasn't off playing Jenny Craig, maybe I wouldn't have to correct papers during my down time. I read the report during the commercial and then faxed it over to Biden. I figured Washington crossed the Delaware. And since Biden was Delaware's senator for decades—let him figure it out.

It's midnight and now I've got to go back downstairs to finish up this health-care meeting. Rahm is dropping the f-bomb every thirty seconds to keep that doddering old fool Reid awake. You always get the feeling that he's one sentence away from pressing the medical alert pendant. Nevertheless, they tell me we've almost got this thing in the bag. Speaking of bags, Pelosi thinks we can deep-six that Stupak language and sneak a few more goodies into the bill for Planned Parenthood. That should get those shrews Rosa DeLauro and Nita Lowey off my back for a few weeks.

---

## A WELL-TENDED IMAGE

*I'm the badass wife who is sort of keeping it real.*
—Michelle Obama, *Daily Telegraph*, October 23, 2008

The Obamas have gone to great pains to project their image as a perfect, normal family. But beneath the self-generated narrative, looking past the swing set and the dog and veggie show, one has to ask, what's really going on here? What is to be believed? And why have we been thrust into the private world of this president and his family as none before? Part of the answer is certainly political. The comforting, traditional images of Mom planning meals and Dad at the soccer game mask the radical policies that are being advanced.

"How could anyone disagree with such great people?"

"That Michelle is the nicest person ever."

These are the reactions that the Obama media offensive was created to produce. It has worked like a charm. In survey after survey, the Obamas top the list for the family most Americans wish they had as neighbors. "They're so warm, so likable—so like us!" Was I the only person laughing when in a May 2010 interview with *Condé Nast Traveler* Michelle Obama bemoaned losing some of her pre–White House freedom and privacy? "I want to get on the Metro," she claimed.

Oh, right, and I bet she wished she didn't have to take Marine One to Camp David on the weekends. She really wishes she could sit in traffic like the rest of us.

In a *Good Morning America* interview in May 2007, Michelle Obama shared her views on family values and once again proudly displayed that designer chip on her shoulder. She told Robin Roberts, "We have spent the last decade talking a good game about family values. But I haven't seen much evidence that we actually value women or families. . . . I think that we as a country have been a little lax in our concern for these issues. We've been nullified by the fear mongers. It's almost as if people have voted against their best personal interest because they've been so afraid of what could happen. You know: 'The terrorists are going to get us.' . . . [a] non fear-based, non-ideological approach is what we need now as a country." Translation: What we need is a country where Michelle Obama dictates the fear—"We can't afford to do nothing on health care," or "Obesity is a national security issue"—where *her* ideology rules.

Michelle Obama's version of family values is to play the devoted housewife while keeping both hands firmly attached to the political levers of power. Her office ruthlessly manages the press coverage of the First Family, doling out exclusive photos, storylines, and personal tidbits to keep her media lackeys coming back for more. The East Wing has become expert at controlling the press. The First Lady's communications director, Camille Johnston, and her press secretary, Katie McCormick Lelyveld, are the media gatekeepers.

They have been so successful, we now know more about the Obamas than people we have known for decades—even our own flesh and blood.

The First Lady shared this endearing story about her relationship with her daughters with *Glamour* magazine (September 3, 2007): "You know, my hope in my gut is that I am just Mommy . . . I mean, so much of our relationship is based on our world at home. It's getting up—you know, we have this ritual in the morning. We get up and they want ten more minutes so they can come in my bed, and if their dad isn't there—because he is too snore-y and stinky, they don't want ever to get in the bed with him—but we cuddle up and we talk. We've talked about everything from the boy that one daughter doesn't like in school to what is a period. . . ."

Can you imagine Dolly Madison telling a reporter that her husband snored and passed gas in bed? Or Nancy Reagan revealing to a magazine that she and Patti Davis had a heart-to-heart about menstruation?

Michelle and her image makers in the East Wing serve up personal tripe that newspapers, magazines, blogs, and broadcasters are only too happy to spread to the world. This type of reportage requires little thought and zero journalistic skill. To them, it's a scoop. To me, it's TMI: Too Much Information. What relevance do these domestic trivialities have on our daily lives or on the president's ability to govern? Still, each is treated by the press corps as if SALT III were just signed.

Here is just a smattering of the White House TMI overload:

- Hair stylist Johnny Wright relocated from Chicago to Washington to keep the First Lady perfectly coiffed at all times. Her personal trainer followed her to D.C. as well.
- The First Lady loves short-shorts. (I am biting my tongue and straining to suppress any and all commentary.)
- Always the supportive wife, Michelle revealed that her husband did not know how to make a bed. He also does not put the butter away after breakfast.

- The president leaves wet towels on the bathroom floor. Can you guess the source of these tidbits? The same First Lady who said, "He's a gifted man, but in the end, he's just a man."

You will notice that the majority of this family minutiae paints the president in a negative light. In addition to trashing America, Michelle can always be relied on to publicly nitpick her husband. When asked about this in the *Glamour* interview, she responded defensively: "Barack is very much human. So let's not deify him, because what we do is we deify, and then we're ready to chop it down. People have notions of what a wife's role should be in this process, and it's been a traditional one of blind adoration. My model is a little different . . ." No kidding.

The release of these intimate details is designed to humanize the Obamas, to take the edge off their radical designs and give them an appearance of ordinariness. This keeps their personal popularity numbers high and has obvious political benefits.

The Obamas are part of a cultural overthrow of discretion and all sense of modesty. Through their nonstop personal disclosures (the president does not replace toilet paper rolls and has the audacity to leave the seat up!), the Obamas, their surrogates, and pop culture are teaching our children to let it all hang out, leave nothing to the imagination. This compulsive need to reveal once-private details now permeates American society.

From the desperate actions of the balloon boy's family to the gate-crashing antics of the Salahis, people are willing to do anything to attract public attention. In this permissive atmosphere, people like musician John Mayer feel entitled to call a former girlfriend "sexual napalm" in public and to expound on the racial preferences of his sexual organ. This habit of untoward self-revelation is now an epidemic and the Obamas are feeding into it.

Obama wannabe Harold Ford, Jr., during his short New York senate run, felt obliged to justify his frequent pedicures (don't ask) to the *New York Times:* "I have severe athlete's foot—feet. I get a foot scrub out of respect for my wife because getting into bed with what I have when I take my socks off isn't respectful to anybody." Though in the age of four-hour-erection ads, I suppose Ford seems almost modest.

The Obamas' love of fame and demand for public adoration apparently knows no bounds, extending to all members of the family. Despite their public decision to shield their daughters from publicity and keep their lives as normal as possible, Barack and Michelle Obama seem to have no problem invoking their girls when it suits them politically.

From their first major appearance at the Democratic National Convention in 2008, to their big interview with *Access Hollywood* on July 4 of that same year, the Obama girls have been trotted out for maximum effect. During their "first interview as a family," Malia and Michelle ragged on the then-senator for sporting "ten-year-old" clothes and leaving his "bag in the middle of the floor." Though Barack barely got a word in edgewise, he did get plenty of abuse from the ladies in the family. No wonder the whole clan has not sat for an interview since. But that doesn't mean that Malia and Sasha have been absent from the scene.

In February 2010, mother Michelle used Malia and Sasha to justify her "anti-obesity initiative or movement." In repeated interviews, she claimed a pediatrician (never identified), alarmed by her daughters' Body Mass Index readings, recommended lifestyle changes to head off an obesity problem. This, Michelle told the world, inspired her national anti-obesity crusade. It is hard to read this as anything other than political opportunism.

Since no one elected Michelle Obama to do anything, she had to insulate herself from potential criticism—so the First Lady ran to the well of personal narrative. Just when her Eva Peron slip began to show, she threw the children out front to mask her meddling in policy. After all, she's just an average mom worried about "the children," right?

It is curious that when the Beanie Baby company, Ty, unveiled its "Sweet Sasha" and "Marvelous Malia" dolls, Michelle Obama thought them "inappropriate" and was so "irked" by their presence, the dolls were eventually withdrawn from the marketplace. But at least Ty created flattering depictions of the Obama daughters and didn't raise public questions about the girls' sizes or body images, which is more than you can say for their mother.

President Obama has also used his daughters as political cover and to advance policy. The most egregious example came during a pivotal May 27, 2010, presidential press conference during the Gulf Coast oil spill. Responding to criticism that he had not been fully engaged during the crisis, he noted that every morning his daughter Malia asks, "Did you plug the hole yet, Daddy?" This was a pathetic and ineffective ploy to engender empathy, to humanize him.

And who can forget the president's open letter to Malia and Sasha in *Parade* magazine during inaugural week (What happened to writing private letters to your children?): ". . . I realized that my own life wouldn't count for much unless I was able to ensure that you had every opportunity for happiness and fulfillment in yours. In the end, girls, that's why I ran for president: because of what I want for you and for every child in this nation . . ."

He went on to cite a laundry list of policy desires. But apparently that concern for "every child in the nation" only includes those fortunate enough to survive the womb.

## "PUNISHED WITH A BABY"

On January 23, 2009, in one of his very first acts as president, Obama overturned the Mexico City Policy, forcing taxpayers to fund groups that promote or perform abortions abroad. This one executive order funneled tens of millions of dollars into the coffers of the abortion industry. When he announced the policy change, the president added: "In the coming weeks, my administration will initiate a fresh conversation on family planning, working to find areas of common ground to best meet the needs of women and families at home and around the world."

This "common ground" line has been a default for President Obama every time the issue of abortion arises. The problem is, the only common ground for children involved in abortion is the soil covering their remains.

How can one expect President Obama to find any semblance of "common ground" when he has surrounded himself with some of the most militantly pro-abortion collaborators in presidential history? Just look at a few of his staff picks:

Ellen Moran, White House communications director, is the former director of Emily's List, a group that bankrolls the candidacy of pro-abortion women who seek national office.

Melody Barnes, director of the White House Domestic Policy Council, is a former board member of Emily's List.

David Ogden, Obama's deputy attorney general, argued in a 1992 brief that women faced no psychological or emotional problems after having an abortion. In fact, he wrote, "The evidence shows that she is more likely to experience feelings of relief and happiness . . . child-birth and child-rearing or adoption may pose concomitant (if not greater) risks or adverse psychological effects." Aside from believing that childbirth poses a greater danger to a woman than abortion, Ogden does have a soft spot for the blind. He sued in federal court to compel the Library of Congress to publish Braille editions of *Playboy* magazine. (Ogden returned to private practice in February 2010.)

Kathleen Sebelius, secretary of Health and Human Services, as well as the former governor of Kansas, is a longtime supporter of late-term abortions. She vetoed a measure that would have limited the grisly procedure, holding firm to her pro-abortion convictions while trying to pass herself off as a practicing Catholic. Owing to her public abortion stance, Archbishop Joseph Naumann of Kansas City asked Sebelius to refrain from receiving communion.

Rahm Emanuel, the White House chief of staff and former congressman, never met an abortion policy he couldn't support. He earned himself an unsurprising zero percent voting score from National Right to Life.

I could go on and on. There is the pro-abortion vice president, Joe Biden; the pro-abortion secretary of state, Hillary Clinton; the pro-abortion solicitor general and Supreme Court nominee, Elena Kagan . . . Although he talks a good game about "seeking common ground," the president hasn't a single pro-life advisor. This perhaps explains, in part, why he is so clumsy in discussing the question of when life begins. Who can forget his telling Pastor Rick Warren that the issue was "above [his] pay grade"?

Forget the canned speeches and the confusing press releases on the issue of life. Where does the president stand on protecting and nurturing the smallest members of our families? For answers, listen to what he says when he is speaking off the cuff. At a Pennsylvania rally in March 2008, Senator Obama told the assembled: "I've got two daughters—nine years old and six years old. I am going to teach them first of all about values and morals. But if they make a mistake, I don't want them punished with a baby."

*"Punished with a baby."*

When an individual considers their own grandchild a punishment, how can you possibly think them capable of creating just or moral policies regarding human life? Of all the deeply troubling remarks made by this president, there is none that I find more offensive or tragic than this one. It reveals President Obama's true feelings about human life and gives us a unique perspective into his notions of family. It also puts in context the many destructive, anti-life policies that we have seen coming out of his administration.

Given that quote, it is painfully obvious why the president overthrew a thirteen-year ban and allowed the federal funding of abortions in the District of Columbia. It makes perfect sense that he would request and receive $648.5 million for international family planning efforts—the lion's share of which will go to contraceptive and abortion services in foreign countries. And if nearly born children are not afforded basic protections, what chance do the embryos have? President Obama permitted federal tax dollars to fund morally offensive, scientifically specious, and destructive embryonic stem cell research. By executive order, he demanded that military hospitals stock the morning-after pill. He invalidated conscience protections for pro-life health workers and even tried to slip abortion coverage into his national health-care overhaul.

And this is "common ground"?

Michelle Obama, on the last day of the Democratic National Convention, in a speech to the Woman's Caucus, said of her husband: "He'll protect a woman's freedom of choice, because government should have no say in whether or when a woman embraces the sacred responsibility of parenthood." The verbal sleight of hand is fascinating. Human life is not sacred, but the responsibility of parenthood is.

## THE DIARY OF FIRST LADY MICHELLE OBAMA

#### MOSCOW, RUSSIA

July 7, 2009

Smokey stepped in it big time today. We have been pounding the story of how he and I met into his head for two years now—and Barack still hasn't learned it! Today, he gets up at a graduation here at the New Economic School and says, "Thank you so much. Well, congratulations . . . to the entire Class of 2009 . . . I don't know if anybody else will meet their future wife or husband in class like I did, but I'm sure that you're all going to have wonderful careers . . ."

What class is he talking about? I sure as hell didn't meet his scrawny ass in school. <u>As if</u> I was his student! Please! Valerie was kicking me so hard when he said that, my left leg is all bruised. I may have to wear stockings for the rest of this trip now—and I hate stockings.

When I heard him tell those Russians that we met in class, I thought, <u>Oh Lord, this thing is unraveling faster than the stimulus bill.</u>

On my orders, Gibbs spent the afternoon making sure the serious correspondents covered the relationship between Russia and America laid out in Smokey's big speech. Desiree got the other idiots to write about Sasha and Malia's matching secret-agent trench coats — we gave them pictures and everything.

Thank God half the graduates and all the reporters were sleeping during Barack's blather. Gorbachev (who was also there) literally had drool running down the front of his shirt. These pundits keep talking about what a great orator Barack is. Truth is, I don't see it. I'm with Gorby; he puts me to sleep too. Reverend Jeremiah he is not! He's a walking, talking AmbienCR. I should have given the graduation speech. I promise you, had I been talking, Gorby would have been wide-awake and taking notes!

---

## LIGHTS, CAMERA, MARRIAGE

It is the stuff of Harlequin romances and Danielle Steel paperbacks. Except in this case, it is being written by accredited journalists.

Christine Simmons, NBC News, May 3, 2009: "The First Couple took full advantage of the cool spring night. After a date night out on Saturday evening, President Barack Obama and First Lady Michelle Obama decided to take a stroll . . . So they began walking on the driveway of the White House South Lawn, holding hands. First they passed the West Wing, then their children's swing set. They kept walking, swinging their hands together."

Associated Press, May 3, 2009: ". . . the First Couple wanted a private stroll. Below an overcast sky Saturday, the Obamas clasped hands and made their way down the driveway of the White House South Lawn. They came back the same way, rounding out their eight-minute walk."

Amazingly, they strolled right past a phalanx of waiting photographers and reporters!

Every calculated move of the First Couple has been analyzed, covered ad nauseam, and drummed into our heads like holy writ: *They are the perfect couple . . . they are the perfect couple . . .* TV correspondents swoon over the thrilling romance of the date nights: the glamour of the First Lady, the gallantry of the president, the way their hands brushed, the moonlit strolls. In between lecturing Americans to "sacrifice," it's nice to know the Obamas are having a good time.

During an official trip to Prague on April 4, 2009, the president snubbed his hosts and decided to spend his only night in the country at a romantic outing with the First Lady. Never mind that this came at the tail end of an international voyage where the First Couple had spent days enjoying dinners and concerts in the United Kingdom, France, and Germany.

"He requested a romantic dinner with a view of Prague, where they can eat the best Czech food," a Czech government source told the *Daily Times* of London. "They have spent days trying to decide on the right restaurant."

Then there was the romantic getaway to New York in May 2009. It took three Gulfstreams, a helicopter, and more street closures than the Macy's Thanksgiving Day parade to pull this date night off.

Days before GM declared bankruptcy, the president issued this defensive statement: "I am taking my wife to New York City because I promised her during the campaign that I would take her to a Broadway show after it was all finished." Someone should inform the president that there is such a thing as touring companies. They routinely bring "Broadway shows" to your hometown. And last time I checked, most of them stop at the Kennedy Center or at the National Theater in D.C. But when Michelle Obama is promised a Broadway show, Michelle Obama gets a Broadway show.

After jetting in from D.C., the first couple ate dinner at the West Village organic restaurant Blue Hill. They then sped uptown to the Belasco Theater to see the opening night of *Joe Turner's Come and Gone.* Streets were closed for blocks, traffic snarled all over the theater district, but the Obamas made their curtain.

The British *Mirror* newspaper estimated that the good-looking couple's New York date, including the "three jets of security staff," cost taxpayers one million dollars. But, hey, it's not about the money, it's about the example.

"It's a reminder that this family is not just two folks raising kids, but it's two folks building a life together," Michelle said of the date nights on *TV One*. She explained to Roland Martin that these dates go beyond her and Barack. "What I've found, which is interesting, is that our girls like it . . . they like the fact that they know that we love each other. That gives them security." (Yet another instance of their using the girls as political shields.)

It is nice that the Obamas carve out quality time to spend together. Special time as a couple *is* important to a marriage. But how much alone time can a couple have when a press pool and the general public are invited to every outing? Does every date need its own press release?

Americans seem to be getting wise to the White House message game. As early as April 2009, a Pew Research Center poll found that a full 53 percent of Americans felt that there was too much coverage of Obama's personal life—and that was before the Manhattan getaway!

The ostentatious date nights are yet another tool used by the White House to garner coverage from the celebrity media while promoting the idea that the Obama marriage is to be emulated and envied. The idea is, if you believe this couple has achieved the ideal, you are more likely to listen to them when they speak out on policies that affect marriage and family life. But before we accept the idea that the Obama marriage is as perfect as it appears, there are some inconsistencies in the record.

The official line on their meeting goes something like this: In 1988, Barack Obama, then attending Harvard Law School, was hired as a summer associate at the Chicago law firm of Sidley Austin. A certain Michelle Robinson was to be his advisor for the summer. "I remember that she was tall—almost my height in heels—and lovely, with a friendly, professional manner that matched her tailored suit and blouse," Obama writes in *The Audacity of Hope*.

The story changed, however, when the president spoke in Moscow on July 7, 2009: "I don't know if anybody else will meet their future wife or husband in class like I did . . ." he recounted. What happened to the law firm and her "tailored suit"? Perhaps this narrative is still taking shape.

The first mother-in-law, Marian Robinson, had similar recall problems at an Education Department event on July 22, 2009, when trying to describe how her daughter met Barack Obama. She hemmed and hawed a bit, repeated the tale of the law firm meeting, and then added, "I think that's how the story went."

Whatever the facts of their meeting and courtship, Michelle and Barack Obama were married in 1992 by that soft-spoken patriot, the Obamas' spiritual father, Reverend Jeremiah Wright. Within a few years, the community activist couple had grown into a family. Soon tensions emerged. They were both so busy with their careers there was "little time for conversation, much less romance," Obama wrote in *The Audacity of Hope*. "Leaning down to kiss Michelle good-bye in the morning, all I would get was a peck on the cheek. By the time Sasha was born—just as beautiful, and almost as calm as her sister—my wife's anger toward me seemed barely contained. 'You only think about yourself,' she would tell me. 'I never thought I'd have to raise a family alone.' "

Barack confided to his grandmother in Hawaii, Madelyn "Toot" Dunham, "I love Michelle, but she's killing me with this constant criticism. She just seems so bitter, so angry, all the time." In his own memoir, *A Game of Character*, the First Brother-in-Law Craig Robinson recounted the hot summer night when his parents saw Michelle and Barry Obama together for the first time, when they stopped by their place on the way to a movie. "Well, he's tall," Marian Robinson remarked. "She'll eat him alive," he recalled his father Fraser saying.

Every marriage has its rocky periods and by all appearances this was the rockiest of the Obamas' union. But one gets the feeling from recent comments by Michelle Obama that the criticism has not exactly waned.

"I've got a loud mouth. I tease my husband," Michelle told *Good Morning America* in 2007. "He is incredibly smart and he is very able to deal with a strong woman—which is one of the reasons that he can be president. Because he can deal with me."

In her crusade to remake her image, First Lady Michelle Obama has sounded more traditional notes. "My first job, in all honesty, is going to continue to be mom-in-chief," she told *Ebony* magazine shortly after the election.

Since then she has offered her advice on everything from what children should eat to how much TV they should watch. Michelle doesn't only hold her children to this standard, but like an evangelist, encourages other families to follow her example. In a March 2010 interview with *Essence* magazine her husband took up the gospel of Michelle: "The girls don't watch TV during the week. Period. . . . "

It isn't that the First Lady's child-rearing ideas aren't laudatory or even without merit. The problem is that Michelle Obama presumes that the entire country needs her to be *our* "Mom-in-Chief."

Even the title seems self-serving, particularly when viewed in the light of an interview Michelle granted *Vogue* magazine in 2007. There, she candidly admitted: "The days I stay home with my kids without going out, I start to get ill."

Luckily for the Mom-in-Chief, since becoming First Lady she has rarely had to spend much time in the residence with the kids. "Everyone should have a chief of staff and a set of personal assistants," Michelle joked at a "Corporate Voices for Working Families" conference in May 2009. But the joke is shot through with truth. This First Lady has the largest staff of any presidential wife in history: twenty-four staffers in all, costing taxpayers more than a million dollars annually. So how could any other American mother compete with or relate to Michelle Obama's situation? And then there is Michelle's greatest aide: in-house babysitter and Grandmother-in-Chief Marian Robinson.

Michelle Obama's mother relocated to D.C. and took up residence in the White House to continue her care of the First Daughters. And though she initially resisted the invitation, her grandmotherly instinct won out in the end. "The whole time I'm raising . . . Michelle [and her brother], I am telling them that, 'Look, you see, I am raising my kids, so don't you all have any kids that you expect me to help you raise,' " Robinson told the *Boston Globe* during the campaign. "And look at what I'm doing!"

Marian Robinson shuttles the girls to school, helps them with homework, but obviously disagrees with Michelle's child-rearing protocol.

"She has them so, I don't know, like little soldiers," Marian Robinson confessed to the *Globe* in one of her only solo interviews. "I've heard [Michelle] say, 'Mom, what are you rolling your eyes at? You made us do the same thing.' I don't remember being that bad. It seems like she's just going overboard." Of the 8:30 P.M. bedtime, Robinson opines: "That's ridiculous!" And what the First Granny says about the one-hour weekend TV viewing: "That's just not enough time." And on Michelle's militant culinary rules: "That's not my thing . . . see when I grew up we had good food, right? . . . If you're going to have fried chicken, have *fried chicken!*" At least somebody in the White House gets it.

"She's just worthless on [*sic*] the discipline area," Michelle said of her mother on *The Tonight Show with Jay Leno* on October 29, 2009. "Just cookies, TV, whatever they want. It's a shame."

I'll take Marian Robinson's spunky, commonsense attitude over Michelle's rigid, holier-than-thou prescriptions any day.

---

# THE DIARY OF FIRST GRANDMOTHER MARIAN ROBINSON

## THE WHITE HOUSE

### August 19, 2009

I almost packed up and went back to Chicago today. This afternoon, Miche caught me in the hallway bringing a stack of cookies to Sasha's room. You'd swear she had busted me with a crack pipe. She hollers, "Mama, I'm the First Lady—and in this house you live under my rules." I turned right around, cookies in hand, and told her, "If you don't stop getting on my case,

I'm out of here, young lady. I don't need this." Then I shoved one of the cookies in my mouth. "Mmmm . . . tastes a lot better than what you're feeding those children from that toxic garden of yours!"

I can't wait for her to get out to Martha's Vineyard. She wanted me to go on vacation with them, to take care of the children all week. I'd have to be nuts. I said, "No, First Lady, you're on the clock now. Have a good vacation!" Back in February, I made a deal with Miche. I told her, "Unless you want me to head back to Chicago and tell the Sun-Times what I really know, you'd better back off and give me some room." So now I get some weekends. I've made them hire a sitter when I go out to a show or something. Monday through Friday my nose is to the grindstone, but on Saturdays and Sundays— that's granny's time.

Oh, I wish the weekend would hurry up and come. Barack and Michelle leave for the Vineyard on Saturday, and then I get the run of the mansion. Martha and Jean and my friend Esther are coming in from Chicago tomorrow, so I guess I can put up with Miche for a few more days. As long as they've got spare guest rooms, free food, and access to that presidential box at the Kennedy Center, I might as well stick around.

Before I go to bed I'm going to sneak my granddaughters some hot cocoa and a little ice cream. They like that at bedtime, and it helps them sleep better.

## UP A FAMILY TREE

The Obamas eagerly offer up all manner of personal details related to their immediate family lives. What is not so well-known but is perhaps more important is the background of their extended families.

It is our personal experience that shapes our concept of what it means to be a family. Particularly important are the models offered to us by our mothers and fathers. In the case of President Obama, this fundamental understanding affects not only his worldview, but his policies. On the surface, the president's notions of family appear solidly traditional, even clichéd—until one glances at the uppermost boughs of the Obama family tree.

Michelle La Vaughn Robinson's family was intact and apparently very loving. Marian and Fraser Robinson were hardworking, proud people with deep roots in Chicago's South Side. Marian was a secretary and later a stay-at-home mother. Fraser, despite suffering from multiple sclerosis, worked for the Chicago Water Department and became a Democratic precinct captain for the Daley political machine. Unafraid of labor, the Robinsons struggled so their children could have security and enough space to grow. Education and personal responsibility were emphasized. The Robinsons taught their children to challenge themselves, furnishing them with a strong sense of confidence that would blossom in later life.

As for Barack Obama's own family—the story is more complicated.

"I have brothers, sisters, nieces, nephews, uncles, and cousins of every race and every hue, scattered across three continents," Barack Obama said in March 2008. And he wasn't kidding.

"When you get my family together, I mean you've got people who look like Margaret Thatcher. You've got people who look like Bernie Mac. You've got, you know my sister, she looks like Salma Hayek," Obama told a Kissimmee, Florida, rally in May 2008, "I don't know if you've seen her . . . she looks Latin."

Have you seen his sister? Hey, Mr. President, time to call LensCrafters!

"[My sister, Maya]'s got a baby, 'cause she married a Chinese Canadian, so she's got a little—I've got a little niece who's a little Chinese baby. So the point is that—that's just how I look at the world is we all have a piece of each other and we can't get caught up in our differences."

Attending an Obama family reunion would be akin to being stuck in "It's a Small World" without the boat and the catchy tune.

Barack Obama's parents were an active pair. Stanley Ann Dunham, an eighteen-year-old girl from Kansas, was attending the University of Hawaii when she met a dashing Kenyan graduate student in her Russian class. She was drawn to Barack Obama, Sr.'s seductive oratory and cocksure self-confidence. He was intelligent, he smoked, and he seemed exotic. Obama had romantic notions of returning home to "shape the destiny of Africa," according to one biography. Months after their meeting, on August 4, 1961, Stanley Ann gave birth to Obama's child, Barack Obama, Jr.

The official narrative is that Stanley Ann Dunham and Barack Obama, Sr., were married in February 1961. But with the Obamas, nothing is as it seems. Barack, Sr., already had a wife of five years in Kenya, Kezia Aoko. She was pregnant when he abandoned her to study in Hawaii. They would have three other children together.

So did Dunham and Obama actually marry? Christopher Anderson, author of *Barack and Michelle: Portrait of an American Marriage*, reports that there are no "official records showing that a legal ceremony ever took place" between Barack Obama's parents. He adds, "There were certainly no witnesses—no family members were present, and none of their friends at the university had the slightest inkling that they were even engaged."

In his memoir *Dreams from My Father*, Obama writes of his parents' nuptials: "how and when the marriage occurred remains a bit murky, a bill of particulars that I've never quite had the courage to explore. There's no record of a real wedding, a cake, a ring, a giving away of the bride. No families were in attendance; it's not even clear that people back in Kansas were fully informed. Just a small civil ceremony, a justice of the peace. The whole thing seems so fragile in retrospect, so haphazard."

Possibly because the wedding never occurred.

Michelle Obama admitted as much during a July 10, 2008, speech at the University of Missouri when she said, Barack's "mother . . . was very young and very single when she had him."

Stanley Ann and Barack, Sr., probably never lived as husband and wife, either. The well-worn story is that Barack, Sr., selfishly opted to study at Harvard in 1962 ("Why should I deny myself the best education?"), leaving his wife and son in Hawaii. But Jerome Corsi at WorldNet Daily uncovered records showing that Stanley Ann Dunham attended classes at the University of Seattle only fifteen days after the birth of her son. She and Junior apparently remained there until at least the spring of 1962. Barry would only see his father one more time, when he was ten years old.

In the interim, Barry and his mother returned to Hawaii, where she met yet another foreign student at the university. (Match.com has nothing on this school!) Lolo Soetoro was an affable Indonesian who married Stanley Ann when Barack was six. The whole clan relocated to Indonesia a year later.

This must have been a difficult period for young Barry. He was the only black person anyone in his neighborhood had seen. He was ridiculed for his pudginess, and being an American surely did nothing to endear him to the locals. His mother later gave birth to a half sister, Maya. Bouncing between Catholic and Muslim schools in this strange land, the boy had to feel isolated and at sea. When he was ten, Barry's mother announced that he would be returning to Hawaii—alone. He would be attending a prestigious school there and living with his grandparents. Barry was being abandoned once more.

When he was ten, both his mother and father visited Hawaii. It would be the first time (since his birth) that Barry laid eyes on his father. It would also be their last meeting. Barack Obama, Sr., had a drinking problem by then, but he still knew how to turn on the charm. During his December visit, he tried to persuade Stanley Ann and her children to return to Africa with him. She declined. She no doubt knew of the ever-blooming Obama family tree in Africa.

Barack Obama, Sr., was a polygamist. He had at least two wives at once

and a slew of kids back in his homeland. Here is the short list of the children
sired if not raised by Barack Obama, Sr.:

> Wife No. One, Kezia, bore him three sons: Abongo (sometimes called
> Roy or Malik), Abo (Samson), Bernard, and a daughter, Auma.

> Wife No. Two, Ruth Nidesand, was a white Harvard classmate who
> moved to Nairobi with Barack, Sr. She had two sons by him: David
> and Mark (Ndesandjo).

> Another woman, named Jael, gave birth to his youngest son, George, in
> Nairobi.

At last count, Barack, Sr., fathered eight children . . . that we know
of. This family tree is so twisted, genealogists have suggested that Barack
Obama is distantly related to Dick Cheney, Scott Brown, President Bush,
and Brad Pitt! If we give Henry Louis Gates enough time, he'll identify you
as Obama's thirteenth cousin once removed.

Barack Obama's extended family is a motley crew. Half brother George,
now living in the slums of Nairobi, has been busted for drug possession.
According to the U.K. *Mirror*, Obama's half brother Abo, who attended
the inauguration, was picked up in Britain for allegedly sexually assaulting
a teenage girl. (He was never charged.) He was living illegally in England at
the time with his mother.

Obama's aunt Zeituni Onyango, the Kenyan half sister of his father, has
been in the United States since 2000. She was ordered deported in 2004,
but she squatted in Boston public housing and continued to plead for
asylum.

## The Diary of President Barack Obama

### The Oval Office

January 12, 2010

Just got a letter from Auntie Zeituni. Immigration is threatening to deport her, and the electric company in Boston is about to turn off her lights. What does she want me to do? Why doesn't she go on eBay and sell the dress and pearls I sent her last year?! She'd make a fortune!

I can't save the world and all my relatives. There are just too many of them.

Reggie gave her a call. He hooked her up with a nearby charity that hands out flashlights and blankets to the homeless. I also asked Rahm to see if we could toss some stimulus money her way. We might be able to set her up as the director of the new "Barack Hussein Obama Immigrant Outreach Center" in downtown Boston. I bet the city would go for it, if we pick up the tab. On second thought, maybe I need to call that immigration judge in Boston. The last thing I need in my first term is an Elian Gonzalez situation with my own flesh and blood!

Then I hear Grandma Sarah has sent word that she's coming over from Kenya to celebrate my first year in office. I hope she doesn't try to bring another one of those ceremonial spears with her. Last night I had a dream that she nicked a pair of Kenyan Airways attendants and her seatmate trying to fit the thing in the overhead compartment. Then things get blurry . . . but Homeland Security called to say Big Janet raised the threat level because the old girl inadvertently poked the checkout clerk at the Dulles Airport Cinnabon with her spear and then knocked over a <u>Dreams from My Father</u> ~~shrine~~ display at Hudson News.

Michelle told me that my brother George in Nairobi is now looking for a handout. He wrote her a letter asking for help to renovate his shanty. Use of the Obama name is one of the most valuable gifts that I could give the man. How much more does he want from me?! Michelle was about to write him a check, but I know if we start giving to one, they'll all be calling: Abo, Auma, Abongo, and those other three guys the press haven't caught wind of yet.

---

On May 17, 2010, an immigration court granted "Auntie Zeituni" asylum. "It's obvious her nephew helped," neighbor Marian Swain told the *Boston Herald.*

Of all of Barack Obama, Sr.'s children, only two of them, David and Mark Ndesandjo, lived under the same roof as their father. David (like his dad) was killed in an accident, but Mark has vivid memories of Barack Obama, Sr. He told the Associated Press in November 2009, "My father beat my mother and my father beat me, and you don't do that." In his semi-autobiographical novel, *Nairobi to Shenzhen,* he writes: "David easily remembered the hulking man whose breath reeked of cheap Pilsner beer who had often beaten his mother. He had long searched for good memories of his father but had found none."

This history had to be difficult for Barack Obama to reconcile with the memory of his father passed on to him by Stanley Ann. In *Dreams from My Father*, he wrote in anguished tones:

> All my life, I had carried a single image of my father, one that I had some-times rebelled against but had never questioned, one that I had later tried to take as my own. The brilliant scholar, the generous friend, the upstand-ing leader—my father had been all those things . . . I'd seen weakness in other men—Gramps in his disappointments, Lolo and his compromise. But these men had become object lessons for me, men I might love but never emulate, white men and brown men whose fates didn't speak to my own. It was into my father's image, the black man, son of Africa, that I'd packed all the attributes I sought in myself, the attributes of Martin and Malcolm, DuBois and Mandela . . . my father's voice had nevertheless remained untainted, inspiring, rebuking, granting or withholding ap-proval. You do not work hard enough, Barry. You must help your people's struggle. Wake up, black man!
>
> Now . . . that image had suddenly vanished. Replaced by . . . what? A bitter drunk? An abusive husband? A defeated, lonely bureaucrat? To think that all my life I had been wrestling with nothing more than a ghost!

President Obama no doubt continues to feel the absence of his father, even in adulthood, as any child in this situation would. This may explain his praiseworthy public service announcements encouraging fathers to "take time to be a dad today." Launched by his Department of Health and Human Services, the PSAs are part of a fatherhood initiative designed to strengthen marriages and family stability. As nice as these spots are, the policies of Obama's administration are out of sync with his message. Strong families and responsible fathers cannot be summoned through legislation or willed via the teleprompter. They can only be raised from within solid, intact fami-lies. Given his tortured lineage, the concept of a solid family may be difficult for the president to grasp fully.

Through his out-of-control spending, President Obama overrules the responsible heads of households, snatching money from America's families and depriving them of their liberty and leisure. While the president trots out idealistic measures to "help families," his economic policies sap stable families of their earned income and redistribute it as he sees fit. By 2015, it is estimated that the U.S. debt will reach $14 trillion—nearly 73 percent of our gross domestic product. This will negatively affect our spending power and erode our way of life. Unfunded entitlement programs are exploding to the point where Medicare is expected to be insolvent by 2017—and let's not even talk about Social Security. Obama's polices are disempowering the family, America's greatest hope, and leaving future generations holding the bag.

- **Welfare:** As the economy contracted, President Obama did manage to grow one thing: the welfare state. He has paved the way for more government dependency than any president before him. The Heritage Foundation reports that within his first two years in office, welfare programs like housing and food stamps will have increased a staggering 30 percent. The tragedy is that only one of the seventy-two government welfare programs actually moves people to self-sufficiency. And when entitlements metastasize, someone must pay. You are that someone.
- **Taxes:** Families will be disproportionately hit by the Obama taxes. Under his 2011 budget, upper-income earners will see their income tax rates rise from 33 percent to 35 percent and 36 percent to 39.6 percent. Those making less than $250,000 a year will assume that these tax increases will have no effect on them. They couldn't be more wrong. These elevated income taxes on upper earners will suppress investment in new and existing companies and jobs will be lost. Middle-class families will be hit hard by the aftershocks.

  Even the dead are not safe from Obama's tax policies. Though the death tax (also known as the estate tax) died on January 1, 2010, President Obama has proposed its resurrection. The president not only wants to revive the death tax, he plans to increase it to a top rate of 45 percent, with an exemption for estates worth $3.5 million. Family business will be torn to pieces by this tax.

  Obama has also endorsed taxing carbon emissions. His cap-and-trade bill, in the name of protecting the environment, will tax everything from gas to home heating oil to the groceries you buy. And when you start taxing carbon emissions, everyone is hit, particularly the middle class and the poor.

- **Abstinence Funding:** A recent study in the *Archives of Pediatrics & Adolescent Medicine* indicated that abstinence-based education programs are effective—more students remain chaste after taking the classes (two-thirds) and young people learn to respect their bodies. In poll after poll, parents prefer that their children learn the virtue of abstinence before marriage. But parents be damned. President Obama defunded abstinence-only education in his first year in office. In 2011, he has proposed routing more than $100 million to new, condom-focused sex ed programs. This is sure to bolster responsible parenthood and inculcate a love of family in the young!

- **Education:** Since 2003, poor families in D.C. had been allowed to send their children to private schools of their choice. The D.C. voucher program was a raging success, with 1,700 children participating each year. Under this innovative scholarship fund, parents 185 percent below the federal poverty line could send their sons and daughters to outstanding parochial schools or exclusive academies like Sidwell Friends, where the Obama girls attend school. President Obama, who claims to care so deeply for the poor, sat back while Congress defunded this program in 2009. He would rather condemn poor children to failing schools than offend the teachers unions. So much for parents making educational choices for their own children. Again, does this help or hurt poor families?

- **Marriage:** In 2008, Obama responded to a Human Rights Campaign (HRC) Presidential Questionnaire with these words: "I do not support gay marriage. Marriage has religious and social connotations, and I consider marriage to be between a man and a woman." But at an HRC dinner in October 10, 2009, the president changed his tune: "I support ensuring that committed gay couples have the same rights and responsibilities afforded to any married couple in this country. . . . And I've called on Congress to repeal the so-called Defense of Marriage

Act. . . ." Now wait a minute. The Defense of Marriage Act, signed into law by Bill Clinton in 1996, merely codifies in federal law the definition of marriage that Obama advanced during the campaign, mainly that "marriage means only a legal union between one man and one woman." But even this elementary view of marriage, embraced by the majority of Americans, is up for grabs in the age of Obama.

Marriage is the foundation of the family, and contrary to President Obama's suggestions, it predates both religion and the state. There are fringe elements bent on trying to turn marriage into a right. But it is not a right. Rather it is a privilege conferred by society upon one man and one woman for the furtherance of the society itself. Marriage exists, primarily, to produce and nurture children. A June 2002 Child Trends study puts it best: "Research clearly demonstrates that family structure matters for children, and the family structure that helps children the most is a family headed by two biological parents in a low-conflict marriage."

---

## THE DIARY OF PRESIDENT BARACK OBAMA

### THE WHITE HOUSE

*October 8, 2009*

This marriage debate is so divisive. Favreau and I were working on this Human Rights Campaign speech, so we decided to read part of it to Rahm, Gibbs, and some of the staffers last night. A couple of the women didn't like my pointed support for gay marriage in the talk. One of the ladies thought I was "flip-flopping on my stated position." I don't think Rahm

appreciated her candor. He jumped up from the couch, called
the woman a "bigoted f*#@ing whore," and stomped out of the
Oval. He's got to switch to decaf.

I can't understand why everyone gets so emotional over this
issue. I mean, I didn't exactly have a traditional Ward and June
Cleaver, Mitt and Ann Romney scene at my house—and look
how I turned out. The most admired man in America two years in
a row! Just ask Gallup.

This morning in the gym, Will & Grace was on TV and Reggie
pointed out that two men could have a relationship just as
strong as any between a man and a woman. There might be
something there. Even after that tiger attack, Siegfried and
Roy are still together. I told Desiree at lunch, the next time we
have a gay event in the East Room, we should invite couples:
Dolce & Gabbana, Mary Chapin & Carpenter, & Rosie & whoever
she's seeing these days . . .

---

In the end, President Obama will be judged not by the image of family
he portrays on magazine covers, but by the policies advocated and enacted
during his term in office. He has within him the possibility of being an incredible role model for fathers and a true advocate for families. But his credibility is damaged by the inconsistency of his policies and the horrendous
effects they are already having on American families. Ultimately, no matter
what the government does, the responsibility to strengthen the family rests
with each of us.

## THE WINNING WAY

Here are some recommendations that might help insulate your family from today's prevailing cultural and political winds:

At dinnertime, my friends Raymond and Rebecca discuss news of the day with their children. They read clippings from the paper, show the family images that relate to the story, and have a spirited discussion. It's a good idea—a way to help children put world events in context, and an opportunity for you to impart your worldview to your family. If you don't form your family's understanding of the issues facing them, someone else will. Best to get your ideas out there early and often.

How we treat one another in our family will inevitably make its way out into society. To keep families strong we have to understand roles and see the goodness that is worth preserving. A dear friend of mine, Pat, always says, "The way you treat your wife at home teaches boys how to treat women." The same is true for the way a wife treats her husband. The girls are watching, too. Modeling good behavior and reinforcing the positive roles within the family creates a living memory that will endure. Don't just tell your children that family is important; show them in ways large and small. Unlike Michelle Obama, try not to undercut your spouse in front of the family or in public. You are the protector (or destroyer) of your children's virtue and the principal architect of their families. They will repeat for decades to come what they see from you.

Don Corleone was right. At one point in *The Godfather,* the don advises a loose-lipped family member, "What's the matter with you? I think your brain is going soft. . . . Never tell anyone outside the Family what you are thinking again." We should all listen to the don and teach the next generation discretion and a sense of modesty. Every family has its difficulties and its failings, but that is no reason to broadcast it to everyone you know. Don't enshrine your family secrets on a blog, and please spare us the endless Facebook updates on your toddler's potty training! Establish rules of discretion and modesty that everyone in the family is obligated to maintain. Too many young reputations have already been harmed by careless images and gossip passed along to the wrong parties. Please, keep it in the family!

Support public policy organizations, politicians, and individuals who are committed to the true prosperity of the family, and give them your support. Beware of politicians who invoke "the children" or "the family"—using them as little more than props. All too often these pols are the ones advocating policies that sap the family of true liberty and limit the freedom of the children they claim to be protecting.

Think about ways that you can help other families in your immediate vicinity. It may be a family in your neighborhood or at church experiencing a health crisis or a job loss. My friend Wendy Long, who has two small children of her own, goes out of her way to help a mother of eight receive the proper lung cancer treatment. Reach out to single people or the widowed, who might not have a place to go on the holidays. This kind of personal, sacrificial concern for others will enrich your family. It will also show young family members the quality of selflessness, which is a wonderful trait to carry into adulthood. (And frankly, something that I need to do a better job of fostering in myself!)

Look around—you will see countless examples of people who go above and beyond to help other families in need. I think of Peggy Hartshorn, who took her outrage and shock over *Roe v. Wade* and turned it into something profoundly positive. As president of Heartbeat International, she has grown this pro-life ministry into a global phenomenon. It has 1,100 affiliates in forty-three countries helping an estimated two million women annually. Heartbeat gives women the option of choosing life for their unborn child by offering complete information and caring support. Now that is truly "pro-family."

But you do not have to run a global charitable effort to make a lasting impact in the most important family of all—your own. Unlike the Obamas, you won't get adoring press coverage when you spend quality time with your children. You do it because you know that the values you instill in them today will serve them well throughout their adult years. Something as simple as reading together after dinner—a "family book club"—will resonate with your children years after they leave the nest. My friend Stephen Vaughn chooses books important to our American heritage—chronicles of great battles and personal courage. Sharing books that reflect your own family's values and interests is a great way to keep connected with your children, and keep them away from the video screens. With younger children, you can read the books aloud. As they get older, everyone can read chapters alone and then discuss as a group.

My great hope is that by the time I shuffle off this earth, I will have left my children with a strong faith, a solid character, and a love of learning. In a world that bombards them with sexualized and violent content 24/7, we as adults must work overtime to fill them up with so much of the "good stuff" that they really have little desire (or time) for the bad stuff.

# CHAPTER 3

# RAZZLE-DAZZLING US TO DEATH

*We have the best brand on earth: the Obama brand. Our possibilities are endless.*

— Desiree Rogers, White House social secretary (retired)

Even if she wasn't humble, at least Desiree Rogers, the Obamas' former White House social secretary, was honest in her appraisal of how this White House and its occupants see themselves. From the very beginning, Barack and Michelle Obama were not merely exposing the public to their individual gifts and ideas, but also marketing a carefully managed brand to the nation and the globe. Rogers described the White House as the "crown jewel" of this relentless campaign to win hearts and minds.

The Obama brand, like any brand, must be constantly reinforced and shaped to keep the public coming back for more. Just as Steve Jobs is constantly innovating to sell all things Apple, so too is the marketing machine that has been pushing the Obama narrative for years. Since the appearance of the Obama logo during the campaign—the blue O riding on a wave of red and white stripes—it was clear that these people wanted to set themselves apart as unique, iconic, and of course historic. Nothing they did would be like anything that preceded it. Through signs, gestures, costumes, and stagecraft, this new political force intended to one-up Camelot by cultivating a level of media and public adoration that would exceed that of any American president who came before.

During his election night victory speech, President-elect Obama looked out at the sea of hopeful humanity gathered in Chicago's Grant Park and boldly announced: "Our union can be perfected." Of course, what he meant was that there was hope for American perfection now that *he* was in charge. The "perfect union" of Barack and Michelle could assist the rest of us poor schlubs in reaching our utopia, too. Lord knows how the country even made it this far without the O-factor.

Central to Obama's governing strategy would be his aggressive—and often brilliant—cultivation of his own pop star status. Being a garden-variety political star just wouldn't do. How many world leaders can boast being commemorated in a Spider-Man comic book and as a Chia Pet all in one year? And what American president still had worship altars displaying his books in airport bookstores when his approval ratings were at all-time lows?

One has to marvel at the scope and the breadth of the nonstop, multi-media marketing offensive waged by the Obamas and their communications team. How did a guy who came from nowhere, with no executive experience and no meaningful private sector bona fides, come to run the largest economy and military in the world? Circumstances certainly contributed: the meltdown of the economy, the nation's growing Bush fatigue. But at the heart of the Obama ascension was a well-oiled PR machine that ruthlessly controlled not only the message, but also the backdrop, clothing, music, staging, and every word that escaped the candidate's lips. Even traditionally private activities for First Families—weekend recreation or holidays—were not immune from being used to hone Brand Obama. And while a disciplined press and marketing operation is essential to any successful political campaign, at some point the marketing has to end and the governing has to begin. Not so with the Obamas, who have given new meaning to the phrase "perpetual campaign" by elevating press manipulation and image control to something approaching an Olympic sport.

I remember being at the 2008 Democratic National Convention in Denver when the media were buzzing that Barack Obama would not accept his party's nomination in the twenty-thousand seat Pepsi Center (which had hosted the entirety of the convention up until that point). Twenty thousand seats? Are you kidding? Obama needed something bigger, bolder, and more impressive. Barack Obama's acceptance speech would be moved to nearby Invesco Field, an eighty-thousand seat open-air stadium and home to the Denver Broncos.

---

## THE DIARY OF SENATOR BARACK OBAMA

### DENVER, COLORADO

August 27, 2008

No time to write today with all the parties, toasts, and Hollywood folks here who want to bask in the glow of "O"! Still can't believe that the DNC originally had me accepting my party's nomination at that puny Pepsi Center! Please! I mean, it was fine tonight for Biden's speech (snoozefest!) and it was okay for the likes of Clinton and Gore (yesterday's news!). But with me we're talking about something truly historic! If John Lennon and George Harrison came back from the dead for a Beatles reunion, do you think they'd be playing to a piddly 20,000 people?

And to hell with those folks who are complaining about the cost. Fund-raising breakfast with Hillary: $1,000. A haircut at John Edwards' salon: $500. Seeing me on stage embrace my destiny before a global audience? Priceless!

The day before the Obama coronation, I needed a song to capture the spectacle that was about to unfold. My pal Raymond Arroyo suggested "Razzle Dazzle" from the Broadway show *Chicago*. It was perfect. The lyrics—"Give 'em the old razzle dazzle . . . razzle dazzle 'em"—described precisely what Team Obama had planned for us. In *Chicago*, the defense attorney Billy Flynn, in song, counsels a client charged with murder on the way to get around the jury. His advice is to "razzle dazzle" the crowd, daze and confuse them with so much glitz and hokum that they allow the murderer to walk. So too for Barack Obama, whose PR team believed that an over-the-top political spectacular would overwhelm the national audience to such an extent that they would ignore the tell-tale signs of his radical policies to come.

The stagecraft used that balmy night in Denver established the tone for all the Razzle Dazzles to come. Some in the British press dubbed it "the Barakopolis": a plaster and plywood masterpiece meant to evoke the Lincoln Memorial, the Parthenon, and the White House all in one backdrop. It was constructed by the same people responsible for Britney Spears' concert stages—experts at creating diversions for those with limited talents. The set was meant to create a feeling of intimacy in the sprawling arena and to convey a few other messages. Christopher Hawthorne of the *Los Angeles Times* described the set: "Obama's campaign produced a full-on neoclassical facade: four imposing Doric columns and ten sizable pilasters all connected by a frieze and arranged in a gently curving arc. From the center of this colonnaded contraption extended a long peninsular walkway, lined with blue carpeting and capped by a circular stage and wedding cake steps." Michelle, Sasha, and Malia would emerge from huge false windows "clearly meant to suggest those at 1600 Pennsylvania Avenue. They were warmly illuminated, suggesting that a family was at home—Obama's." We should be suspicious of any candidate needing this much artistic reinforcement.

*Rocky Mountain News* columnist Mike Littwin had no such reservations. He enthused: "Obama, standing before tens of thousands of people . . . joined under a Rocky Mountain sky, where possibilities seem as endless and luminous as the many Bronco's skyboxes shining from above." And that was written *before* Obama had uttered a word. Behold the power of the Razzle Dazzle. All hail the Emperor of Hope and Change!

To prepare the way for the Messiah, there was enough entertainment for four Super Bowl halftime shows: Sheryl Crow, Stevie Wonder, will.i.am, John Legend, Jennifer Hudson, and Michael McDonald all whipped up the crowd before Obama took the stage. Of course, he started his speech by reveling in his favorite subject—himself. Then it was the usual references to the "failed presidency of George W. Bush," telling the enthralled masses: "America, we are better than these last eight years. We are a better country than this." This from a man with virtually no real-world experience to qualify him for the most important job in the world.

During Obama's rhetorical exercise in breathtaking narcissism and historical revisionism, the media treated the television audience with frequent cutaways of weeping girls and mesmerized young men. These were the loyal O-subjects who had waited for hours to see their king. The congregants of the Church of Obama offered testimonies to their faith. "I cried my eyelashes off," Oprah Winfrey attested. "I think it's the most powerful thing I have ever experienced." "It was amazing," exclaimed the "performer" Fergie of Black Eyed Peas fame. And that renowned philosopher, actress Jessica Alba, expressed her sentiment in words that will be oft quoted and remembered. "Incredible!" she gurgled.

The Mile-High Razzle Dazzle had news anchors combing their thesauruses for new honorifics to sustain the interest of forty million viewers who were watching on television. Yes, Barack Obama was the first African-American to accept a major party's nomination for president, but restating that fact only takes the marketing so far. The $3 million extravaganza—an Obamapalooza for the ages—was absolutely essential in the overall battle plan, which was to distract voters and divert their attention from the hard truth that they were on the verge of electing the most inexperienced and one of the most left-wing people ever to have run for the presidency. How did Barry Obama go from passing out leaflets on a Chicago street corner to standing a few feet away from the nuclear football? Sheer Razzle Dazzle, baby. And this was only the beginning.

One of the chief architects of the Obama public relations blitz was

Desiree Rogers. A native New Orleanian and descendant of the voodoo queen Marie Laveau, the Chicago socialite was a close friend of the Obamas and a fund-raiser. She also enjoyed an intimate friendship with Valerie Jarrett, the president's senior advisor. Rogers was named Social Secretary and Special Assistant to the president, with privileges in the East and West Wings of the White House. More than a party or event planner, Desiree Rogers saw herself as a brand manager, a visionary executive on site to "promote the Obama presidency." She made herself indispensible to the political and policy wing of the Obama White House and was only too happy to advertise her ingenuity on the pages of *Vogue,* the *Wall Street Journal Magazine,* and *Capitol File.* Of her Razzle Dazzle, Rogers said, "We are trying to do different types of things that can leave imprints in people's minds and show them that we can be the best with some of the simplest things." By "simple," she meant, of course, selling Brand Obama by enlisting the full force of the East and West Wing staff along with a parade of visiting Hollywood celebrities.

---

## THE DIARY OF WHITE HOUSE SOCIAL SECRETARY
## DESIREE GLAPION ROGERS

### EAST WING

*January 19, 2009*

*The People's House. That's what I've convinced Miche to call the White House. And I will be its custodian, so help me God. With its whitewashed elegance and stately manner, this home will bear witness to some of the most notable events in America's history—I am the maker of that history.*

Each time I walk up the drive, I can almost hear the limestone whisper, "Thank you, Miss D. Thank you." It's a wonder that this house survived those Bushes! I told the staff today: if I ever see Lee Greenwood or Charlie Daniels on an entertainment request sheet, expect the pink slips to start flying.

We are going to make this truly the People's House—at least for the people we know! Ha-ha. Oh, we'll let the average citizens roam around the property, and the president and First Lady have agreed to surprise the tourists once a year. (Miche and I spent half a day in the White House screening room, rolling on the floor watching footage of those slovenly tourists gasping and giggling when they realized the Obamas were there to personally greet them in the Blue Room. One man actually started to brush his teeth as he approached them. Lord, it's like our own West Wing version of Candid Camera.)

My mission is to return a sense of art and elegance to this house not seen since the days of Jackie Kennedy. Of course, we'll put her amateur efforts to shame because we actually know how to have fun. Our Easter Egg Roll is going to be fantastic this year—and historic. Fergie just agreed to sing at the Egg Roll, and Miche and I are going to totally revamp how the staid program is usually done. Peeps *and jelly beans are out this Easter—yoga and cooking demonstrations are in. That's what children need to learn at Easter anyhow: how to move their bodies and cook healthy meals. We're also going to have our own high-octane sports competition. I bet we can sell it as an exclusive to the Disney Channel: "The White House Easter Games, live from the South Lawn—here is your host Desiree Rogers . . ." The staff tells me we must have an Easter Bunny; it's tradition. But given our health-conscious theme, I think I'll ask Taylor Lautner from Twilight to be the bunny—and just wear the furry head without a shirt. I mean, the men have that tramp Fergie. We mothers need something to look at, too!*

## BIPARTISAN RAZZLE

It began, like most parties, with cocktails. Obama tried to turn the White House to his advantage early on by hosting a series of bipartisan Wednesday night cocktail hours. These were designed to soften up resistance to his policies and build personal relationships between ideological foes. Friends of the Obamas told Politico that Desiree Rogers was the perfect person to "replicate the same kind of environment" that Michelle and Barack had enjoyed in Chicago.

Only days after taking office, the Obamas hosted an informal, bipartisan Super Bowl party. They passed around cookies, shared hot dogs and pizza, and watched then-Republican senator Arlen Specter wrestle the popcorn bowl from fellow squish Republican representative Charlie Dent in the

White House screening room. (Does a Super Bowl get-together attended by Arlen Specter and D.C. congresswoman Eleanor Holmes Norton actually qualify as a "party," let alone a bipartisan one?)

Republican Trent Franks of Arizona said of the affair: "I think the value of social interaction like this is not so much that it co-opts anyone in any way. It certainly didn't in my case. I think it humanizes and personalizes opponents. We can diminish politics and try to work together for what's right for the country."

This demonstrates the danger of getting sucked into the Razzle Dazzle for even a moment. No doubt Congressman Franks soon saw the light. But for a Republican to believe that Barack Obama's goal is to "work with Republicans" to do "what is right for the country" demonstrates staggering ignorance. Despite the temporary spell cast on some of the participants, Obama's charm offensive did nothing to gain any meaningful bipartisan support for his major initiatives. In the end, Obama's $800 billion stimulus bill was only supported by three "Republicans"—the trio I called, "Spe-col-snow" (pronounced "Specklesnow")—the soon-to-be Democrat Arlen Specter and the two Maine senators, Susan Collins and Olympia Snowe. These votes gave the Senate Democrats and the White House the filibuster-proof cushion it needed in the final 60–38 vote.

Following the first six or seven Wednesday night mixers, the White House stopped hosting the parties—no doubt due to their ineffectiveness. Plus, when you can kick back with the likes of George Clooney and Brad Pitt, why bother schmoozing with conservative Republicans, the lowest figures on the celebrity food chain?

---

# THE DIARY OF FIRST LADY MICHELLE OBAMA

### THE WHITE HOUSE

February 26, 2009

Exhausting day as usual, working on the details of our next Wednesday night cocktail party. Barack loved our Stevie Wonder event the other night. He even mentioned that Stevie's music was the "essence of our courtship." Unfortunately, he said the same damn thing to Earth, Wind & Fire on Sunday night. Axe has to whip that speechwriting department into shape—they have got to start writing some new lines for this man!

We are putting together an amazing lineup of performers to entertain us throughout the year. Desiree has been terrific at spinning these weekly command performances as part of our effort to make this "The People's House." That is, if the people happen to live at the Kennedy Center! Politico, the Washington Post, and now the AP have their own puff pieces: "Obama kicks up White House entertaining." Obama?! Do they think he plans these shindigs?! Never mind. Desiree will fix that in the next article.

They tell me that right-wing radio is calling our events "inappropriate" given the economy and all. The nerve! Are those people giving up their fat steaks and wine cellars in order to better commiserate with the average folks?! Besides, we are working our fingers to the bone here and deserve to kick up our heels when we damn well feel like it. Is Joe Blow in Columbus who lost his job on an assembly line going to feel better if we just sit around the White House and turn all the lights off? I don't think so.

Axelrod wanted to see Tony Bennett, so we worked him into the Stevie Wonder event. Rahm keeps asking about the Bolshoi Ballet (maybe we can book them for May Day or something). And Valerie wants me to invite the First Lady of Soul in for a concert (I'm thinking we'll lure her with a Kennedy Center honor or the Gershwin Award next year). As a surprise for Desiree, I'm going to extend an invitation to Wynton Marsalis and maybe his father, the piano player, to perform for us. They're from New Orleans, so I know she'll enjoy that. Now Sasha's asking if the Wiggles can come in for a show. I think I'll book those Aussies when I'm away on one of my anti-obesity trips. All those bouncy, kiddy pop beats make me ill.

---

## DAZZLING DINNERS

Some of the Republican governors attending the first big postinaugural evening soiree were harsh critics of the president's boondoggle stimulus plan, going so far as to refuse to accept the funds. But the Obamas had a trick up their sleeves: Earth, Wind & Fire. Reportedly one of Desiree Rogers's favorites, the '70s mega-hit band was booked to perform at the

February 2009 White House Governors' Dinner. Given the political tensions of the moment, Earth, Wind & Fire was more than the evening's
entertainment. Desiree Rogers hoped the group would help set the mood,
help break the ice, and help woo the unwooable. After all, "Shining Star"
could be the Obamas' theme song.

Before the governors noshed on Maryland crab and Nantucket scallops,
the president announced that this first event was a "great kickoff of what we
hope will be an atmosphere here in the White House that reminds everybody that this is the people's house." After dinner, the governors were led to
the East Room, where the social secretary's office had erected a dance floor
for the 130 guests. The six tables around the dance floor were clogged with
Obama staffers, forcing the governors onto the dance area. Rogers and company thought they could sway the political intransigents by literally forcing
them to sway to the music. By the time the first strains of "Boogie Won-
derland" began to sound, the governors had formed a conga line. (To this
day I am haunted by a disturbing vision of Bobby Jindal and Tim Pawlenty
busting a conga move.) But group dancing will only get you so far, and the
limits of socializing soon became painfully clear. Hours of the Electric Slide,
disco dancing, and the Hustle, and what did the Hustler-in-Chief have to
show for it? Not a single Republican governor; the president failed to win
over even one convert to his big-government spending plans. But at least
now everyone knows that Governor Bill Richardson can out-twist Chubby
Checker.

Fast-forward to November 2009, when the White House hosted its first
state dinner for India's prime minister. It was a spectacular affair, produced
within an inch of its life. It was to be so special, so groundbreaking, that
even the White House executive chef Cristeta Comerford had to step aside.
She was deemed unfit to prepare food for the head of state of this key American ally. So Chef Marcus Samuelsson of the restaurant Aquavit in New
York was brought in to create a mostly vegetarian menu, showcasing some
of the treasures of Michelle Obama's vegetable garden. Samuelsson had the
distinction of being the first guest chef in history to cook for a White House
state dinner. No expense was spared outside the kitchen, either. Desiree
Rogers erected a bulletproof tent capable of seating four hundred guests,

outfitted with dangling chandeliers and magnolia branches lining the walls. Jennifer Hudson and A. R. Rahman, of *Slumdog Millionaire* fame, provided entertainment for a guest list that included Steven Spielberg, David Geffen, Katie Couric, and Sanjay Gupta. The Obamas had truly opened the White House to the people . . . even those without invitations.

The immediate criticism of the lavish White House partying raised concerns about taste and sensitivity. Sure, Desiree had whipped up a hip Bollywood party, but was it appropriate during an economic downturn? Desiree Rogers told *Capitol File*, "*Laissez les bon temps rouler* [let the good times roll]. It's been part of my life all along, that it's extremely important that our lives are celebratory, that we do have joy in our lives. And I think it's particularly important as all of us go through difficult times." So feel better, out-of-work Americans! The people in the "People's House" are having a grand time for you.

## MENTORING WITH THE STARS

The Obamas owe much of their success to the celebrities who are forever rubbing elbows with them. Whether on the campaign trail or in the White House, wherever the Obamas are, some celebrity is certain to be within reach. The image of these stars fraternizing with the president and his staff telegraph dual messages: 1) The Obamas are cool like us. 2) You love us and we love them—so you should love them, too.

Walking through the White House on certain days can be like walking through Madame Tussauds. You'll find more celebrities in the West Wing than at a *Vanity Fair* Oscar party.

Most of the time, Barack and Michelle Obama operate as First Fans, booking favorite actors and musicians to "play the East Room." One of the first acts to perform for the Obamas was Stevie Wonder. In February 2009, he was presented with a Gershwin Prize by the president. The Obamas sounded like groupies throughout the event, and in what would become their pattern, managed to use Stevie Wonder's music to draw attention to themselves.

Michelle regaled the crowd with the story of being introduced to

Wonder's music by her grandfather. Later she said that she had "discovered what Stevie meant when he sang about love. Barack and I chose the song 'You and I' as our wedding song." The president paid the singer even greater tribute when he said Wonder's songs were "the soundtrack of my youth . . . I think it's fair to say that had I not been a Stevie Wonder fan, Michelle might not have dated me. We might not have married. The fact that we agreed on Stevie was part of the essence of our courtship."

Except for Stevie Wonder, none of this historic magnificence would have been possible.

Wonder was the first in a long line of celebrities encouraged to perform for invited guests and offer workshops to the young at the White House. This allowed the stars to feel as if they were giving back to the community, while Michelle and Barack squeezed intimate concerts out of them for free. Even ex-Beatle Paul McCartney couldn't escape the long arm of the Obamas' Razzle Dazzle. On June 2, 2010, McCartney performed in the East Room and all he got for it was a Gershwin Prize. This was all fitting since McCartney penned the Obama immigration theme song, "Let 'Em In."

The "Poetry Slam" was an odd evening by any standard. James Earl Jones recited a selection from *Othello*, and then Lin-Manuel Miranda, the rapper and composer of the Broadway show *In the Heights*, performed an original rap on the life of Alexander Hamilton. He intoned: "How does a bastard orphan son of a whore and a Scotsman dropped in the middle of a forgotten spot in the Caribbean rise to prominence?" The president must have loved hearing that reflection.

Jazz was celebrated at the White House in June 2009. Once again, Michelle introduced the performers by referencing a personal story. She spoke of her father, who played jazz loudly around their house, and added, "So it means so much to me to bring this music here to the White House."

Listening to Michelle, you'd never know that Dizzy Gillespie, Pearl Bailey, Eubie Blake, Charles Mingus, Joe Williams, Frank Sinatra, and Wynton Marsalis (whom the Obamas brought in for their jazz night) had all performed at the White House at the invitation of former presidents. Perhaps their fathers did not play the jazz as loudly as Michelle's.

There would be celebrations of country music, Latino music (which required the erection of a tent on the South Lawn), classical music, and music from the civil rights era, complete with Joan Baez and Bob Dylan. Even Easter became an occasion to book big-name talent. Fergie sang at their first Easter Egg Roll and the cast of Fox's hit show *Glee* performed in 2010. Few acts escaped the Obama parlor, and if the celebs weren't performing, they were drafted into Michelle's mentoring program.

Starting in March 2009, Michelle Obama hosted the first in a series of mentoring events: a chance for girls to mix and mingle with successful women in government and the private sector. Alicia Keys, Sheryl Crow, and Olympic medalist Dominique Dawes attended the first dinner. Hang around enough high-powered celebrities and you start to look like one—at least that's what the White House press machine was hoping. After she hosted exactly one mentoring dinner, *Glamour* magazine awarded the First Lady "special recognition . . . for her commitment to mentoring young women," according to Lynn Sweet at the *Chicago Sun-Times*. Michelle also appeared on the magazine's cover.

In the ensuing months, Michelle Obama would show up at schools and special mentoring dinners with Fran Drescher, Susan Sarandon, Alfie Woodard, and others. The generosity and concern of the Razzle Dazzle never ends.

---

## THE DIARY OF FIRST LADY MICHELLE OBAMA

### THE WHITE HOUSE

*March 19, 2009*

*Another nonstop day. My feet are killing me! I was up late shooting the breeze with Sheryl Crow and Alicia Keys, who came into town to help me with a White House dinner for 110 young women students from D.C. schools. I like Alicia but could've done without Sheryl Crow—as if the fourteen-year-olds in Northeast are sitting around rocking out to "If It Makes You Happy" on their iPods! Please. Still, Desiree reminded me that Sheryl showed up to sing in Denver and at the Lincoln Memorial concert during the Inauguration. (will.i.am should've dropped her from that duet of "One Love"!) Desiree also pointed out that since Stevie Wonder and Sweet Honey in the Rock had already performed here, we needed Sheryl for "diversity purposes." I guess it's fine and the staff says it's good for my image. But how do they expect me to dance to "All I Wanna Do"? At what point can we stop trying to "soften my image" and just let me start being myself again?!*

---

This White House is so star-crazed, it cast an actor as the associate director in the Office of Public Liaison. Kal Penn, the actor best known as Kumar in the *Harold & Kumar* movies and for his role on the hit Fox show *House*, took a break from acting to play the part of a West Wing apparatchik for the Obamas. According to the *Los Angeles Times*, Penn's job is to provide "outreach to young people, the artistic community, and the Asian-American community." As if the Obamas need help reaching out to the "artistic community." Half of the community is being commanded to perform for them!

George Clooney, the Academy Award–winning liberal, met with the president and vice president in February 2009. Given the extensive coverage, it was as if the Chinese president had come to forgive the U.S. debt. Clooney's mission was to ensure that Darfur was a priority for the administration. During the meeting, Obama promised to appoint an envoy to Darfur, who would report directly to the White House. Good night and good luck.

Clooney's *Ocean's Eleven* costar, Brad Pitt, blew into Washington a month later and tried to turn his "Make it Right NOLA" foundation into a model for the nation. The foundation builds cheap, green housing in Katrina-ravaged sections of New Orleans. Pitt met with Speaker Nancy Pelosi and Majority Leader Harry Reid before being invited to the White House for a sit-down with the Big Man and the Big Mouth.

---

## THE DIARY OF VICE PRESIDENT JOE BIDEN

### U.S. NAVAL OBSERVATORY

February 22, 2010

Shakira . . . Shakira . . . it's true, her hips don't lie! Today that Colombian songbird stopped by the Oval to say hello to Barack and me. She was on the Hill pushing education in the developing world. (And boy is she developed!)

Poor thing had to spend the morning in the company of Nita Lowey (I guess we all have to do penance from time to time). This gal was a knockout. If I were four or five years younger . . . I frankly couldn't take my eyes off her, but Barack was all business. He was talking Shakira's ear off about promoting his immigration reform bill later this year.

Honestly, if they all looked like this hot tamale, I'd tear down the border fence myself.

---

For too many Hollywood stars, this kind of social activism is a fun sideline—a chance to gain access to the most powerful man in the world and come away feeling like the most important person in town. Others are simply looking for a few snapshots they can later post on Facebook.

Rap mogul and Obama booster Jay-Z and his megastar wife Beyoncé dropped by the White House in March 2010. Like other high-flying celebs, when they land in D.C., they expect to see the man in charge. Truth is, Jay-Z had some time on his hands before a concert and decided to make the most of it. The Jay-Z posse got an all-access pass to the West Wing, including access to the Situation Room.

Looking at the posted photographs, Jay-Z and Beyoncé could be auditioning to be the Obamas' understudies. Perhaps during the next foreign trip, they could house-sit for Barack and Michelle—or perhaps play them in a BET made-for-television movie. One thing is certain: the White House is always open to Jay-Z and his wife. Any star can worship Obama, but how many have commemorated him in song the way Jay-Z has? Remember his famous remix of "My President Is Black"? Who can forget the poetic line "No more war, no more Iraq, no more white lies, the president is Black."

For celebrities, the Obamas represent a possible dream. No matter their background, no matter their experience, Obama showed them that anyone with a little star power, some style, and a few designer duds could run the country. In turn, the president needs the stars to give him street cred, connect him to the pop culture, and provide White House Razzle Dazzle on demand.

President Obama showed his affection for Hollywood at a revealing, splashy fund-raiser on May 27, 2009. According to the *Los Angeles Times*, Steven Spielberg, Jeffrey Katzenberg, Seth Rogen, Kiefer Sutherland, Ron

Howard, Jamie Foxx, Antonio Banderas, Melanie Griffith, and more than two hundred other glitterati crowded into the Beverly Hilton to pay homage to the One. Katzenberg introduced the president in worshipful tones usually reserved for religious leaders: "If you look in the dictionary under 'grace under fire,' it will say Barack Obama."

When Obama reached the podium, he gushed to Katzenberg, "If it weren't for you, we would not be in the White House."

## THE GARDEN OF PLENTY . . . STORIES

On March 20, 2009, Michelle Obama, in designer boots and black stretch pants, surrounded by legions of public school children, broke ground on what would become the mother of all Razzle Dazzles—that 1,100 square-foot horticultural hamlet of hype: the White House vegetable garden. This could well be the most discussed garden since Eden—and one thing is for sure: it is anything but secret.

"The whole point of this garden for us is that I want to make sure that our family, as well as the staff, and all the people who come to the White House and eat our food, get access to really fresh vegetables and fruits," Michelle Obama told the *Wall Street Journal* the day she broke ground for her crop.

Consistent with her vision that she must model behavior for all of America, Michelle Obama insisted that children should eat more organic foods, and that families should strive to make them more available. When asked by the media to explain her foray into gardening, she conveniently turned to her daughters Malia and Sasha for cover. She told the *New York Times* on March 19, 2009, that the idea for the garden "came from her experiences as a working mother trying to feed her daughters, Malia and Sasha, a good diet.

"I wanted to be able to bring what I learned to a broader base of people," Michelle explained. "And what better way to do it than to plant a vegetable garden in the South Lawn of the White House?"

When I first heard Michelle talk about the garden, it was clear to me where she was headed. The fertile patch on the South Lawn was intended to grow into the First Lady's personal public policy platform—a feel-good, picture-ready project that would help position herself as a policy advocate. Michelle's policy advisor, Jocelyn Frye, told reporters following the ground-breaking that the garden fit into the First Lady's overall health message. Frye added: "She and the president thought hard about it." I bet they did.

---

## THE DIARY OF FIRST LADY MICHELLE OBAMA

### THE WHITE HOUSE

*January 23, 2009*

*Desiree, Jocelyn, and I spoke with my old boss at the University of Chicago Medical Center, Susan Sher. Susan always has the best ideas. She thinks I need to do something bold that gets me into the policy game, early on. No literacy campaigns for me. I'll be damned if all this fabulosity is going to go to waste reading Dr. Seuss to snot-nosed kids all day. I know I'm supposed to be the Mom-in-Chief, but I gave at the office . . . I've got important work to do for America.*

*As we were talking, I gazed out of Desiree's window and it hit me: a garden. I'll launch my own vegetable garden! I'll leave my stamp on the White House and generate some good publicity at the same time. Desiree and Katie (my press secretary) think if we can scare up some poor kids to pick at the dirt, we could land the* cover of the <u>New York Times</u>. I'll be kind of a fashionable, toned, and tall Mother Teresa with a rake.

Susan had the best idea of the day. She said we should use the garden to establish me as a children's health advocate. It's a great touchy-feely issue for me to hit before moving on to my formal health-care role once the reform bill passes. That Susan is a winner! Maybe I should bring her on as my Chief of Staff. Hmmm . . .

The only problem is planting the damn thing. I don't know squat about gardening and I don't care to learn. I sprung the plan on Barack tonight. He was a little reluctant at first, but I wore him down until he saw things my way. I told him that since the White House is a national landmark, the Park Service should plant my garden for me. Smokey agreed. I mean the American people should have a garden that they can be proud of. It's going to be great. Desiree's already selecting my outfits for the first garden photo shoot. I told her I'm game for anything except gardening clogs and sunhats.

---

Michelle Obama never gardened in her life, nor did she have a garden in Chicago. But in Obamaland, experience need never be an obstacle to political advancement (just ask the president). Michelle found others to do the heavy lifting while she took all the credit.

We've all seen the pictures on the nightly news and in the magazines: the Bancroft Elementary School children digging in the garden with the

First Lady. They moved some dirt around, dropped a few seeds here and there, and jubilated as Michelle led the merry band. The raw feed of the event was something to see:

MICHELLE   Let's hear it for the fruits!
CHILDREN   Yay. (unenthusiastic)
MICHELLE   Let's hear it for the vegetables!
CHILDREN   Yay. (still unenthusiastic) Boo! (sheepish)
[The First Lady scans the faces of the children all around her, looking for the Tea Party offspring in her midst.]
MICHELLE   Who said "boo"? I'm going to take away your shovel cookie.

That's right, the woman who continues to lecture the entire country about healthy eating habits (while filling her pie hole with ribs, burgers, and fries) served designer cookies to the children who helped plant the garden of health and fitness! Anytime you gaze intently upon the Obamas' Razzle Dazzle, the hypocrisy moves to the fore—so do the lies.

With Michelle's green advocacy, the garden has been sold as "organic" and portrayed that way in the media. Multiple reports describe it as such. But the First Lady's office quietly admitted to Reuters's David Alexander on June 2, 2009, that it "has never made [the organic] claim. It takes three years to certify an organic garden, with different standards applying," they conceded.

Based on the press coverage, one would assume that Michelle, the First Family, and twenty-five public school children planted the garden and would maintain it themselves. The First Lady herself even told the press that her family would be weeding the garden "whether they like it or not."

But anyone watching the White House's own online video, "Inside the White House: The Garden," can see that it was actually National Park Service employees who, using heavy equipment, tilled the soil, seeded the South Lawn plot, and "assisted" the Bancroft kids in planting the garden. What the video makes plain is that the children did not plant seeds, but fully grown blooms in most cases. To my eye, the garden was not planted, so much as replanted.

---

## THE DIARY OF FIRST GRANDMOTHER MARIAN ROBINSON

### THE WHITE HOUSE

October 29, 2009

Up again at 4:43 a.m.! With all this noise, how is a person supposed to sleep? It's that big dump truck the Park Service brings in every other day. When they back that mother up, it beeps—loudly! This morning I had enough. I threw my robe on and went outside. The Secret Service stopped me at the back door. "You should stay in the house, Mrs. Robinson," the agent said.

"You stay in the house. I got business in the yard, young man," I told him. "You best get out of my way"—and he moved. The agent followed me out to Miche's garden—and what a shock I got there.

I was wondering how that garden grew so quickly. I mean, they pull wheelbarrows full of vegetables out of that patch almost every day. Now I know where all the produce comes from.

When I went to complain to the truck driver about the noise, I looked to my right and there were all these people out in the garden—dozens of Park Service workers bent over their hoes in the dark. Let me tell you, they froze when they saw me. And in the back of the truck: vegetable containers stacked to the roof! And these vegetables were <u>huge</u>! Tomatoes like basketballs! Potatoes, big as Robert Gibbs's backside. They must do this every week, right before they bring in another group of public school children to "harvest" Miche's garden. Those poor children will get hernias trying to pull those gargantuan veggies out of the dirt. If they're smart they'll make the fat ones carry the produce. Though if Miche has her way, cutting out calories and fats, they'll all be rail thin!

Who knows, maybe this will create another national security crisis for her to cure. I can hear her now: "Save the children's backs!" "Let's Move Your Spine!" "We need to protect our children's spinal health!" That girl never could leave well enough alone. Damn, I wish I could get to sleep.

---

It isn't enough to be the most glamorous, smart, wise, and healthy First Lady. Michelle Obama must be first in everything. Even her garden has to be historic. She told CNN's Larry King on February 9, 2010, "As you know, this year I planted this wonderful garden—the first ever White House garden. . . ."

I hope Abigail Adams wasn't listening. Hard as it is to imagine, long before anyone had even thought about Michelle Obama, there were vegetable gardens at the White House. Abigail and John Adams planted the first one in 1800. Andrew Jackson built a hothouse to grow tropical fruit on the site of today's West Wing. Eleanor Roosevelt planted the famous White House Victory Garden. And even Hillary Clinton tended a veggie garden on the roof of the White House. She and Bill had originally wanted to plant vegetables on the property, but were advised that it would destroy the formality of the White House. With a swing set, an expanded basketball court, and Michelle's garden, formality is obviously no longer an issue.

The White House and the First Lady have repeatedly bragged about how inexpensive the vegetable garden was, encouraging citizens to follow their example. They claim that a mere two hundred dollars' worth of seeds produced the never-ending bounty (and never-receding headline). More than a thousand pounds of produce have been yanked from the White House garden in less than a year's time. What a bargain! You could probably plant one on your own lawn—particularly if you have several hundred thousand dollars at your disposal to pay for all the National Park Service employees to maintain the crop, a full-time cook like Sam Kass to oversee it, and a battalion of chefs ready to create whatever organic dish you desire. You might also want to allocate some funds for replacement crops and heavy equipment so the Park Service can keep the garden stocked and looking bountiful. Oh, and if you can bring in some unpaid public school labor, that always helps in a pinch.

Look to your First Lady as an example. She has even turned fieldwork into something chic. Michelle told the *New York Times*: "There's nothing really cooler than coming to the White House and harvesting some of the vegetables, and being in the kitchen with Cris and Sam and Bill, and cutting and cooking and actually experiencing the joys of your work."

Given the resources required to launch Michelle's garden project, media coverage was not left to chance. The *Los Angeles Times* reported that the First Lady's staff struck a deal with the *New York Times*, giving them an exclusive first look at the garden and an interview with Michelle. So in March 2009, as a financial crisis gripped the country, a photo of the First Lady in her garden dominated the front page and heralded the arrival of green Razzle Dazzle. It would spawn hundreds of media stories and create a perfect backdrop for Michelle's "Let's Move" anti-obesity initiative. Something tells me the full harvest of this garden has yet to be tallied.

## The Diary of First Lady Michelle Obama

### The White House

*April 30, 2009*

I am out killing myself: visiting federal agencies, creating event after event in that garden, sweating like a pack mule, doing the hula hoop to promote fitness — and what do I return home to? On the cover of the first <u>Wall Street Journal Magazine,</u> wearing nothing but a black trench coat and a pair of Cartier earrings in all her haughtiness — was <u>Desiree Rogers</u>! Axelrod brought it over to show Barack and me just before dinner. He was very concerned about the impression this could leave with the voters. You'd think the <u>Journal</u> would have the good taste to have one of us on the cover! My breath literally left me when I saw Desiree's face staring up at me from the cover of that magazine.

Who does Ms. Glamorpuss think she is? One minute she's in New York sitting next to Anna Wintour, the next she's going to some MTV dinner representing the White House. Valerie dropped that bomb on me a few days ago. She'd better get back to planning parties and picking my wardrobe or she'll find herself looking for another job. And in this economy, that's going to be rough.

# BO THE WONDER DOG

*That dog is going to be something else. I am not certain what the*
*girls have in mind, but we'll think of something.*
                                    —DESIREE ROGERS, *VOGUE*, FEBRUARY 2009

If there is one story that epitomizes the Razzle Dazzle of the Obama White
House, it is the media frenzy caused by Bo, the First Dog.

During the campaign, Barack Obama promised his daughters that if
he won the White House, he would buy them a dog. This minor political
sidebar became a major story for cable, broadcast news, and serious papers
of record. For months, the media tried to guess which breed of dog the
Obamas might bring to 1600 Pennsylvania Avenue. Then the new president upped the ante by suggesting that it had to be a shelter dog, but one
that didn't exacerbate Malia's allergies. While two wars raged on and the
U.S. economy teetered on the brink of collapse, the U.S. media investigated
hypoallergenic dog breeds and speculated about which one would make the
White House cut.

Politico reported that the *Washington Post* even negotiated exclusive
access to the First Pup with the White House. But they were scooped by
TMZ.com, where photos of the dog were released first. Finally, in April
2009, the Obama family trotted out "Bo," their Portuguese water dog (so
much for a mutt from the shelter), for all the world to see.

This particular story and the way the White House controlled it drew
the attention of the *Los Angeles Times*. In an April 20, 2009 story, it revealed
how the East and West Wings manage stories and dictate terms to the press:

> Administration officials have even weighed the economics of paparazzi
> photography, strategically releasing images of the family to diminish the
> monetary value of unauthorized pictures and give the White House con-
> trol over how the family is portrayed. In return for access, celebrity news
> outlets must refuse to publish unauthorized pictures—or risk being cut
> off by the White House. "If there are no images, then you create a supply-
> and-demand problem where the supply is none and the demand is huge,"

White House Press Secretary Robert Gibbs said. "If there is at least some supply that continues in a way that is respectful to who they are—you drive down the price and the paparazzi is not part of the equation."

With Bo there were no mistakes. The White House planned Bo's coming-out party and the media played along beautifully. The president went so far as to offer evidence that the dog was truly a member of the family. "He's a star, he's got star quality," Obama told the adoring reporters at the party. Over the next few months, media stars from Oprah to Brian Williams were only too happy to pet the First Pooch and pretend that this was all somehow newsworthy. Upon seeing the dog during a Christmas special on ABC, Oprah gushed, "Bo, it's Bo!" And Brian Williams looked as if he had never seen a dog before when the First Lady dragged Bo into the frame of his *Inside the White House* NBC special. Distinguishing just who was the lapdog in the aftermath of these televised encounters is a tall order.

---

## THE DIARY OF PRESIDENT BARACK OBAMA

### THE WHITE HOUSE

April 14, 2009

When you hear that Ted Kennedy's giving you a dog, you envision something regal—majestic. We never imagined that he would bring us a dog that looked worse than its droppings! Apparently he's got several versions of this ugly thing at his own house. There's no accounting for taste, I guess.

Since we couldn't return him (or drop him at the pound), Desiree and Miche decided to use the dog for some publicity. So Bo had his coming-out party today. We told the press that

the girls named him after some cousin's cat. (These girls have
so many cousins on my side, I figure we're safe from press
scrutiny . . . it's easier to find the cat than all the cousins!
After I leave office, I should write a multivolume book titled
"Children from My Father." That man spread more seed than the
Park Service on the South Lawn.)

When we went out to present Bo to the press this
afternoon, Michelle comes up with this line about the dog being
named Bo to honor her father. I almost did a double take. I was
thinking: <u>How is she going to connect the dots on this one?</u> I'll
be damned if she didn't come up with a whopper. She told the
scribblers that they named the dog Bo because her Daddy's
nickname was Diddley. Bo Diddley, get it? I just smiled. On the
way back to the House I told her, "I haven't heard a story that
good since you told them you were planting that vegetable
garden to teach kids how to eat." She punched me in the arm
and went on with the girls.

Back at the office, even Reggie had to ask me why we named
the dog Bo. I said, "What do you think?" He kind of made that
funny, crooked smile he makes when something dawns on him
and said, "I'll be damned. You made those girls name that ugly
dog after you?" I said, "If I've got to trip over that thing every
day, the least they can do is name it after me. Truthfully, the
most redeeming thing about that mangy mutt is his name." He
high-fived me and we headed out to a hair appointment. He's
been calling me Bo all afternoon. I told him if he didn't stop I was
going to start calling him Diddley. There's nobody like Reggie . . .

# WHO ARE THE PEOPLE IN YOUR NEIGHBORHOOD?

Sooner or later, the First Lady's staff had to inject the fashionable mom next door into official policymaking. They couldn't just have Mrs. Obama announce some initiative one day and send her up to Capitol Hill demanding policy changes the next. They opted for the Razzle Dazzle approach: introduce Michelle Obama to the federal scene, while bolstering her image as First Mom. Turning the negative, angry, anti-American harpy of the campaign into the funsy Mom-in-Chief was hard enough, but to insinuate her into the political machinery of Washington, without drawing a foul, was heavy lifting indeed. Their solution was neighborhood visits.

On February 2, 2009, the First Lady told employees of the Interior Department, according to the AP, that her neighborhood visits were "a great way for me to get to know our new community and to meet you, our new co-workers and our new neighbors." It was as if the First Lady had just wandered over to the federal agencies to borrow a cup of sugar and have a chat. The reality was far different.

Like Mr. Rogers welcoming new puppets to his neighborhood, Michelle Obama began a series of tightly scripted "drop-bys" at government departments, large and small. The First Lady bounced from one federal bureaucracy to another as a sort of goodwill ambassador for the White House. Each visit looked like all the others. Federal employees were herded together, velvet ropes were set in place and then flanked by long-serving bureaucrats, as the First Neighbor addressed her adoring supplicants from a lectern.

One wonders if any of these career bureaucrats had the sense to stop and ask themselves, "Why is this woman welcoming me to the neighborhood? I've been here for twenty-six years and she just blew in from Chicago! Shouldn't I be welcoming her?!"

But they probably had no such thought. This is the chief effect of the Razzle Dazzle: logic is crippled and all partakers are rendered speechless by the display. And speechless they were. The other question that nobody bothered to ask is exactly why Michelle Obama needs to "learn, listen" and "know what's going on" at federal agencies? She wasn't elected to do anything—and the last time I checked, the government is not running a vo-tech school for the politically ambitious.

More monarch than First Lady, Michelle continued to visit each federal agency with a straight face, warmly welcoming them to her kingdom—er, neighborhood. The departments of Education, Health and Human Services, Interior, Homeland Security, Agriculture, Veterans Administration, the Environmental Protection Agency, etc., all played host to the First Lady in the early months of the administration.

*Time* magazine called Michelle's shameless bureaucratic ingratiation a "thank-you tour." Darlene Superville of the AP said that the First Lady's visits had provided "rare recognition and inspiration for the often neglected" government worker. What about the "often neglected" American taxpayer? In fact, Michelle was only fulfilling her husband's promise "to make government cool again." By spreading her celebrity and a little Razzle Dazzle to the bureaucrats, she was also preparing the way for her own political agenda and building bridges of goodwill that she would use in the days ahead.

## LOCK UP THE CHILDREN

In March 2009, the cable network Nickelodeon unveiled a politically charged animated segment within its programming dedicated to toddlers. The extended spot was an homage to the president with one goal in mind: to inculcate love of Obama among the young, even if much of the audience was in Huggies. The animated Barack Obama bounced around the screen like a hopped-up Johnny Quest, as the childish voiceover lovingly cooed:

> Nickelodeon celebrates President Barack Obama and some of his favorite things. Barack Obama is the first African-American to be president. That is what's called a historic event. Leading a country is no easy task. So what does he do to relax, you may ask? He loves shrimp linguini and the chili he cooks. He also plays Scrabble, collects comic books. He likes classical and hip-hop and jazz music, too. He always goes shopping for the same type of shoe. He reads lots of books and writes wonderful speeches. He goes on vacation and takes walks on beaches. He loves basketball; it's his

favorite sport. In the White House backyard, he'll have his own court. He reads bedtime stories to his daughters at night. The president in pajamas? What a sight! Now you know the president better than before. Which leaves just one thing: when he sleeps does he snore?

Thanks, Nickelodeon, but Michelle Obama had already solved that enduring mystery.

Meanwhile, on PBS, Michelle Obama crashed onto *Sesame Street* to deliver a bit of toddler Razzle Dazzle. As a way to push her childhood anti-obesity scheme, she helped Elmo and some children plant vegetable seeds. In the segment, she urges the kids to eat vegetables and (never able to resist a reference to herself) promised that if they followed her advice, they would "grow up big and strong just like me." I suppose Cookie Monster was forbidden from appearing on the street that day. Though, in an odd pairing, he did appear with Agriculture secretary Tom Vilsack to promote children's nutrition and exercise. Maybe they should have had Miss Piggy tag along.

Elmo is practically a cabinet secretary in the Obama White House at this point. In addition to encouraging children to eat well, Health and Human Services secretary Kathleen Sebelius used Elmo to teach children how to protect themselves from the swine flu. On May 22, 2009, they too appeared together.

The swine flu public service announcements showed Elmo advising tots: "Wash your hands with Elmo. Wash, wash, wash. . . . Sneeze into your arm with Elmo." With no vaccine in sight, at least Sebelius offered children something to combat the flu.

On September 8, 2009, the president sans Elmo addressed millions of students on the first day of school. The mere announcement of the speech caused a firestorm among parents who felt that the White House was forcing their children to listen to the president's propaganda. Some school boards decided to block the address. A lesson plan issued before the pep talk by the Education Department suggested that school officials instruct students to write an essay describing how they could help support the president.

Despite the controversy, the president proceeded with his plan. Though the talk was boilerplate "stay in school and study" stuff, he did manage to work in a health-care reform plug. A student in the crowd (a plant) asked him why the country had no universal coverage, and the president was delighted to respond. I'm sure that's what your kids are up nights thinking about.

⟜✕✕✕⟝

## The Diary of White House Social Secretary Desiree Glapion Rogers

### East Wing

*November 30, 2009*

*I only created the most stunning state dinner in American history. (No small feat, considering that we were dealing with the Indian head of state. You try planning a party around a country known only for its street urchins and curry!) Who else could have perfectly balanced Bollywood, Hollywood, and Barackwood! Who else would have thought to seat Brian Williams, Bobby Jindal, and the cast of Slumdog Millionaire at the same table? I ask you.*

*But I suppose all this glamour, beauty, art, and wonder comes at a price. Oh, the heavy cost of civilizing America.*

*Now I stand accused. Like my ancestor, Marie Laveau (the so-called voodoo queen of New Orleans), I now* understand that bringing magic to the masses can take a heavy toll. After remaking a nobody from Hawaii into the president of the United States . . . after turning a spiteful woman with all the fashion sense of Al Roker into the most celebrated First Lady of all time . . . this is the thanks I get?! Desiree stands accused. Desiree is the petal condemned to fall so that the tree may survive . . . But this petal ain't falling, sugar.

Two uninvited reality show contestants from Virginia crash my event and I'm to blame?! Oh, this is rich. The press is calling for my head. Valerie tells me that Two-Ton Gibbs, Rahm, and Busted Axelrod have joined the lynch mob. I've got one question for them: without my marketing know-how, without my event engineering, where would the Obama brand be? I'll tell you where: forty points down in the opinion polls like their man!

It is I alone who have shielded Michelle from the popular free fall. I've picked each gown and plotted each star turn. It was the reviled Desiree who staged the harvesting ceremonies in that fake garden! It was Desiree who instigated the bipartisan conga line at the Governors' Dinner—Desiree who convinced Ted Kennedy to give them that goddamn water dog! Yes, I did all that and so much more. The neighborhood visits to the government offices—_me_! Michelle's Photoshopped image on the cover of _Vogue_—_me_! The J. Crew coordinates that helped connect Her Royal Thighness with the little people—_me_! It's all me! I _am_ the real First Lady! (Only far more alluring and five dress sizes smaller.)

The press and those vultures on Capitol Hill have no conception of just how much I mean to this place. If the Obama family is a brand—honey, I'm the Must-See. E.O.! I'm sure Michelle knows all this, but just in case, I'm taking out an insurance policy tomorrow night. The First Lady, Valerie, and I are going to Acadiana for gumbo and spare ribs (I know the way to the First Lady's heart). Over dinner I'll tell them how just this week I convinced Green Giant to be a partner in our garden promotion campaign. Who isn't gonna love Miss D after I unveil a new line of frozen, prepackaged White House Garden Vegetables? Can you say Barak-O-li? Miche-Celery? And the kids' favorite: mini-Valerie Carrots . . . (I had to work Jarrett in somehow.) If that doesn't grab them, I've designed a whole line of Michelle Obama Fitness Apparel with Under Armour. It uses an all-new material called Expandex. As Big Mama back in New Orleans used to say: "If the gumbo tastes bitter, throw more sugar in the next roux."

# WHEN RAZZLE DAZZLE GOES WRONG

Though they have expertly played the Razzle Dazzle game, there are times when even the Obamas' manufactured glitter takes a tragic turn for the worse. And though their friends in the media conveniently cover for them, some of us have long memories.

## *Olympic-Size Disaster

The First Lady, Oprah Winfrey, Valerie Jarrett and other White House officials flew to Copenhagen in the fall of 2009 in an effort to persuade the International Olympic Committee to select their hometown of Chicago as the destination for the 2016 Olympics. Madrid, Rio, and Tokyo were all in the running for host city, but Michelle Obama was confident that she alone could win the global popularity contest. Add Oprah and some big media attention to the mix—and it was all but in the bag for Chi-town. Before leaving for Copenhagen, the First Lady promised CNN: "It's a battle—we're going to win—take no prisoners."

To seal the deal, the president decided to suspend his push for nationalized health care and fly to Copenhagen to make a personal plea on behalf of Chicago. What globalist could resist?

"What a dynamic duo they will be. I think it will be high impact," Valerie Jarrett, the senior presidential advisor, said.

The Obamas pulled out all the stops, weaving their personal narratives into the final Olympic sales pitch. Michelle tugged at foreign heartstrings by invoking her father, who suffered from MS: "Sports were a gift I shared with my dad, especially the Olympic Games," she told the IOC members. "Some of my best memories are sitting on my dad's lap, cheering on Olga and Nadia, Carl Lewis, and others for their brilliance and perfection. But I never dreamed that the Olympic flame might one day light up lives in my neighborhood." (Keep dreaming, sister. If you believe this story, Michelle's father must have had a very strong lap. As Michelle Malkin pointed out, Mrs. Obama was *twenty years old* when Carl Lewis won the gold in 1984!)

After a speech by mayor Richard Daley, President Obama rose to secure the Olympic games for Chicago by recalling *his election:* "Nearly one year ago, on a clear November night, people from every corner of the world gathered in the city of Chicago or in front of their televisions to watch the results of the U.S. presidential election. Their interest wasn't about me as an individual; rather, it was rooted in the belief that America's experiment in democracy still speaks to a set of universal aspirations and ideals . . . There is nothing I would like more than to step just a few blocks from my family's home and, with Michelle and our two girls, welcome the world back to our neighborhood." Glad it wasn't about him as an individual.

After all the artful lies, the star power, and the emotional speeches, the Obama gang left Copenhagen empty-handed on October 2, 2009. The Obamas were upstaged and beaten by Lula da Silva, the president of Brazil. And the U.S. came in dead last in the ballotting.

## *The Toxic Garden

For all the ink spilled over Michelle's vegetable garden, there is one story that barely got any coverage. In July 2009, the National Park Service discovered that the soil of the White House garden had been fertilized, years ago, using sewage sludge. When they tested the ground it yielded elevated lead levels of 93 parts per million. The EPA recommends not planting crops in any soil that reaches 300 ppm or higher. No wonder those dignitaries were glowing when they left the White House dinner parties. And we all thought it was reflected glory from the Obamas . . .

The *Guardian* newspaper in Great Britain was one of a handful of news organizations that even carried the story, which is surprising given the media obsession with this garden from the start. "It is advised for young children to be tested for exposure to lead if they play in areas where lead concentrations exceed 100 parts per million," the *Guardian* reported on July 2, 2009. "Children are especially vulnerable to exposure to lead, which can cause neurological and kidney damage and stunt their growth."

The White House refused to comment on whether the Obama girls or all those public school children romping in Michelle's garden were ever tested for lead exposure. They did assure the *Guardian* that they were committed to serving fresh and healthy food. Given their track record, this is less than assuring.

## *Veggiegate

The Razzle Dazzle was on full display when the East Wing used the garden to score Michelle Obama an appearance on one of Food Network's most popular shows: *Iron Chef America*. The First Lady emerged from the White House to lecture the country (again) about eating healthy food, then revealed the "secret ingredient" for the cooking competition: "anything from the White House Garden . . . take as much as you need," she said. For several minutes, viewers watched super chefs Emeril Lagasse, Bobby Flay, Mario Batali, and White House Executive Chef Cristeta Comerford flounce through the garden filling their baskets with produce. The more than seven million viewers who tuned in to the January 3, 2010, broadcast were led to believe that the cooks were using the White House garden goodies in their cooking. Wrong. Assume nothing in Obamaland.

Turns out, the Iron Chef competition was shot a week after the White House harvest party—and not in Washington, but in New York. The "stunt vegetables" used in the broadcast were purchased at a New York supermarket. The problem is not that the producers of the show purchased greens for the recording, but that Michelle Obama misled the viewers in her big reveal. She should have said, "The secret ingredients tonight are vegetables *like those found* in the White House garden—or whatever is available at D'Agostinos." But since when is honesty a requirement for the Obama Razzle Dazzle?

## *The Fall of the Queen of the Razzle Dazzle

It was actually during a bit of staged Razzle Dazzle that Desiree Rogers may have signed her White House death warrant. The *Wall Street Journal Magazine* recounts an event that took place in the White House kitchen back in February 2009. Desiree and Michelle Obama appeared before the media to preview the desserts to be served at the Governors' Dinner that evening. The delectable treats were placed on the Truman china. After the First Lady introduced the china and began speaking about the food, Desiree Rogers casually cut in:

"One correction. It's Wilson. This plate is Wilson."

"Oh, no, it's not Truman," Mrs. Obama said.

This may have well been the beginning of the end for Desiree. Razzle Dazzle is all about featuring personalities. For Michelle Obama, having the brand manager correct or outshine the brand in any way may have been more than she could accept. The *New York Times* reported on March 12, 2010, that David Axelrod had a "long conversation" with Rogers about her "interviews and photo shoots." Her apparent honesty about "the Obama brand" was more than the West Wing could swallow. Robert Gibbs shut down a photo shoot with Rogers wearing an Oscar de la Renta gown in the First Lady's garden. Susan Sher, Michelle's new chief of staff, began to question and scrutinize Rogers's events. And then the Salahis showed up.

In what should have been the highlight of Desiree Rogers's White House career, her first state dinner was marred by a pair of Virginia social-ites, Michaele and Tareq Salahi, who crashed the party. Rogers was blamed for seating herself during the dinner rather than paying attention to who was entering the White House gates or properly manning the checkpoints. Desiree defended her decision to seat herself at the gathering, explaining to the *Wall Street Journal*: "What better way to see the flow of the evening?"

The gate-crasher controversy provided the Obamas with a good excuse to show their stylish friend the door.

In their official farewell statement on the Desiree Rogers departure, the Obamas wrote: "When she took this position, we asked Desiree to help make sure that the White House truly is the People's House, and she did that by welcoming scores of everyday Americans through its doors—from wounded warriors to local schoolchildren to NASCAR drivers." Reading between the lines, we envision the statement that Michelle wished she could have released: "Good riddance to a woman who approached official White House social events like a heat-seeking missile, aimed at whatever two-bit celebrity crossed the threshold. She was content to leave our White House doors unmanned so that gaudily dressed fame-seekers and self-important entrepreneurs like herself could waltz through. In the end, Desiree could never get past the fact that she is not, and never will be, as glamorous and as revered as First Lady Michelle Obama!"

## THE DIARY OF FORMER WHITE HOUSE SOCIAL SECRETARY DESIREE GLAPION ROGERS

### EAST WING

*February 27, 2010*

*A gray cloud hangs over the republic. The color and life that once reigned at the People's House have faded. Desiree retreats and her magic goes with her. I "resigned" my post yesterday. Tubby Gibbs went out and told the press that I "personally informed" the Obamas of my decision in January. Honey, it was the other way around. Michelle Obama personally informed* me *that Smokey thought I should depart and that ever since the Indian state dinner, her mother didn't "feel safe in the White House." With Desiree gone, I can assure you they'll be safe from one thing—popularity! I haven't picked an outfit for Michelle since late January and the effects are apparent. I flipped past Fox last week and there she was on that Huckabee show looking like a chimney sweep on food stamps. Nothing matched. It was a shame. Without me doing the clothes shopping, that poor woman's closet will look like Candy Crowley's before long.*

I met my successor today. People have been asking what I think of her. Two words: Frumpy Disaster. They may as well bring Bush's social staff back. What kind of name is Julianna Smoot for a White House social secretary? She's supposedly some sort of fund-raiser. Give me a break. That dame couldn't raise twenty dollars in Warren Buffett's bedroom! But I can't say anything now. I'll save it for when I'm sitting across from Barbara Walters—she owes me for letting her shoot that Most Fascinating Person thing in the Green Room anyway . . .

I bumped into Rahm yesterday. He comes skipping down the hall and had the gall to say, "Well, I hear the voodoo queen is leaving us." I smiled and said, "You better keep an eye on your tutu, Rahm. I have a little doll on my nightstand with your name on it." I laughed and played it off as a joke. What he doesn't know is, I was serious. I've got a voodoo doll for everyone in this building. Child, I'm breaking out my long pins! This is going to be a rough year for these people. They may have driven Desiree away, but once I finish my book, launch my lifestyle and couture show on cable, and start writing my _Vogue_ column, I'll make 'em all pay. As Big Mama used to say during Mardi Gras, "Enjoy the parade while it's rolling, 'cause you'll be shoveling horse shit when it's over." For the Obamas, the parade is coming to *an end. And Desiree will give them a shovel-ready project they'll never forget!*

---

The Razzle Dazzle is really one huge shell game. It is mostly made up of glittery distractions meant to divert your attention from the destructive policies and warped intentions of Obama and his crew. It has also helped the administration get its message onto nontraditional, even offbeat media platforms that otherwise would give the president no coverage at all. Nothing is accidental. All of it is ruthlessly planned and orchestrated by the political operation in the West Wing. Anita Dunn, who for a time served as Obama's communications director, offered up the secret of the Razzle Dazzle at a forum in the Dominican Republic in January 2010: "Very rarely did we communicate through the press anything that we didn't absolutely control." You can say that again.

## THE WINNING WAY

We can make light of the Razzle Dazzle (God knows I have). But if there is one thing that conservatism could use right now, it's a little Razzle Dazzle. We may never have Hollywood set dressers or fashion mavens running about, but we should spend a bit more time thinking about things like presentation, setting, tone, visual reinforcement, and beauty. These concepts are never far from the Obamas' thoughts and shouldn't be far from ours. The way we present our ideas to the public, the form and fashion will expand or limit the reach of those ideas. And most of the time style does matter.

In May 2009, Jeb Bush, Mitt Romney, and House Minority Whip Eric Cantor convened a "solutions summit" meant to resurrect interest in the Republican Party. They held the kickoff event at a pizza parlor in Arlington, Virginia—a pizza parlor literally inside the Beltway! Three politicians sitting on bar stools in a pizza joint is not the sort of Razzle Dazzle that the party needs. A year later, the GOP launched its America Speaking Out Web initiative, billed as "your opportunity to change the way Congress works by proposing ideas for a new policy agenda." Members who participate can "earn badges." It quickly became a laughingstock on the right and left. Bravo! Suddenly, the pizza parlor conclave sounds inspired.

Because of his acting background and ease before an audience, Ronald Reagan innately understood Razzle Dazzle in its best sense. He married style and substance effortlessly without resorting to cheap theatrical distractions. Reagan also surrounded himself with smart advisors like Michael Deaver and Roger Ailes, both visionaries who understood the power of broadcast media and how to use it.

Today a new breed of media innovators is making a major impact. Following the path forged by the original new media powerhouse Matt Drudge, folks such as Andrew Breitbart (breitbart.com), Michelle Malkin (hotair .com), Erick Erickson (redstate.com), and Lila Rose (liveaction.org) are all using new media in fascinating ways—taking the conservative message to whole new sectors of the population. Florida's Republican upstart Marco Rubio built his entire senatorial campaign by using nontraditional media— starting on my radio show!—and created national name recognition for himself.

Technology offers conservatives remarkable opportunities. But to seize them we must be bold, daring, and sensitive to the way in which we shape the message in this shifting culture. Now is the time to marshal our creative resources and partner with others to advance conservative principles in the media and throughout the culture at large.

## WON BY ONE

Conservatives, demoralized after the 2008 elections, needed a little of their own Razzle Dazzle to jump-start their movement and inspire the resistance to what would be Obama's sweeping agenda of "change." The Tea Party organizers took a page of the Obama playbook and used social networking and the conservative media to help them organize rallies and publicize their views. There are thousands of people responsible for the Tea Party movement that has swept the United States and transformed American politics.

But most people forget that it was a blogger in Seattle and the lone voice of a television business commentator who helped spark the revolution.

When Obama and his democratic cronies were shoving his stimulus bill down the throats of Americans, a blogger named Liberty Belle (Keli Carender) cried foul. In desperation she organized a protest, quickly dubbed a "tea party," in Seattle. On the day of the party, she wrote on her blog: "Make no mistake, the president will be signing that bill tomorrow; I have no illusions that he will actually listen to us. But, maybe, just maybe we can start a movement that will snowball across the nation and get people out of their homes, meeting each other and working together to redirect this country towards its truly radical founding principles of individual liberty and freedom. Maybe people will wake up slowly at first, and then quickly when they realize the urgency needed." And wake up they did.

Two days later, on February 19, 2009, CNBC cut to analyst Rick Santelli on the floor of the Chicago Mercantile Exchange. He was critiquing Obama's mortgage bailout and the stimulus package. Suddenly in the middle of his analysis, on live television, he turned to the traders on the floor all around him: "This is America. How many of you people want to pay for your neighbor's mortgage, that has an extra bathroom and can't pay their bills? Raise their hand." "*Booo,*" the traders responded. "President Obama, are you listening?" Santelli yelled into the camera lens. Like Braveheart, he ended his segment with a rallying cry: "We're thinking of having a Chicago tea party in July. All you capitalists that want to show up at Lake Michigan, I'm going to start organizing!" There were cheers on all sides.

These two individuals, in their own ways, used Razzle Dazzle for the common good. They used their voices and their platforms to reach others and made a united point: the government is out of control and it has to stop. The impact of these two people, a blogger and a TV commentator, sent shock waves through the nation that are still being felt in Washington and all over the world. This is what each of us must do: creatively raise our voices to defend American freedom whenever it is attacked, and draw as many to our cause as possible. This is the Razzle Dazzle capable of moving mountains and hearts.

CHAPTER *4*

# YOU'RE THE NEXT GOVERNMENT TAKEOVER

Only a month into his presidency, Barack Obama traveled to Fort Myers, Florida, for a town hall event. Among the thousands who arrived early for "ringside" seats was Henrietta Hughes, a sixty-one-year-old homeless breast cancer survivor. She knew this was her moment and did her best to get recognized. Her perseverance paid off. She caught the president's eye.

"Okay, this young lady has been standing here very patiently, and making me look a little guilty," the president, pointing to her, said. "Go ahead."

Henrietta covered her mouth as if Bob Barker had just called her to "come on down" as the next contestant on *The Price Is Right*.

"I first want to say, I respect you and I'm grateful for you, been praying for you," she began, her voice quivering with nervous excitement. "But I have an urgent need—um, unemployment and homelessness, a very small vehicle for my family and I to live in, we need urgent—and housing authority has two-year waiting lists, and . . . we need something more than the vehicle and the parks, we need our own kitchen and our own bathrooms. Please help."

Without skipping a beat, the empathizer-in-chief asked, "Well, listen, what's your name?"

"It's Henrietta Hughes."

"Okay, Ms. Hughes. We're going to do everything we can to help you, but there are a lot of people like you, and we're going to do everything, all right?" he said, and kissed her cheek. "I'll have my staff come up to you after the town hall. All right?" Her prayers answered, Henrietta shook her head appreciatively, slowly mouthing, "Thank you, thank you."

Afterward, reporters and others from the audience swarmed around Henrietta, who had suddenly become Queen for a Day. She told the scrum she had maxed out on her government benefits and that local charities were not forthcoming. She was showered with business cards, job offers, even cash. Eventually she was given the keys to a new house—all because she begged the president for help on national television.

Of course, we should be happy when Americans who hear stories of loss and poverty are moved to help other Americans like Henrietta. But in this case, she was rewarded because she *begged* for the *government* (Obama) to rescue her. Henrietta was, in a sense, one of Obama's first bailouts. The manner in which he handled Henrietta's "domestic policy challenge" was emblematic of the Obama agenda to come. If someone or some industry has a problem, Obama's knee-jerk response is "write a check" (courtesy of U.S. taxpayers).

Obama should have used the town hall moment not to patronize, but to apologize to Henrietta. After all, she suffers from the entitlement mind-set created and incentivized by Obama's political heroes and mentors. In the warped mind-set that is modern-day liberalism, panhandling in front of a national audience is now acceptable and encouraged behavior.

## THE DIARY OF PRESIDENT BARACK OBAMA

### AIR FORCE ONE

February 10, 2009

I've got to hand it to Axe. He pulled off something today at our town hall in Fort Myers that was brilliant. For weeks he's had staff scouring Florida looking for a destitute person with a heartbreaking story to parade before the cameras during our big event. He found a winner! This Henrietta Hughes was right out of central casting. She tearfully begged me for a car and a house and everything. So I blessed her with a kiss. It was great TV!

I told Axe we need to do one of these at the end of every town hall. First off, it makes me look like Santa Claus (only with nuclear codes and snappier clothes). And secondly, it teaches the people that if they work really hard (to get to my rallies) they can take home some great swag. I was even thinking we could turn this into a regular town hall contest. I'll pick names of two poor folks from a lottery bin and let them compete for prizes: cars, homes, scholarships, and high-end medical treatments. Whoever can name the schools I attended and the places my mother lived, gets a prize. The other contestant receives a signed picture of me. So everyone's a winner—and they'll learn something, too.

Obama and his forefathers have advanced a vision where government assistance is a lifestyle choice. They have wrecked economies, sapped initiative from the people, and lowered our national expectations. If we keep following Obama's lead, we'll all be begging politicians for houses and cars. Which is exactly what he wants. Obama instinctively believes that every problem has a government solution. This heavy-handed autocratic approach was most apparent in his obsession to "reform" health care.

## ONE NATION, UNDER OBAMACARE . . .

*We know we spend a huge amount of money in that last year of life. . . . The most important thing we can do with end-of-life care right now is to encourage people to look at hospices as a legitimate option.*

—BARACK OBAMA IN AN INTERVIEW WITH DR. JON LAPOOK
ON CBS's *THE EARLY SHOW*, JULY 16, 2009

Once upon a time, in a faraway land called America, there was a health-care system beloved by its patients and admirers from around the world. These clever Americans somehow managed to find cures for horrible diseases and save more lives than any other health-care system in the world.

Along came a man named Barack Obama, who insisted America's old-fashioned ways were all wrong. "America's health care costs too much," he claimed. A trusting lot, the American people elected him president and eagerly awaited his promised savings. Immediately he started to advance his agenda, but soon ran into trouble. The people listened and decided these new ideas were not what they had hoped for and said they preferred the old way better. But the president flicked them off like a flea on beautiful Bo's curly coat. Protests rang out across the country. The president tried quieting them, but to no avail. He pressed forward, undeterred by the pesky people and their frivolous concerns.

Americans soon discovered that patient care would no longer be the priority. The president decreed that doctors would be judged not by the number of lives saved, but by how much money they saved the government.

Yet someone had forgotten to remind the president that the government of the United States had no money, so no matter how much money his new system saved, even the most basic services were suddenly unaffordable. Care deteriorated. Doctors retired early. Medical school enrollments plummeted. There seemed to be fewer elderly people around. And . . . everyone suffered miserably after all.

Thinking of the ObamaCare saga as a fairy tale helps soften the horror by making it less personal. And like all good fairy tales, perhaps there really is some small chance for a happy ending.

Obama seized on the economic downturn to make health-care reform about "lowering costs," reducing the deficit, and reining in insurance company profits. During his innumerable sales pitches the president avoided promising that the level of care would *improve* after the law was passed. But how could it? Simply put, America's health care is (or at least was) among the best in the world. According to Stanford University Medical Center's Dr. Scott Atlas:

- Americans have better survival rates from common and rare cancers than Europeans (*Lancet* Oncology Study)
- Americans have better access to treatment for chronic diseases than Canadians (National Bureau of Economic Research, NBER)
- America's impoverished receive better care on average than Canada's (NBER)
- In the United Kingdom and Canada, patients waiting to see a specialist wait far longer (often twice as long) as Americans (Health Affairs)
- More than 70 percent of German, Canadian, Australian, New Zealand, and British adults say their health systems need either "fundamental change" or "complete rebuilding" (Health Affairs)
- The vast majority of medical innovations come from the United States (U.S. Department of Health and Human Services)

With that kind of data, it is not surprising that every major poll found Americans to be overwhelmingly satisfied with the health care they were receiving. A *Washington Post*/ABC News poll in June 2009 found that

83 percent of Americans were either "somewhat" or "very satisfied" with their health care. Eighty-one percent felt the same about their insurance. It is rare that Americans are this unified on any issue—not that it mattered to Obama.

To bolster his thesis that health care costs too much, the president cited and relied upon one Dartmouth Atlas of Health Care study. It rated hospitals by how much they spent on patients who died while under their care. He used these "findings" to demonstrate that more money does not necessarily lead to better results. So he argued that health-care dollars should not go to places that "spend too much" on health-care services. The president ignored the two other major studies that severely undercut his main argument. In February 2010, a University of Pittsburgh report confirmed what should have already been conventional wisdom: hospitals that spend the most on tests and care generally save the most lives. The second, also in February, was a *New England Journal of Medicine* analysis that savaged the Dartmouth Atlas study for trying to measure efficiency by looking only at costs, not outcomes in the health of the patient. The Dartmouth Atlas Project's Dr. Elliott Fisher basically agreed with the criticism. According to the *New York Times*, he insisted that "he and his colleagues should not be held responsible for the misinterpretation of their data."

This devastating data, on top of the unrelenting town hall opposition, should have scuttled Obama's grand health-care scheme. Many of us thought the surprise Scott Brown Senate victory in Massachusetts, which deprived the Democrats of their filibuster-proof majority, would have put the final nail in the coffin of ObamareidpelosiCare. But no. The Democrats knew that health care would be their platform for radical change. The people would have "health-care reform" whether they liked it or not.

## FIRST, DO NO HARM

Unable to indict the quality of the American health-care system on the facts, Obama turned to emotional manipulation. He began peddling a series of sob stories, elevating individual tales of misfortune into national cries for action. Usually the victims went unnamed, although occasionally he revealed the identity of his campaign prop. Eleven-year-old Marcelas Owens stood at Obama's side throughout the bill's final week. Marcelas's mother had died a few years earlier of pulmonary hypertension after being laid off as a fast-food manager and losing her insurance. Yet it was never clear how ObamaCare could have saved her. The truth is, her home state of Washington *does* offer care to the poor, and Mrs. Owens did in fact receive care throughout her illness.

Ohio cancer victim Natoma Canfield also became a late-game stump-speech addition. Canfield had written to the White House about her struggle. She had paid significantly out of pocket for care when her premiums rose 25 percent in 2008. Then in 2010 she learned rates were to rise again, and she decided to cancel her policy. Shortly thereafter, she was diagnosed with leukemia, and wrote a letter about her predicament to President Obama.

Obama used the letter as emotional evidence that his health-care bill was desperately needed. At ObamaCare rallies, he boasted of reading her letter to insurance company CEOs. Team Obama arranged for Natoma's sister to attend his final health-care rally in Strongville, Ohio. "She was very sick," Obama reported. "She expects to face more than a month of aggressive chemotherapy. She is racked with worry not only about her illness, but also the costs of the tests and the treatment that she's surely going to need to beat it." In other words, without ObamaCare, she is going to die. These people will stop at nothing.

## The Diary of President Barack Obama

### The White House

March 23, 2010

Right now, I gotta admit feeling a lot like my man LL Cool J: "Rockin' my peers and puttin' suckas in fear . . . explosion, overpowerin' / Over the competition, I'm towerin'!" How you like me now, Roger Ailes!

I actually had a genius idea for the signing ceremony for the health-care reform bill. Picture this: As the crowd waits with gleeful anticipation for me to enter the room and sign this bad boy into history, that dry-ice fog starts pouring into the room. Then, lasers! Lasers flashing every which way, when suddenly Jay-Z emerges from the smoke, hyping the crowd with one of his numbers (or maybe Bow Wow—we'll consult the charts tomorrow to see who's the most popular). Then, the man they've all been waiting for—me! Except I don't just walk to the podium, I moonwalk to the podium! In fact, why not turn this entire event into another Michael Jackson tribute? We've invited that little kid Marcelas, who provided us with an incredible sob story to market the bill, to attend the signing. I'm thinking he can stand beside me—like my own Emanuel Lewis! The new social secretary, Smoot, extended an invitation to Janet and Tito, but I'm not sure they'll make it. It's probably too much, but if Desiree Rogers were still here, she'd know how to pull it off.

# A MANDATE TO MANDATE

In the law's immediate aftermath, attorneys general in more than a dozen states filed lawsuits against Washington, arguing that the new mandate that requires every American to purchase health insurance or pay a fine is unconstitutional. Their citizens' constitutional rights were being trampled by ObamaCare's individual mandate. Equally troubling is the fact that this new health-care regime empowers the federal government to ration care based on "cost effectiveness," which ultimately intrudes upon our personal medical choices and the doctor-patient relationship.

Republican Senators Pat Roberts, Tom Coburn, and Mike Enzi offered separate amendments banning the use of "comparative effectiveness research" to restrict care. Democrats shot each of them down.

---

## THE DIARY OF DIRECTOR OF
## THE OFFICE OF MANAGEMENT AND BUDGET
## PETER ORSZAG

### WASHINGTON, D.C.

*April 8, 2010*

*I am now convinced that no one in D.C. really reads legislation (phew!). But since we passed the health-care bill, I figure it's time a little credit flowed my way. During my Q&A*

at the Economic Club today, I shone some light
on my brainchild—the Independent Payment
Advisory Board, the new commission created by
the health-care bill. (Adhering to Gibbs's rule,
I did not refer to it as a "death panel." But how
I wanted to scream to all those economists, "We
got the death panel through the door and nobody
even noticed!") The power we now have via this
panel is remarkable. They will set fees for doctors
and hospitals, ration individual treatments
and care. And best of all, the president makes
the panel appointments with no congressional
oversight! This is a killer panel! And I mean
killer!

Every financial model indicates that the only
way to restore fiscal sanity to this country is
for people to die. After all, they've got to die
sometime! This one panel will allow us to quickly
and quietly shove the unfit down the hospice

chute, reap a bounty of inheritance taxes, and end wasteful spending on the care of people already in the process of dying. Some reporter worriedly asked me as I left, "You mean this panel's recommendations could alter the health care of millions of Americans—and unless Congress and the president reject it by law, the recommendations automatically take effect?" "You've got it," I told him. "Ha ha ha haaaaaa." The congressional inertia actually plays in our favor! I know once our "elder reduction program" kicks in, the pitiful stories will begin trickling out, but they'll have to work damn hard to stop us. Keep your sob stories! We've got a debt to bury—and a lot of old folks, with big retirement accounts! The HuffPo can now refer to me as "nerdy Sexy Savvy." I better call Arianna.

---

Democrats love to talk about how their law will help Americans with "preventative care"—HIV tests, anti-obesity programs, and countless other bureaucratic initiatives that are supposedly going to make us live longer, healthier lives. If only we could have a prevention initiative against bureaucracy. ObamaCare creates more than 150 new bureaucracies, each uniquely empowered to shove Americans through our new national health-care machinery. Here are just a few examples of the nanny state initiatives in H.R. 3590, the "Patient Protection and Affordable Care Act":

- **Section 4204: Immunizations.** Grants funds to encourage more prolific immunizations, including grants to provide home visits for "education, assessments of need, referrals, provision of immunizations, or other services."

- **Section 4201: Community Transformation Grants.** Provides funds to "promote healthy living"—an expansive section that specifies such activities as "creating healthier school environments, including increasing healthy food options, physical activity opportunities, promotion of healthy lifestyle, emotional wellness, and prevention curricula, and activities to prevent chronic diseases," as well as "creating the infrastructure to support active living and access to nutritious foods in a safe environment." (Can someone say *food deserts!*) Measuring Section 4201's success will be determined, in part, by a representative of the state who monitors "changes in weight; changes in proper nutrition; changes in physical activity; changes in tobacco use prevalence; changes in emotional well-being and overall mental health; other factors as determined by the Secretary." All of which will be reported back to the government.

- **Section 4202: Healthy Aging, Living Well; Evaluation of Community-Based Prevention and Wellness Programs for Medicare Beneficiaries.** This particular grant's success will in part be determined by Medicare beneficiaries "reduc[ing] their utilization of health services and associated costs under the Medicare program for conditions that are amenable to improvement under such programs."

- **Section 4205. Nutrition Labeling of Standard Menu Items at Chain Restaurants.** Restaurants with at least twenty franchises are required to post menu items' calorie count, "a succinct statement concerning daily caloric intake," and "ranges" or "averages" for trickier offerings, "such as soft drinks, ice cream, pizza, doughnuts, or children's combination meals."

The list continues for nearly as long as the transcript of a typical off-the-cuff Obama response to a straightforward question. And buried within each, you usually find a special clause requiring the secretary to further elaborate on whatever the preceding section actually meant. We can count on the Obama administration to elaborate with a vengeance.

What can Americans expect under ObamaCare? Who knows—the law grants powers so vast, almost no aspect of our personal autonomy is off-limits. Everywhere we look, every doctor's visit, every shopping trip to the grocer, every romantic night at a restaurant, every trip to a vending machine, every IRS form, *everywhere*, we'll confront the long, judgmental hand of Obama, pushing us one way or the other.

## LOAN SHARKS

Health care is not the only area where Obama has sought to expand government authority. For much of the past three decades, liberals have insisted that home ownership is a right, not a privilege.

It became government policy to encourage and facilitate home ownership among those lacking the financial means. To ease the way, Washington mandated "relaxed lending standards" through laws such as the Community Reinvestment Act, which went through several iterations since its establishment in 1977, getting worse with each revision. Banks could choose to either be labeled racist—and incur very loud, angry, and public protests from the likes of ACORN—or lower standards and extend loans to homebuyers who couldn't even afford a down payment.

Fannie Mae and Freddie Mac, the tax-exempt, government-insured firms charged with buying and securitizing mortgages, exacerbated the problem. Fannie Mae's chief from 1991 to 1998 became the government's main instrument in achieving racial justice through home ownership. All of this came to a head in 2008, when loan defaults started spiking. Turns out not every American is entitled to a home, nor qualified to take on the massive debt involved with purchasing one. The home mortgage fallout roiled the economy, as many banks were heavily involved in the subprime market. Fannie and Freddie have since been fully nationalized and provided, at last count, with a taxpayer bailout topping $200 billion.

And what of James Johnson, Fannie Mae's chief during much of the lending boom, who infamously said, "Every American who wants to get a mortgage will have their [sic] loan approved"? He left Fannie in 1998, after taking home $6 million in his final year. At least that's what he told shareholders. A 2004 congressional investigation found that during his tenure as CEO, Fannie secretly deferred pay, so that in 1998 he actually paid himself $21 million. So naturally Obama named him chairman of his vice presidential search committee. He bowed out after reports surfaced that disgraced former Countrywide CEO Angelo Mozillo had given him a sweetheart loan.

## HERE WE GO AGAIN

The horrendous collapse of the housing market notwithstanding, President Obama's zeal for social engineering via home ownership was undiminished. On Tax Day 2009, Obama unveiled yet another gimmick: an $8,000 giveaway plan to any first-time homebuyer. In many cases, this meant that purchasers needed no down payment whatsoever. Obama told a gathering at the Old Executive Office Building, "I think it's wonderful to see that this is already prompting some willingness for people to go ahead and make the first-time purchase, where they thought maybe it was out of reach before."

Yeah, it was out of reach because most of these people couldn't afford their monthly cable bill, let alone a mortgage. You know what else is "out of reach"? Me buying a Gulfstream 550. Maybe Obama should create a First-Time Gulfstream Buyer Tax Credit, so that I get suckered into massive debt I can't afford. If someone had just taught the president one simple lesson—*Don't buy what you can't afford!*—America might have been spared most of his harebrained schemes.

# STIMULATING AMERICA?

Obama kicked off his presidency by taking out an $800 billion loan against our country's future. Democrats promised that the American Recovery and Reinvestment Act would stimulate the economy, create jobs, and return Americans to work.

The "stimulus" bill consisted of three basic categories: federal spending projects of all types, expanding the social safety net, and tax cuts. Obama warned that without his "stimulus," America's unemployment rate could reach as high as 9 percent. But if we just spent $790 billion, he'd ensure unemployment remained closer to 8 percent. Unfortunately, what happened next was the worst of both worlds: as Washington recklessly wasted hundreds of billions of dollars, the unemployment rate skyrocketed past 10 percent anyway.

It has been an unmitigated, budget-busting failure. Ask yourself: What have *I* received from that $800 billion? Chances are, unless you work for the government, weatherized your home, or were already impoverished, the answer is: Nothing.

Because no meaningful statistics exist, it is impossible to say whether any of the jobs attributable to the "stimulus" bill were "saved," "created," "invented," or merely just "theoretical." Here is just a smattering of who and what was stimulated with our money:

- A $25,000 check went to In the Heart of the Beast Puppet and Mask Theatre in Minneapolis.
- Washington state's Parks and Recreation Commission received $50,000 for its Asian-style rod-puppet show, according to the *New York Post.*
- And the Pig Iron Theatre Company (a "dance-clown-theatre ensemble") in Philadelphia received $25,000 to help pay for its production of *Welcome to Yuba City,* which is a "cowboy/clown odyssey, presenting hilarious fragments of a mythic American desert-scape."

---

## The Diary of Vice President Joe Biden

### U.S. Naval Observatory

February 25, 2009

The Boss put me in charge of administering the "stimulus" money (whatever the hell that means). You know Barack just comes out and says these things, and it's the first I've ever heard of it. Don't get me wrong; he's great with the public stuff—very complimentary. At the State of the Union, when he announced my new position (which is the same thing Jill calls me at home)— Stimulus Czar—I was flattered. "Nobody messes with Joe," Barack said. <u>Sure</u>, I thought, trying to hold that smile on my face. <u>Joe can mess it up all by himself because he doesn't know what the hell you are talking about.</u>

Next thing I know, around midnight, I get a one-page stimulus briefing and I find out they're launching a website so the public can track how the money is being spent. I'm supposed to be in charge of this thing! I don't even own a computer!

To tell the truth, aside from spending a s*#tload of money, I don't see what this stimulus bill accomplishes. But like it or not, Barack sends me out to sell the spending plan in the a.m. I appeared on <u>CBS This Morning</u> (which, saints be praised, no one was watching), and Maggie Rodriguez (a spicy dish) asked me how the stimulus will "help small business." "Sh#t if I know," I wanted to tell her. But it's a morning show and kids might have been watching, so I came up with some malarkey about how the stimulus is good because it'll fix bridges and roads that allow people to reach small businesses. But the more I think about it, that's like telling people that a tsunami is good because the flowers will get watered.

---

Other "stimulus" beneficiaries include people with no obvious need for taxpayers' money. Nearly $6 million in stimulus funds went to two PR firms run by Hillary Clinton's pollster, Mark Penn, to promote awareness of the switch to digital TV. The grant "saved" three jobs. According to the *Hill*, an advisor to Obama's 2008 campaign, Alfredo Balsera, "received nearly $70,000 to help alert viewers in difficult-to-reach communities that their televisions would soon no longer receive broadcast signals." (You can see why this project was of particular importance to President Primetime.)

There seems to be no end to the stimulus boondoggles. Consider the measly $5 billion weatherizing initiative. That's a lot of weatherstripping. Improving home insulation would, in Obama's reckoning, have two major benefits. First, it would put people back to work (gluing rubber stripping to windows and doors?), and second, it would advance Obama's energy agenda by increasing home energy efficiency.

But as usual, Obama's ideas just don't pan out. The Associated Press reported on March 28, 2010: "In Indiana, state-trained workers flubbed insulation jobs. In Alaska, Wyoming, and the District of Columbia, the program has yet to produce a single job or retrofit one home. And in California, a state with nearly 37 million residents, the program at last count had created 84 jobs."

All this spending only added to our national debt. Reducing our crushing budget deficit requires a serious commitment to cutting spending. Obama lacks even an unserious commitment to cutting spending. But make no mistake: the president does have a plan to tackle the deficit—following the ingrained liberal instinct to raise taxes.

---

## THE DIARY OF PRESIDENT BARACK OBAMA

### THE WHITE HOUSE

February 18, 2010

I don't need Congress to reduce the debt. We'll do this the Chicago way. The Senate refused to establish a Debt Commission to get our financial house in order—fine. I just announced the appointment of my own Debt Commission! It's good to be the president.

The eighteen-member bipartisan group was chosen entirely by me! Thank God there are still a few progressive Republicans out there willing to take up space around a table. If it wasn't for Alan Cranston, we would have had to make Arlen Specter switch parties again. Here's how this deal's going to work: The commission will offer me their debt reducing ideas, and then I'll force Congress to accept them before year's end. Pelosi has already agreed to fast track all ~~my~~ the commissions' recommendations during the lame-duck session. So even if we get our clocks cleaned at the ballot box in November, we'll give those ungrateful voters something to remember us by.

Look, there's only one way to knock this debt down: we need to suck more money from the wealthy and everybody else working for a living. With the spending contained in that health-care bill and the ever-rising entitlements, we're going to need to "spread the sacrifice." (That may be my new slogan as I sell this to the people.)

Though we just announced the commission today, the report is already completed. My budget chief, Orszag, economic whiz Romer, and Rahm have been working on the report for months. After the commission meets for a few weeks, we'll slip the report in their folders and they'll rubber-stamp it. Most of the commissioners already know about the report anyway. It's all in there: a value-added tax, a new national sales tax, we're going to raise the Social Security age to seventy-two. And to really reduce spending: anyone who contracts a deadly disease after the age of sixty will get an all-expense paid, quickie visit (we hope) to the hospice. I know there'll be gnashing of teeth over a few of these changes. But the voters need to listen more closely when I speak. I told them I wouldn't raise <u>income</u> taxes on people making less than $250,000 a year. I didn't say anything about all the other taxes.

---

Obama loves to brag about the tax cuts he gave out as part of the stimulus. This is one of the biggest lies of his first year in office. These so-called tax cuts were as illusory as the jobs created by the "stimulus" bill. "More than a third of Obama's 'Make Work Pay' goes to people who do not pay income tax," the Heritage Foundation found, rendering it little more than glorified welfare. For those who do work, the "tax cut" amounted to eight to fourteen dollars a week. Most of us never even noticed the change in our paycheck. As for his four-hundred-dollar tax rebate in 2009, the important thing to note is that no tax rates are actually being cut.

If this is Obama's new deal, we'll take the old one. And speaking of FDR, Obama reportedly believes that the only reason that the New Deal failed was that it didn't go far enough (i.e., the spending programs were too modest). He bemoaned the fact that Roosevelt "pulled back toward a balanced budget." Perish the thought.

Thanks to Obama's reckless economic policies, America's national debt is skyrocketing. According to the Federal Reserve, the share of what we owe nationally now tops $690,000 per family. And yet no matter how loudly we protest the policies fueling the debt, we are still forced to sacrifice our personal prosperity to help shoulder the government's bills. There used to be a popular term for that: indentured servitude.

With so much of our money to burn, the administration also ordered the relaxation of rules to determine eligibility for federal food stamps. The *Daily Caller* unearthed a letter from the associate administrator for the food stamp program, Jessica Shahin, who instructed regional food-stamp distributors: "Applicants will not need to provide documentation verifying their resources . . . mak[ing] most, if not all, households categorically eligible for [food stamps]." Asset and gross income limits were tossed out the window. Who needs eligibility rules when we have a "stimulus" to implement?

With the gates to the public feeding trough thrown open to all comers, Obama added $17 billion to the 2010 budget (a mere 30 percent of the entire federal food stamp program!).

## GOVERNMENT TO THE RESCUE!

The way Obama tells it, he's never been much of a fan of the Troubled Asset Relief Program (aka TARP), the $700 billion bank bailout. In his 2010 State of the Union address, he told America, "We all hated the bank bailout. I hated it. You hated it. It was as popular as a root canal." So why has his administration been so obstinate about keeping TARP alive? So he could use the money for all manner of liberal mischief, that's why.

Remember what then-senator Obama promised taxpayers would happen once TARP completed its goal? In a fall 2008 Senate debate, he said, "This is not a plan to just hand over $700 billion of taxpayer money to a few banks. If this is managed correctly, we will hopefully get most of, if not all of, our money back—and possibly even turn a profit—on the government's intervention, every penny of which will go directly back to the American people."

Fast-forward to December 2009. Obama told an audience at the Brookings Institution that after all's said and done, TARP will "only" cost $141 billion. That rules out taxpayers making a "profit" off TARP. But hey, things could have been worse—we could have lost the entire $700 billion, right? We consumers should start trying similar gimmicks. The next time you're eyeing a purchase but just can't afford it, put something even more expensive on your shopping list. When you prudently come to your senses and realize there's no way you can afford that more expensive item, presto! You just "saved" enough money to buy whatever was originally on your shopping list.

These TARP "savings" were obviously burning a hole in Obama's pocket, so he decided to pour billions into other projects. When Obama bailed out Chrysler and GM, he used TARP funds, despite clear legislative language restricting funds to banks only.

In October 2009, with the congressional battle over ObamaCare heating up, the administration announced a new idea for TARP. Below-market loans would be extended to small banks with ideas for expanding lending to small businesses (never mind that small banks are by definition not "too big to fail," the supposed criteria for TARP funds).

Not surprisingly, a study by two University of Michigan economists, released on December 21, 2009, found that banks that shelled out the most money for political contributions and lobbying received more federal cash. Banks located in the district of a House Financial Services Committee member are also 26 percent more likely to receive TARP funds.

The one obstacle to the administration's use of TARP as its own socialist piggy bank was the TARP inspector general, Neil Barofsky. Charged with monitoring the ongoing administration of the program, he was reviled by the Obama economic staff for his brutal assessments. So the White House quickly moved to neutralize him. No longer would he have oversight of the small business loan program. This "curious change," Barofsky wrote to the Treasury Department, "would be terribly wasteful and lead to duplicative efforts and, at worst, could lead to significant exposure to waste, fraud and abuse." Mission accomplished!

---

## The Diary of President Barack Obama

### The White House

February 24, 2010

Spoke to the Business Roundtable guys today. When I looked out at the roomful of CEOs at the St. Regis, I thought to myself, <u>These guys think they're so special, running multibillion-dollar companies.</u> Big whoop. I could do that in my sleep! I'm running an enterprise worth <u>trillions</u>! They all seem a little cocky to me.

Axe and Rahm said that I needed to appear more "business-friendly" before we bring the hammer down on these people. But I think we're going way overboard with the sweet talk. Today, I actually became physically ill at a few points during my speech. <u>"I am an ardent believer in the free market. I believe businesses like yours are the engines of economic growth in this country."</u> And the gushing didn't stop there! <u>"You create jobs. You develop</u>

new products and cutting-edge technologies. And you create
the supply chains that make it possible for small businesses to
open their doors." At this point, even Mr. T (one of my pet names
for my old friend the teleprompter) started to break into a
digital sweat. "So I want everyone in this room to succeed." Well,
there is some truth to that. I need them to make money . . . so
they can send the bulk of it here to Washington!

Thankfully, the rest of the speech was filled with real
substance, and set the stage for how Geithner, Romer, and I are
going take over . . . everything!

You know what's funny? No matter how hard I slam these fat
cats, they still keep writing checks to the DNC!

---

The administration also uses TARP to exert influence through "pay
czar" Kenneth Feinberg. Once a matter left to bosses, shareholders, and
review boards, private sector salaries at TARP-recipient firms are now
regulated by the Treasury Department. Feinberg's first round of cuts came in
October 2009. Slashing wages by an average of 90 percent, Obama's payroll
overlord targeted 175 employees. Many complained, arguing their companies were being disadvantaged against non-TARP recipients. *As if* Democrats
hadn't already thought of that!

Senator Charles Schumer, Representative Barney Frank, and a few
other Democratic undesirables are currently incubating plans to broaden
Feinberg's domain to include *all* publicly traded companies—TARP recipients or not. And Feinberg actually viewed his mandate as far more expansive
than just micromanaging employees' pay. He also insisted that, henceforth,
chairmen and CEOs shall be separate positions, boards shall be required to
create "risk committees," and the process of "staggering" board elections
would hereafter be banned.

But Obama's TARP mayhem was just getting started. Initially a tool for "saving" big financial institutions, Obama found TARP even more useful as a club to bash the banking industry. Thus Obama positioned himself on the side of "Main Street," and against Wall Street. This, he believed, would help convince the American people that a stronger federal hand was needed. (Read: more taxes, fees, and regulations).

Obama claims that he never wanted to micromanage the internal operations of private banks. However unpleasant the undertaking, he contends it was necessary in order to protect the larger economy from another financial crisis. According to Politico, the president laid down his demands to CEOs of finance during a White House gathering in April 2009. His approach was Chicago-style:

> "These are complicated companies," one CEO said. Another offered: "We're competing for talent on an international market." But President Barack Obama wasn't in a mood to hear them out. "Be careful how you make those statements, gentlemen," the president intoned. "The public isn't buying that. . . . My Administration is the only thing between you and the pitchforks."

In a January 2010 radio address, Obama got down to business: "We have now recovered most of the [TARP] money we provided to the banks. That's good news, but as far as I'm concerned, it's not good enough. We want the taxpayers' money back, and we're going to collect every dime."

Whether banks actually took TARP money made no difference. Obama proposed a tax targeting any financial firm with at least $50 billion in assets: "This week, I proposed a new fee on major financial firms to compensate the American people for the extraordinary assistance they provided to the financial industry."

Left unmentioned is why TARP *lost* money. The banks paid off their loans. Yet the companies now under federal control—GM, Chrysler, Fannie Mae, and Freddie Mac—failed to pay up. For this, they were *rewarded* by President Obama with exemptions from his proposed "Financial Crisis Responsibility Fee."

Obama used TARP to garner new tax revenue, a billion-dollar slush fund for political boosters, and increased power over private companies. Not bad for a single government program. And when the plan was winding down, Senate Democrats proposed a "Wall Street reform" bill to make permanent their favorite parts of TARP.

Riding a populist wave of anti–Wall Street sentiment, Team Obama pushed their financial reform package through the Senate in spring 2010. To galvanize public support and overcome a Republican filibuster, Democrats orchestrated a bit of political theater on April 27. They hauled Goldman Sachs executives before a Senate subcommittee, subjecting them to eleven hours of grilling. The intention was clearly to paint the financial services industry as a dragon in need of a government slaying.

---

## THE DIARY OF PRESIDENT BARACK OBAMA

### THE WHITE HOUSE

April 26, 2010

If we want to take over Wall Street and pass financial regulatory reform, we've got to set the stage. Tomorrow Carl Levin is dragging a gaggle of Goldman fat cats before his Senate Subcommittee on Investigations. He's got to make piñatas of these boys! The only hang-up is that Levin and Claire McCaskill (the Democrat leads on the committee) know squat about finance. I had Larry Summers come in today to give them a little finance and investment (for dummies) tutorial.

This all reminds me of my days as a community organizer. If we're going to control Wall Street, we need an inciting incident, some drama to draw attention to our cause and expose the enemy investors for what they are. It's all up to Levin and McCaskill. Problem is, those two are about as exciting as a C-SPAN 3 weekend special on Mark Twain.

But I have to say, when I dropped in on them earlier, they were responding very well to Larry's coaching. They'll knock it out of the ballpark—and for some extra insurance, I'll hold a few rallies to let my people know who the real enemy is.

---

## THE DIARY OF DIRECTOR OF
## THE WHITE HOUSE ECONOMIC COUNCIL
## LARRY SUMMERS

### WASHINGTON, D.C.

*April 27, 2010*

*These people are in way over their heads—idiots from top to bottom. The hearing today was a total bust. I didn't think it was possible, but Levin and McCaskill actually made Goldman Sachs look good. If it wouldn't send the markets into a tailspin, I would go public with what I know.*

*First, the president calls me in the other day to get my views on "shorting" in the financial sector. True to form, I could tell he had his own fixed opinions on the matter before I ever opened my mouth. I tried to explain to him that these large institutions routinely short their investments to hedge against losses. Had they not done so, the economic tumult would have been even more severe. "Larry," he says, "I don't need a lecture on hedging. The Park Service does that every day right outside that window. Save the undergraduate seminar for the senators." That's when he brought in Levin and McCaskill.*

*For the next two hours, I tried to familiarize them with the basics of investment and finance. I knew when McCaskill started drawing stick figures with dollar-sign faces that we were in trouble. I give up. These people wouldn't know a derivative from a security if Charles Schwab himself broke it down for them. And this crowd is going to run the financial services industry?!*

---

On April 28, the president took to the road to sell his financial regulatory overhaul, telling a crowd in Quincy, Illinois, "I want to be clear; we're not trying to push financial reform because we begrudge success that's fairly earned. I mean, I do think at a certain point you've made *enough money*." Demonizing wealth creators is a cute trick for a man who made $5 million in 2009. I wonder if that was "enough money" for him and Michelle?

By the end of April, Obama had worn down Republican resistance, and they allowed his financial services power grab to proceed unimpeded.

—◈—

## THE DIARY OF PRESIDENT BARACK OBAMA

### THE WHITE HOUSE

April 29, 2010

Suckers! I can't believe these Republicans McConnell and Shelby fell for a "bipartisan" compromise on financial regulatory reform. Don't they know how we operate?

We now control cars, health care, banks, and soon the entire financial services industry. Next stop: the global market! I really should have transferred from Harvard Law School to the Business School. Who would have imagined that a community organizer would someday be a captain of _every_ industry?

I just got off the phone with Holder. We've got to keep the pressure on Goldman Sachs if we're going to pass this bill. Holder's announcing a major criminal fraud investigation tomorrow, examining Goldman's investing practices. We had to do something after Levin failed to draw any blood during that loooong hearing the other day. But it's all right—Barack is back on the scene. After we take down Goldman, I'm thinking we can reconstitute it as "Obama Sachs." That's one firm that is absolutely too big to fail!

# FIAT-IFYING THE AUTO INDUSTRY

By 2007, General Motors and Chrysler were hemorrhaging money—GM alone had lost $38.7 billion, and another $30.9 billion in 2008. Both companies entered bankruptcy in spring 2009, but instead of allowing the normal process to play out, Obama seized the moment to assert federal control.

"We are acting as reluctant shareholders—because that is the only way to help GM succeed," said Obama, as he excitedly snatched control of the company. "What we are not doing—what I have no interest in doing—is running GM." For that he had someone else in mind. Obama turned to his friends, the United Auto Workers. The UAW was given 55 percent ownership of Chrysler and 17.5 percent of GM. This was obvious payback for the $24 million the UAW contributed to Democrats between 2000 and 2008. (By comparison Republicans received less than $200,000.)

This act of brazen crony capitalism had severe repercussions. Delphi, the Troy, New York–based auto parts maker that entered bankruptcy when GM failed, was just one casualty. In November 2009, Delphi dumped its pension plan on the federal Pension Benefit Guarantee Corporation as part of its restructuring, which typically means reducing pension checks.

Luckily, Obama saved the day. Sort of. With GM under his thumb, Obama forced the automaker (which once owned Delphi) to absorb Delphi's 46,000 union employees, so that their pay and pensions would be preserved. As for Delphi's nonunion workers? They were out of luck.

"I am absolutely committed to working with Congress and the auto companies to meet one goal: The United States of America will lead the world in building the next generation of clean cars," Obama heroically proclaimed on March 31, 2008. But why should "clean" cars be Detroit's number-one focus? What about the novel concept of building cars Americans actually want to buy and drive?

Dumb questions, I am sure. Obama knows best. In his first speech before Congress, Obama claimed, "Everyone recognizes that years of bad decision-making"—i.e., building too many trucks and SUVs—"pushed our automakers to the brink." He brokered a deal with Fiat so that Americans could learn how to build those tiny death boxes so popular in Europe, proudly announcing: "Fiat is prepared to transfer its cutting-edge technology to Chrysler and, after working closely with my team, has committed to build—building new fuel-efficient cars and engines right here in the United States." No matter that in 2008, eleven of GM's twenty top-selling cars were pickups and SUVs. In 2009, the top two best-selling cars in America were the Ford F Series and the Chevy Silverado pickup trucks.

To help advance his eco-friendly vision for GM, Obama replaced the company's chairman with Edward Whitacre, Jr., who memorably remarked, "I don't know anything about cars." Perfect, neither does Obama. But he did know how to convene yet another government study group—the "Auto Task Force." Its mission was to produce a report detailing why GM failed and how it should operate in the future. The report was a slapdown of Obama's dream for a new green American auto industry. "[GM had] little margin for error" and its turnaround would be "very difficult," it concluded. The report went on to highlight how GM's bottom line would suffer tremendously if higher Corporate Average Fuel Economy (CAFE) standards were mandated. Less than a year later, Obama's EPA announced the most stringent CAFE standards ever.

Let them drive clown cars!

---

## THE DIARY OF PRESIDENT BARACK OBAMA

### THE WHITE HOUSE

June 4, 2009

Some of these so-called businessmen are getting on my nerves. They keep insisting that I don't understand the way the car industry "operates." They keep whining that Americans don't want to buy tiny "clown cars." "Americans want big cars, fast cars," they keep telling me. Listening to these guys, you'd swear the whole country just bought front-row seats at a truck and tractor pull! You know what I told those fat cats? Some things are more important than what Americans want to buy. Things like community and climate change and that episode of <u>Entourage</u> where Drama thinks he has no friends until the guys throw him a big surprise party at the end. We have to be concerned about each other and buy things that advance the common good. (I've always identified with Vinny on <u>Entourage</u>, though I can relate to Drama, too. People don't always recognize talent at first glance, but in time they learn to appreciate it.)

To make sure those car nuts got the message, I had the EPA write up some new rules to ensure that, in short order, every American will be driving one of those European-style golf carts. I love those little things. Who said automobile CEOs were all powerful?!

---

I think of bailouts the way I think of charity. Sure, giving away five bucks to someone on the street might make you feel good about yourself, but are you really helping anyone in the long term? Have you ever seen someone with a "will work for food" sign and actually tried to give the person food? I tried this once with an old woman sitting on the curb outside a Starbucks. She was rattling her empty Caramel Macchiato plastic cup. When I attempted to give her my untouched cinnamon scone, you might have thought I had thrown acid on her! She started screaming, "Take it away! Take it awaaaaay!" It was such a scene that other patrons thought I was harassing her. Frankly, I have more respect for the smelly panhandler I ran across in New York recently, who was holding a piece of cardboard that read: "Actually, I just want a beer."

If only the Obama administration had been this candid about the true objectives of the auto bailout and the union influences that shaped it. The Auto Task Force conveniently neglected labor costs as a contributing factor to GM's downfall (the first step on the road to recovery is admitting you have a problem!). But Americans knew better. In April 2009, Gallup found that 72 percent of Republicans, 66 percent of independents, and 42 percent of Democrats opposed the auto bailouts. Who, besides Democrats, enjoys subsidizing failure?

By propping up organized labor at the expense of smart business, tax-payers aren't the only losers here; the core American principle of honoring valid contracts has also suffered a bruising defeat. In 2007, investors shelled out $6.9 billion to purchase Chrysler bonds that they expected would produce a decent return. The bond agreement contained a stipulation that once Chrysler returned to profitability, these investors would be repaid first. Obama did not think twice about disregarding the contract, dismissing them as "a small group of speculators." (The group actually included public teachers, pensioners, and retirees.) "I don't stand with those who held out when everyone else is making sacrifices," Obama argued. He claimed their pleas amounted to "an unjustified taxpayer-funded bailout." In the end, Obama tossed the bondholders just under one-third of their original invest-ment: $2 billion.

This one episode should terrify every American who has ever made an investment in any U.S. company. In an effort to "save" a company or an industry, Obama has no qualms about trampling the contractual rights of American citizens.

—ᴖ—

## THE DIARY OF PRESIDENT BARACK OBAMA

### THE OVAL OFFICE

May 7, 2009

A measure of a man is whether he stands up for his friends when the world is against them. When the chips were down for Barack Obama during the primaries, the union bosses were there for me. Now it's time to return the favor—Obamastyle! Some in the press are trying to paint the UAW as the bad guys, while making the CEO profit-mongers out to be America's white knights! They just don't get it.

This morning, I read a column by that sourpuss paleocon George Will that made light of my bold plans to restore balance to the UAW contract talks. Captain Bow Tie had the nerve to write: "The UAW will own 55 percent of Chrysler, so perhaps the union will sit on both sides of the table in negotiations. They should go smoothly, although the UAW may think it has made sufficient concessions, such as the one that says henceforth overtime pay will not begin until the worker has toiled 40 hours in a week."

Will just doesn't get it. It's not like I won't be there representing the American people in all negotiations. As I told UAW chief Ron Gettelfinger the other day, "With you and Barack Obama on both sides of the negotiating table, the UAW will get anything it wants. Let's melt these big boys down and help the worker for a change, shall we?" And I meant it, too, because these labor organizers have suffered for years and they could not be sweeter guys.

Case in point: this afternoon, after weeks of haggling with the corporate overlords about how much of their companies they'll be allowed to retain, Gettelfinger dropped in for a visit. Would you believe that this man actually took time out to review every word of my plans for the auto industry! He even pitched in and added a few lines of his own. That's sacrificing for America. The man's a patriot. Not only is the UAW offering to help finish writing up the plan, they're actually willing to take the reins and run these companies on my behalf! These guys are saints!

---

Meanwhile, as Obama wrapped his tentacles around everything from health care to automobiles, the real issues the federal government should be handling—such as immigration enforcement—are treated as an afterthought. While his Homeland Security Department has carried out some high-profile workplace raids, the president has generally failed to take border enforcement seriously. President Obama might as well say what we already know: enforcing the federal immigration laws (i.e., removing those here illegally) is an impediment to achieving one of his top priorities—his reelection. In the undocumented-alien population Democrats see millions of potential new voters who will be reliable supporters of their big-government agenda. Every deported alien is one less vote for Obama in 2012.

When Arizona decided to do the job the federal government won't do, and passed its own tough immigration enforcement measure in April 2010, the president dispatched his legal and PR machine to slam the law. The law, wildly popular in the state, calls for Arizona police to verify the legal status of individuals they come in lawful contact with. What an outrage! People who live and work in America must be here legally?!

At a town hall meeting in Iowa, Obama characterized the Arizona effort this way: "Now, suddenly, if you don't have your papers and you took your kid out to get ice cream, you're going to be harassed, that's something that could potentially happen." This was a particularly despicable instance of Obama fearmongering, given the fact that the law's language explicitly prohibits using race or ethnicity as the "sole factor" in prompting a request for identification. Attorney General Eric Holder held a press conference to register his disapproval, and Homeland Security secretary Janet Napolitano told a congressional panel she was "deeply concerned." Amazingly, both were forced to admit to Congress that they had never actually read the law.

Hey, Janet, we're deeply concerned, too. Deeply concerned that you, Holder, and the rest of the cabinet are totally incompetent.

---

## THE DIARY OF PRESIDENT BARACK OBAMA

### AIR FORCE ONE

April 27, 2010

Just got word from Rahm that the Arizona law is already having its intended effect! He tells me that many of the undocumented citizens there are already starting to self-deport back to their home countries! This is a nightmare. Plouffe says we need all the newly registered Democrat voters we can get in 2012, and that includes the 460,000 estimated to live in Arizona. By the way, somebody's falling down on his job—that number should be up to at least a million at this point!

We have to do something, pronto! I know, I'll have Gibbs coordinate with La Raza. I'm sure we can help set up a few great reverse sting operations to make those xenophobes in Arizona look really bad. We can also orchestrate a scenario with some sympathetic figures—maybe an attractive pregnant Latina or an army veteran, who can claim they were called names and manhandled by local police. I also need to get our immigration rights advisors to organize huge, disruptive, May Day protests. We've got to maintain our momentum. I've decided to shelve my comprehensive immigration plans until next year, so I can focus on taking over the financial markets. But we can't let up. We've got to lock down these cities across America—if only to keep my future voters from leaving! Until we get this law repealed, I'm boycotting Arizona Iced Tea.

---

# A CULTURE OF DEPENDENCY

Winston Churchill once described an appeaser as someone who hopes that "if he feeds the crocodile enough, the crocodile will eat him last." The same is true of businesses only too happy to cut deals with a predatory government. In August 2009, I had a spokesman on my radio show from America's Health Insurance Plans, the trade group for the health insurance industry. AHIP had repeatedly expressed interest in working with Obama to craft compromise health-care legislation. I warned him that insurance companies were a mere speed bump along the way to the industry's gradual nationalization under ObamaCare. He maintained that AHIP is smarter to hammer out a deal than oppose "reform" outright.

After his initial failure to sell America on his utopian health-care vision, the president retooled the message, turning insurers into bogeymen ("the special interests who profit off the status quo," as he so gently referred to them). Before long, I saw the same spokesman complaining in a newspaper article that insurers "do not deserve to be vilified for political purposes." So much for the fruits of playing nice.

Within a week of the health-care reform bill's passage, AT&T, Verizon, Caterpillar, Deere, Valero Energy, AK Steel, and 3M warned how the law would hurt their employees and customers. Democrats still high on their "historic" achievement went nuts. Beverly Hills Democrat Henry Waxman fired off a demand for these companies' executives to explain themselves and beg forgiveness before his House Committee on Energy and Commerce. Fortunately for them, Waxman ultimately canceled the hearing once he realized that the forum could be used to showcase ObamaCare's horrors.

"Some people regard private enterprise as a predatory tiger to be shot," Churchill once said. "Others look on it as a cow they can milk. Not enough people see it as a healthy horse, pulling a sturdy wagon." I think Obama falls into his own category: he sees private enterprise as prey to be hunted and its corpse to be feasted upon.

But private enterprise is not the only part of American society affected by a culture of dependence. Such a culture will hurt all of us. Surrendering to a life of government dependence saps the soul of its independent spirit.

Remember Henrietta Hughes, the starstruck town hall attendee who pleaded on national TV for Obama to give her a house? In 2004, Henrietta lived in Rochester, New York, with her son Corey, a computer programmer. When Corey began suffering pains in his thyroid gland, he received free care from Dr. Carolyn Mok at the Mercy Outreach Center, a clinic for the uninsured and underprivileged, operated by the Sisters of Mercy.

"There isn't many doctors that will see you if you don't have insurance," Henrietta then told the *Rochester Democrat and Chronicle.* "There's doctors, just out of the compassion and goodness of his heart, that will give his service or her service, and I'm very grateful to God."

Henrietta and Corey eventually packed up and moved to Florida, where they again fell upon hard times. By her own account, she used government assistance until the tap went dry. When Obama visited, she said no local charities were willing to help. But that's not what the director of We Care Outreach Ministry, Tanya Johnson, says. Johnson said her faith-based charity gave Henrietta food and money and offered job-training courses for Corey, according to a report by southwest Florida's WINK News. "We would have allowed her to stay for the first ninety days, no income. You know, free," Johnson said. Henrietta said, according to WINK, that We Care Outreach Ministry "couldn't meet her needs."

What about Natoma Canfield, whom we last heard Obama invoking at one of his final health-care rallies? Turns out she too had no reason to pen a personal appeal to the president. "She may be eligible for Medicaid," said Lyman Sornberger, executive director of the Cleveland Clinic's patient financial services. "And/or she will be eligible for charity [care] of some form or type. In my personal opinion, she will be eligible for something."

The Cleveland Clinic has personal guides to help patients find a program to assist paying medical bills, FoxNews.com reported. Even if Natoma failed to qualify for Medicaid, "there are probably eight to ten options that a patient has."

Far from spurring national cries for action, Henrietta Hughes and Natoma Canfield each exemplified success stories in American charity. Selfless acts fortify our society, as highlighted by the gratitude Henrietta expressed after her son received free care in New York. In Florida, we know she turned to state-provided social handouts; soon she was eschewing private charity and displaying the traits of an entitlement mentality.

America is powered by millions of self-reliant individuals pursuing their own American Dream. Expanding the welfare state is like putting sugar in the gas tank.

## THE WINNING WAY

A March 2010 poll from Xavier University found that 60 percent of Americans believe the American Dream is harder to achieve than it was for their parents' generation.

A growing economy that churns out jobs and opens new opportunities for wealth creation is the best antidote for Americans' current unease about their economic future. We all must be actively engaged in the political process, supporting candidates who stand up for free market principles and reject the Obama takeover mentality. The stakes are too big for us to fail.

As shareholders, we should urge companies to refuse the "helping hand" of government, so that they may remain competitive, free, and profitable. If you work in the business world, or own your own business, then we need you out there advocating on behalf of economic liberty and the capitalist system. Too many in business rolled over for the big takeover artists in Washington, and we are all now paying the price.

Government will always take more than it gives. Liberals of President Obama's stripe will always spend instead of cut. It is the only way they can cultivate a dependent constituency, which in turn perpetuates their power. So it is up to us to oppose their efforts with the same zeal that Barack Obama has brought to his own radical initiatives. The alternative is not an option. Doing nothing, waiting for others to act, or hoping for the best will ensure only one outcome: *you* will be the next government takeover.

CHAPTER **5**

# FIT TO SERVE?

*Our growing softness, our increasing lack of physical fitness, is a menace to our security.*

—JOHN F. KENNEDY

It was 11 P.M. on a Friday and the blizzard of 2010 was bearing down on the mid-Atlantic states. Washington, D.C. was in the bull's-eye. For days, local news had warned of a massive, paralyzing snowfall. In the nation's capital, that meant impassable roads (you have a greater chance of seeing Bigfoot in D.C. than a snowplow), power outages, and general hysteria. When I walked outside to shovel, we must have already had ten inches on the ground. And no, it wasn't that light, airy, cotton-candy-type stuff—it was wet, heavy, heart-attack snow. An hour into it, my heart was racing, my turtleneck was drenched in sweat, and with my car still not totally dug out, my mind began to wander.

*I'm pretty fit, but man, this is harder than it was twenty years ago! My forearms, my back, my legs—everything hurts. What about tomorrow—how will I possibly dig out my car when two more feet have piled up? Heaven forbid, what if something happened to one of my kids during this blizzard? An ambulance couldn't make it down my street. Am I strong enough to carry them through the snow to a main road? If we lose electricity, do I have a "survival kit" handy in case we need it to ride out the storm?*

Realizing how vulnerable I was, even in a state of solid physical fitness, I started wondering about my preparedness for other potential crises.

*What if there is another terror attack in Washington? What's my "family plan" for rounding up my children and, if need be, getting out of town? If things got really rough, would I be able to provide for my family in a catastrophe? Eat off the land? I'm still traumatized from running over a squirrel on the way to taking my SATs! Could I build a makeshift shelter? Unless it was made out of Lego blocks, unlikely . . . uh-oh.*

By the time I finished my driveway, the snowfall had become blinding. But for me it was a moment of clarity about what I need to do to protect my children in an emergency. When 9/11 hit, I was childless and carefree. Things are different now. We live in a time of great peril. It isn't all about me anymore; it is about them. So on a beautiful snowy night, I vowed to start taking preparedness more seriously.

---

## THE DIARY OF PRESIDENT BARACK OBAMA

### THE WHITE HOUSE

February 6, 2010

Man, Hawaii's looking really good right now. This snow is really getting to me. Dying for a smoke. Cooped up here again with Miche, the kids, and Mother Robinson, who feels the need to bark out the latest weather news at awkward times. The woman insists on calling the National Weather Service herself at least twice a day—wants to "hear the weather from the horse's mouth." Whatever. And Miche . . . love her . . . but boy, if I have to hear one more thing from her about the latest drop in my approval ratings. "Do this, Barack." "Fire this person, Barack." "If you had only listened to me, Barack." My head is going to explode. If I wanted this type of abuse, I could tune in to Rush Limbaugh!

Wow, the snow is still coming down. How am I supposed to blow off steam when the b-ball court is covered by a foot of snow? Call me crazy, but I thought groundskeepers were supposed to take care of the <u>grounds</u>! Thought about shoveling it myself, but in case anyone hasn't noticed—I am not just the president, I'm an <u>international celebrity</u>! Does Denzel shovel his own driveway?

Actually, on second thought, anything to get me out of this place for an hour or so—and it's the perfect cover to grab some smokes! Maybe a little manual labor would help me with the blue-collar types, too. They sure do get huffy about this whole jobs thingy. This unemployment issue is being blown out of proportion. I can think of worse things than getting paid to do nothing! Kind of like community organizing! LOL! Back to the b-ball court—I better ask the Axe. He's great at managing the snow jobs. Get it? Snow jobs?! Man, I'm good.

---

## ARE YOU READY FOR THE NEXT CRISIS?

Just because you don't wear a uniform doesn't mean you shouldn't be fit to serve. We all have a responsibility to our families, neighbors and, yes, to our country, to be as prepared as possible for whatever life throws at us. Weather emergencies, other natural disasters, terror attacks, severe illness, accidents, crime—whatever it is, none of us can afford to be passive.

Let's face it, there won't always be someone there to help you—especially if you are waiting for timely government response. Plus, why should any of us put ourselves in a situation where we have to depend on the government for a rescue? (Unless, of course, you're AIG.) Invariably, a government "solution" means less power and money for the people, and more power and money for Washington.

I know what you are thinking. How on earth can she turn a discussion on fitness and preparedness into a critique of the Obamas? Think of Michelle, with her toned arms, anti-obesity initiative, and vegetable garden. Or the president, with his daily workouts and weekend hoops and golf games. (And who can forget that campaign photo of His Buffness, shirtless in the Hawaiian surf?) The First Couple represents the epitome of fitness and seeks to spread the message of healthy eating to the masses. They are setting a positive example for the rest of us, are they not?

―――――――――――――――⎯⎯∞∞⎯⎯―――――――――――――――

## THE DIARY OF PRESIDENT BARACK OBAMA

### THE WHITE HOUSE

February 15, 2010

They call me "No Drama Obama," but I am on the verge of losing it. <u>Miche is driving me nuts!</u> I agreed to give her this anti-fat fiefdom so I could get help on health-care reform, not so she could be on my back 24/7 because I grab a few fries every now and then. Just because she's an obesity czar doesn't mean she's suddenly Megan Fox! You know, if you live in a glass house . . .

Every time I turn around, she's braying on about how the

country needs to start eating healthy, do more exercise, etc. Oh, please—a few training sessions with her overpaid personal trainer and now she's Denise Austin? And as for the eating part, who's she kidding? Is she sleepwalking when she orders those late-night quesadillas and nachos from the White House kitchen? She acts like she's sacrificing when she says "hold the guac"! For fun, I told Sam Kass (the White House chef) to keep a list of what she eats on a daily basis. Here's the rundown for today:

BREAKFAST
*3 fried eggs
*bagel with "low-fat" cream cheese
*plate of bacon (too many strips to count)
*grits (double order, drenched in butter)
*smoothie (if you consider a chocolate malted milk shake a "smoothie")

LUNCH
*slab of baby-back ribs
*bowl of jambalaya
*"salad" (the garnish on the plate)

AFTERNOON SNACK
More ribs

DINNER
*Veal Parmesean w/ double baked potato (low-fat margarine—oooh, what restraint!)

*green beans (untouched)

*chocolate volcano "virtue cake" (it used to be called "sin
  cake," but she made the kitchen staff rename it
  because she said it was "too judgmental")

*washed down with (1) cosmo and (1) glass of organic
  chianti

BEDTIME SNACK:
The last 3 ribs

And she's on my case every time I have a burger?! Next time
she nags me, I'll serve her up some steamed Baraccoli! Oh, am I
good or what?

---

Yes, it is great that they exercise, and yes, it is laudable that the First
Lady uses her celebrity to encourage us to live a healthy lifestyle. But if the
president and First Lady are going to lecture the rest of us about what we in-
gest, shouldn't they live by the same rules? Months before she kicked off her
fat fight, Mrs. Obama chatted with school children at a Cinco de Mayo event
and spilled the beans about her favorite type of food. "I love beans and rice.
I love mole. I love all the mole sauces, I love beef and lamb and quesadillas," she laughed. "I mean, you name it. The question is, what don't I like?
I like it all." Indeed. A few days later, the First Lady took her staff to a place
called the Good Stuff Eatery for lunch. The fare included the "Prez Obama"
burger (natch), regular burgers, smokehouse burgers, bacon cheeseburgers,
and two types of fries. (Are they heart-friendly if "dusted" in sea salt, thyme,
and rosemary?) The *Washington Post* reported that this was one of "several"
outings Mrs. Obama and her aides had made to local burger and barbecue
joints. "Sometimes you just need a burger," staffer McCormick Lelyveld
told the *Post*. "It was her idea."

For a couple that is supposed to symbolize health and fitness, there seems to be no end to their own fast-food noshing. Who can forget when the press pool followed the president and vice president to Ray's Hell Burgers during their first months in office? It was supposedly a spur-of-the-moment food run—not that they had anything else to do. Barack Obama advanced the narrative of his historic presidency when he ordered the classic cheddar burger with Dijon mustard. Other burger runs followed with similar fanfare, including a particularly embarrassing trip to Five Guys with NBC anchor and lunchmate Brian Williams, who was doing a "day in the life" love-in with the president. (Shhh! Don't tell the kids that *Men's Health* magazine rated Five Guys Fries the "worst regular order of fries" in America—1,464 calories, 71 grams fat [14 grams saturated], 213 milligrams sodium.)

---

## THE DIARY OF VICE PRESIDENT JOE BIDEN

### WASHINGTON, D.C.

May 5, 2009

Hey, being vice president is f---ing cool! The Prez invited me out for some quality time—even though it was POTUS & VPOTUS (I love that acronym!), we were just two guys goin' out for cheeseburgers. (By the way, none of the people who waited on us had Indian accents. I still don't get why they gravitate toward 7-Elevens.) Anyway, we did some great male bonding today—for forty-five minutes or so I was able to forget all that Recovery Act gibberish I'm supposed to be tracking. And as I sat at that burger joint, watching this young, bright, nice-looking guy in shirtsleeves across from me, I felt vindicated. The kid didn't so much as drip one drop of grease or Dijon mustard on himself! Hardly needed a napkin! I knew I was right when I said he is a "clean" African-American!

But that Michelle, she's something else. We get back to the White House and she was on Barack like white on rice. I couldn't hear much of what she was saying other than "I told you I wanted a <u>double</u> cheeseburger, extra fried onions, you fool!" Man, she's tough. Kind of like a black Hillary Clinton. I mean that in a good way.

---

Then my personal favorite: six weeks into the First Lady's childhood obesity campaign, she and the girls headed to New York for spring break, and made headlines when they made a beeline to the legendary pizza joint Grimaldi's. The Obamas and three school chums ordered four pies—no word on whether the sausage and pepperoni were low-fat varieties.

As usual with liberals, the rules and edicts they insist on saddling the "little people" with don't apply to them. Remember, they're special. They're historic.

## FOR THE OBAMAS, IT'S ALWAYS PERSONAL

George and Laura Bush were also extremely fit, but we weren't subjected to a constant barrage of news stories and profiles featuring mind-numbing details of their exercise regimens. I had the grueling pleasure of mountain biking with President Bush a few times. For him it was about the personal challenge, camaraderie, and friendly competition—never about selling an image of himself to further a political goal.

With the First Lady's battle against the bulge, there is more going on than meets the thigh. As with so much of what the Obamas advocate, their fitness and healthy eating push is one part federal boondoggle, one part vanity project. We the people are supposed to be thrilled to ride along on their ego trip, oohing and aahing about how they look, how they act, and just their overall awesomeness. By pushing stories about Mrs. Obama's physical strength, her toned arms, and workout routines, her handlers were determined early on to establish her as an authority on health and fitness. That way, when the time came for her debut as policy advocate on these issues, it would seem to many like a natural fit because her credibility was already established. By that logic, anyone with a ThighMaster or Gold's Gym membership—or snow shovel, for that matter—qualifies as an expert.

---

## THE DIARY OF FIRST-LADY-IN-WAITING MICHELLE OBAMA

### CHICAGO

*November 19, 2008*

*Another grueling day: media interviews, hair styled, wardrobe review, talked for a few minutes to the girls. But the AP finally caught up to most every other media outlet and ran a great piece about my arms. (Yeah, they mentioned Smokey's workouts, too — but I'm ticked that they didn't even drop in the detail Desiree leaked about how he's still sneakin' cigs with Rahm!) Wait until they see the designer one-of-a-kind dresses that Desiree has lined*

up in my closet—every single one of them sleeveless! A plum one
for the Joint Session of Congress speech in February. A fuschia
one for the <u>Vogue</u> cover. I can really get used to this part of being
First Lady.

I did tell Desiree that under no circumstances do I want the
public to know what she calls my biceps, although "Brad" and
"Angelina" are the perfect nicknames! (After all, only Brangelina
gets covered more than these sleek, sensuous lovelies!) These
reporter fools are so easy to lead around by the noses. They're
all writing up a storm about how we are fitness role models and
such. I hear freaking CNN is doing a segment titled "How to Get
Michelle Obama's Toned Arms"! Hilarious! (The young lady
reporter was begging the press office for some scrap about how I
manage to look so gorgeous, so I told Cornell to give her a few
of our secrets. Hell, after nearly two thousand personal training
sessions together since 1997, we have this down to a science.)

But honestly, average citizens shouldn't get their hopes up. It's
going to take a lot more than some hammer curls and tricep pull-
downs to look as good as me! After all, as Mama always says, I
started with a perfect foundation!

# GOVERNMENT, THE ULTIMATE "PERSONAL TRAINER"

What the Obamas get wrong on fitness and health care is what they always get wrong. Like all left-wingers, they believe that for every problem there is a government solution. (Remember, as Rahm Emanuel famously said, "Never let a crisis go to waste"—or, as the case may be, "waist.")

On February 9, 2010, Michelle Obama launched her much-hyped anti-obesity initiative, called "Let's Move!" which was orchestrated with the planning and precision of the D-day landing. Cabinet secretaries, congressional leaders, celebrities, star athletes, business leaders, and select schoolchildren were brought in as human props to mask the fact that this was yet another heavyweight body slam by the nanny state. Mrs. Obama marshaled the full force of the White House, complete with an executive order signed by the president to "create a ninety-day plan that allows optimal coordination as we move forward." And, of course, since Democrats can't breathe without spending billions in tax dollars, the Obama administration also asked Congress for $10 billion over ten years to improve the quality of school lunches and breakfasts.

Of course, congressional authorization was a mere formality. Who, after all, would deny Michelle? Even as the president's own approval ratings tanked, hers remained enviably high. So whatever Sleeveless wants, Sleeveless gets.

---

## THE DIARY OF PRESIDENT BARACK OBAMA

### THE WHITE HOUSE

March 2, 2010

Now I've had it. This "Let's Move!" sideshow of Miche's is really starting to cramp my style. The press is having a field day with the results of my medical checkup. How can someone with my stellar physique have elevated cholesterol?! I don't believe those numbers. Who did the blood testing—Rasmussen? And then to add insult to injury, they're getting on me for eating a little fried chicken and mac & cheese at Mrs. Wilkes' Dining Room in Savannah today. I told the reporters not to tell Michelle— the last thing I need is another lecture from her. Man, they usually keep my secrets, but not today.

---

Of course, liberal elites are loath to admit that anything they do is overtly political: "This isn't about politics . . . I'm talking about common-sense steps we can take in our families and communities to help our kids lead active, healthy lives," the First Lady said on February 9, 2010, when she launched her "Let's Move" initiative in the state dining room.

Any time the Obamas say, "It's not about politics," it's definitely about politics. The First Lady clearly believes in a government-managed, top-down approach to pretty much every issue facing America. And no, I was not dissuaded of this notion by Mrs. Obama's interview with *Newsweek* editor John Meacham (March 17, 2010), where she said that government cannot mandate healthy eating: "You can't tell people what to do in their own homes, nor should you." If she really meant that, of course, she would not be using the power of Congress, the White House, and HHS to help her with her pet project. Her approach to everything is statist. "[We] need to make sure that we pass legislation that makes sense, that sets clear basic nutritional guidelines, not just in the school lunch lines, but in the vending machines and a la carte lines," she told *Newsweek*. So much for not being able to legislate healthy eating.

So if we have too many fat people in America, it's up to the Obamas and their elite friends to force-feed us their views and policies on nutrition, exercise, and healthy living. And when Michelle barked, "Let's Move!" it wasn't just government types that stood at attention. American corporations and professional associations did, too. Their eagerness to "cooperate" with the First Lady, like the hospital groups and drug companies that leapt to work with President Obama on health care, seemed counterintuitive. After all, the Obama administration wants to control them, and dictate the terms of their corporate existence.

Consider Mrs. Obama's speech on March 16, 2010, to the Grocery Manufacturers Association, where she basically ordered the companies in attendance to shape up or else: "We need you not to just tweak around the edges, but entirely rethink the products you are offering, the information that you provide about these products, and how you market those products to our children." Look at the language—*"entirely rethink the products you are offering."* The implicit threat is there—do this now, or get ready to deal with a raft of new federal regulations. And if that weren't intrusive enough, she described her own version of *The Price Is Right*, intoning "there needs to be a serious industry-wide commitment to providing the healthier foods parents are looking for at prices they can afford." Mrs. Obama is not only going to dictate ingredients but also prices? There's a place where that approach to governance is very popular—it's called Venezuela.

Sadly, not one executive from Coca-Cola, Kraft, or any of the other big food manufacturers had the guts to stand up and question this excessive governmental interference. In fact, not only did no one from the food industry publicly resist the warnings of Mrs. Obama, but the food business sycophants lined up. The American Beverage Association promised new calorie labeling. Major food suppliers pledged to cut sugar, salt, and fat in school cafeterias and offer healthy alternatives. Pepsi announced it was pulling its soda from schools worldwide. Even Burger King pledged its support. My personal favorite: the American Academy of Pediatrics urged its physician-members to regularly check the Body Mass Index (BMI) for children two years of age and older. Two-year-olds?! Tubby toddlers, beware!

# SELL THE AGENDA, USE THE CHILDREN

"A couple of years ago—you'd never know it by looking at her now—Malia was getting a little chubby," President-elect Obama said, according to ABC News. It seems he then gave his wife a little push to do something about it, which she did.

———————————— ❧❧❧ ————————————

## The Diary of First Grandmother Marian Robinson

### The White House

April 12, 2009

I liked the idea of moving out of Chicago for a while, but living full-time at the White House with President Prissy is becoming less and less attractive to me. I went to the dentist today and picked up a November 2008 copy of <u>Parenting</u> magazine in the waiting room. As if I need to read another interview with Barack and Michelle! How dare Barack tell them that my granddaughter was ever "chubby"? And I can't believe that Michelle took him seriously. The girls are not now and never were fat. And excuse me, but Barack wasn't exactly a featherweight in some of <u>his</u> kiddie photos!

At dinner tonight, Barack asked if I could pass the salt, and I said, "Congratulations!" "For what?" he said. "For asking me to pass the salt without your teleprompter!" He got all snippy with me after that, but he was just grouchy because no amount of salt could make that bland, free-range, skinless chicken dish tasty. Sasha just pushed it around her plate. Malia ate a few bites but was miserable. The girls begged me to get Sam and the crew to whip up a pepperoni pizza for them after dinner. I had it delivered up to the third floor, they snuck up before bed, and we each gobbled down a few pieces. Take that, Mr. and Mrs. Party Pooper!

---

So Michelle marched her daughters into the pediatrician's office. According to the First Lady, he "was concerned something was getting off-balance" with the girls' weight. The doctor "cautioned me that I had to take a look at my own children's BMI," she remarked, adding, "In my eyes, I thought my children were perfect. I didn't see the changes." Little by little, she changed her daughters' diets—less fruit juice, more water; smaller portions; apple slices in their lunch boxes; bright veggies at the dinner table; and no TV during the week. (Call the Nobel committee! He gets the Peace Prize for not being George Bush and she gets the Peas Prize for taking the fat out of our land.) Then, as Mrs. Obama tells it, at the next checkup, their pediatrician was astounded by the change in the girls. In other words, thanks to Mom's ingenious nutrition plan, the girls had avoided waddling farther down the road to fatdom.

This set off a flurry of debates on the Internet and cable television, with some health advocates questioning whether the president and First Lady were actually doing harm to the body image of girls across America by invoking their perfectly fit girls as examples. Paul Campos, writing in the *New Republic*, expressed the disgust many people were feeling:

> [O]ne wonders if the First Lady has considered that putting her pre-teen daughters on diets is far more likely to make them eating disordered rather than permanently thin. (If the kind of obsessive monitoring of food and activity choices Obama recommends to parents actually "worked," there would be almost no fat kids in America today, at least in the middle

and upper class families where Obama's anxieties about her daughters' weight are all too common).

Also, by invoking their daughters' weight travails to justify their latest adventure in nanny state politics, the Obamas are violating their own cardinal rule that children of politicians should be off-limits. Candidate Obama made the point on more than one occasion, including in defense of Bristol Palin: "I think people's families are off limits, and people's children are especially off limits. This shouldn't be part of our politics. . . ." In February 2010, Michelle Obama told CBS News that when it comes to being with their girls, the White House is a "politics-free zone." The instinct to keep children out of the messiness of politics is, of course, right. But how exactly is telling the story of the chubster daughters shielding them from the public glare? Once again, the rules the Obamas want everyone else to live by don't apply to them.

---

## THE DIARY OF FIRST GRANDMOTHER MARIAN ROBINSON

### THE WHITE HOUSE

February 17, 2010

If I've said it once, I've said it a thousand times—Michelle really is the one who shoulda been president. Has President Spindly Legs looked at his numbers lately? Goodness gracious, Iran's Mahmoud Shrimpy is more popular here than he is!

Then Barack has the nerve to tell some reporter that I am "becoming quite the lady about town"! Why doesn't he keep his uppity nose in his own business? Even au pairs get nights off every now and then—and by the way, they get paid more than

I do . . . which is easy since I get paid with only the privilege of living with Mr. Historic.

Oh, and His Highness is supposedly miffed because I told the same reporter that I don't eat dinner with them every night because I want to give them their "private family time." The truth is, he bugs the living daylights out of me with his cocky attitude about everything from politics to fitness! If I hear him bragging again about how he's in much better shape than W was when he was president, I'm gonna lose it!

"Reggie says my calves are getting stronger." "Reggie says my golf swing is improving." "Reggie says my ab workout rocks." You know what Reggie should also say? That you reek of cigs, Smokey! Or is half a pack a day also recommended in the Body by Reggie workout DVD?

---

## YES WE CAN . . . DICTATE EVERYTHING

No matter how "down home" the president and First Lady try to act or sound, they are, at their core, elitist snobs. Maybe they weren't always this way, but somewhere along the line they both developed a metropolitan snootiness that they just can't shake. Don't be fooled by the phony southern accent that Mr. Obama puts on when he's "fired up" in front of an audience outside the Washington–New York–Los Angeles orbit. Don't be taken in by Mrs. Obama's "I-was-once-struggling-out-there-just-like-you" charade. Remember, she's still the woman who, during the campaign, said, "For the first time in my adult lifetime, I'm really proud of my country." And he is the same fellow who remarked that bitter Pennsylvania voters "cling to their guns or religion." The bottom line is: they are both disdainful of NASCAR voters, who might like to kick back with a bowl of ice cream or a beer at the end of a hard day.

This condescension was on full display when the First Lady headed to Philadelphia to promote Let's Move! on February 16, 2010. It was there that she launched her ground war against "food deserts." The Let's Move! website defines a "food desert" as a place where a grocery store is more than a mile away. (Gee, to think I didn't even know that I grew up in a "food desert" in Glastonbury, Connecticut!) The First Lady managed to bring not one, but two cabinet secretaries with her to the Fresh Grocer store in North Philadelphia. (USDA Secretary Tom Vilsack makes sense—but Treasury Secretary Geithner?)

The $15 million store had opened recently in a poor area in North Philadelphia, with money from the Pennsylvania Fresh Food Financing Initiative. The aim of the public-private partnership is to give low-income areas easier access to grocery stores. Isn't obesity mostly a behavioral and lifestyle-related problem? Is it really an issue of people's *proximity* to "healthy food"? And as to the criticisms that have been leveled at grocery stores for supposedly "abandoning" inner-city neighborhoods across urban America—does the First Lady ever consider the possibility that the grocery stores that closed in Detroit, Los Angeles, and Newark, etc., did so because they weren't profitable? Or that the areas had become so crime-ridden that doing business there became untenable?

The Obamas, of course, don't really care about American business unless it's dedicating itself to achieving one of their inane social welfare goals—whether it's "universal health care" or cap-and-trade or the fight against fat. Apparently the government even has the key to unlock the fitness secret. In his 2011 federal budget, Obama asked for a whopping $400 million to launch a national effort based on the Pennsylvania model.

This shows just how out of touch the Obamas are. Poor people buy things like Ramen noodles and boxed macaroni and cheese because they are cheap and filling—not because they're sold around the corner at a convenience store. (By the way, both are tasty!) Who out there actually believes that once we blow $400 million that we don't have on food cooperatives, poor people will start buying baby arugula, acai juice, and artisanal cheese? Has Michelle Obama ever really looked at what is distributed at a food pantry? Writer Matt Labash has, and during an appearance on my radio show, described it this way:

> Guess what I didn't see there? I didn't see Swiss Chard, I didn't see exotic Daikon radishes or whatever they are. I saw canned Dinty Moore beef stew and the other foods that make Malia and Sasha fat. Because poor people can't afford the things that Michelle Obama is talking about. So it's basically an insult. It's a classist argument, it really is. It's just a level of snobbery that makes me very uncomfortable. These people are lucky if they can afford iceberg lettuce. I don't know if they understand there is a recession going on. Poor people can't afford the food they are talking about.

Maybe poor people can't, but left-wingers like the Obamas will do what they always do in their quest to achieve a socialist utopia—they'll ask working Americans to pick up the tab. There aren't enough rich people in our fifty states to pay for all the garbage they are trying to sell us. The fact is, now that we've seen the cost to our wallets and our freedom, more of us just want the government to leave us alone. We are tired of being lectured about everything from the amount of carbon we emit, to how high we set our thermostats, and now to what we put in our stomachs. What happened to the line that the government should keep its hands off our bodies? *Our Bodies, Ourselves,* etc.? Oh, that's right, that applies only when a woman wants an abortion. Cheetos bad, abortions good.

## FITNESS WITH A PURPOSE

Why should we even care about being fit? Especially when we reach adulthood, and are beyond most competitive sports, what's the point? Sure, it makes us feel better, look better, and often live longer, but are there other, perhaps more compelling, reasons to get ourselves in decent shape? The answer is yes.

First, primal instincts compel us to do everything in our power to protect and care for our families. That job gets more and more difficult (and more dangerous) if we are carrying around an extra thirty or so pounds of fat on our bodies. I'm a bit of a fitness freak, yet I still feel like I get tired too easily when I am carrying my twenty-five-pound son on my hip while making breakfast. And I wonder whether I am conditioned enough to keep up with two children at a Saturday afternoon soccer clinic. Here's the un-PC skinny: the more overweight and out of shape we are, the more difficult it will be for us to respond optimally in an emergency, and the tougher it will be to carry out everyday tasks and responsibilities. So why handicap ourselves this way if we can do something about it?

Second, maintaining a base level of fitness is also—pardon me for sounding corny—the right thing to do for the country. Yes, you read that correctly—*for the country*. Right about now you're thinking, *What? If I want to sit on my couch all day and pound Dove bites and root beer, that's exactly what I'll do. If I want to be a fat slob, I'll be a fat slob.* Certainly, that's true. We are free to be as soft and out of shape as we want. We are also free to become maniacally obsessed with exercise for vanity's sake. (You know, the people who constantly stare at themselves in the gym mirrors.) Or we can decide to reject both of the previous two options and simply commit to being as strong as we can be in the event that we are needed to stand in the physical defense of the country.

Think of the people trapped on the ninety-first floor of World Trade Center's north tower who had to walk down ninety flights of stairs. Think of the firefighters walking up. What if one asked for your help? Could you get out of such a difficult situation alive? Or have you let yourself go to such an extent that you wonder if you would have the stamina or strength to survive?

Sometimes people don't believe me when I tell them that I have had my own struggles with weight. In college, my cheeks were so big I looked like I had a perpetual case of the mumps. Diets never worked for me—things evened out when I started treating food as fuel, not as an indulgence. If you are driving, you don't need to fill up with gas every time you're down a quarter tank. When I started writing down every bit of food and drink I put into my mouth, it was shocking to realize just how much I was consuming when I wasn't the slightest bit hungry. I was a classic college grazer. If a Snickers bar was lying around, I'd eat it. If a bunch of friends were going out for pizza and I had already eaten dinner, I'd join them and eat again. For the most part, I survived on Diet Coke and heavy, high-calorie, processed foods.

By age twenty-three, I had turned my eating dysfunction around. It wasn't anything dramatic. I just made a conscious effort to fill up on the natural stuff—salads, lean meats, fish, whole grains, lots of water. Reorienting my food intake made all the difference. Oh, and I still ate junk food (and still do), but just didn't (and don't now) subsist on it.

No matter how old you are, no matter where you live, no matter how busy you are, you can, with a little dedication, increase your strength and fitness level in a relatively short period of time. This will vastly improve the likelihood of your making it through an emergency situation and helping those around you, too.

As Michelle Obama said—and didn't believe for a nanosecond—we cannot legislate fitness. Each of us must individually commit to putting in the time and effort to make ourselves freedom forces of nature. This does not require the self-absorbed and narcissistic attitude that we've come to expect from the Obamas. All that is required is your personal resolve to invest some time and effort for the sake of your family and our nation. Eating right, exercising, getting enough sleep, drinking plenty of water, drinking alcohol only in moderation, not smoking—these are all important for our physical and mental well-being.

This isn't a fitness or diet book, so this is not your resource for the perfect exercise routine. Unlike Michelle, I don't claim to be an expert. But if you are reading this and feel like you want to do more to get in shape, then, as Nike would say, just do it. Consult with your doctor first—especially if you haven't been exercising for a while—then develop a plan of action to reach your own patriotic fitness. With the resources available on the Internet, including social networking sites that cater to every conceivable fitness level, there's no excuse.

Personally, I love the new group exercise trend of boot camps. They usually take a "whole body" approach to fitness, attract a wide range of ages and backgrounds, and make fitness fun. I'll never forget the Navy SEAL boot camp I did in Richmond, Virginia, with a college friend and his son a few years back. What a blast—we ran up hills and through the woods and over rocks, and did sit-ups and push-ups. It was an advanced boot camp (find one for beginners if you are just starting out) and really tough, but everyone was encouraging to this newcomer and committed to finishing the hour strong. Friends in Dallas rave about the Coppell Fitness Boot Camps—thousands have had fun getting in shape and meeting new friends in the process. Not a bad deal for fifteen dollars per session. Odds are, with a few clicks on the Web, you can find a local exercise boot camp appropriate for your fitness level. Try it. Unless you really despise being with other people, you'll like it.

As for your diet, take the same approach. Do some homework and use some common sense. Research your age group and weight loss goals and start talking to others about their own experiences with strategies that work and those that do not. It sounds cliché, but there really is comfort in knowing that you are not alone. Don't get discouraged because you don't see immediate progress. Like anything in life that's meaningful, it will take time and you'll have setbacks along the way. Just remember that we need to keep our bodies tuned up and strong if we want to be active participants in the fight to keep America strong.

## THE WINNING WAY

It was not until I had a child of my own—about seven years *after* September 11—that I actually started to put together my own survival plan in the event of a natural disaster or terror attack. This is particularly embarrassing given the fact that I stood a few hundred yards from the Pentagon in flames on the morning of September 11.

Being prepared for every conceivable contingency may not be possible, but there is a lot we can do to avoid the worst consequences of inaction. Look at what happened during Hurricane Katrina. Thousand of folks waited for the government to rescue them, instead of doing everything in their power to evacuate when told to do so. The sad truth is, through the Great Society's social welfare state, we have enabled a generational dependency on government that has left millions of Americans vulnerable in an emergency. We must do everything in our power to reclaim that rugged individualistic spirit that helped us settle this nation and develop the world's most powerful economy. We don't want to be a nation of roof squatters.

The White House website recounts then-senator Obama's commitment to rebuilding in New Orleans and his support for "legislation requiring disaster planners to take into account the specific needs of low-income hurricane victims." How condescending. Poor people don't have legs and brains?

There are many great sources for survival planning information available online, at no charge. The American Red Cross website has a helpful checklist of what you need to have in the event of different types of emergencies, such as in the event of a terrorist attack. Log on to the website and print out the list. Share it with your spouse, children, friends. For instance, regarding the "emergency preparedness" or "survival kit", there are dozens of reputable Internet sources (too many to list here) where you can purchase everything from portable water filtration devices to solar blankets. You will have to spend some money to be in a state of preparedness, but remember, what you spend today could save your life or your family's lives in the future. What you don't know and are unprepared for can literally kill you.

We don't need more government lectures or mandates or reports on healthy eating or exercise. The answers to any shortcomings we might have in either area won't come from hypocrites in Washington, who think they know what we need better than we do. We are a strong, patriotic, practical-minded, and resilient people. We can, and should, become "fit to serve" on our own.

# CHAPTER 6

# WILL THE REAL MESSIAH PLEASE STAND UP?

—◈—

## THE DIARY OF PRESIDENT BARACK OBAMA

..............................................

### HONOLULU, HAWAII

December 24, 2009

Axe just called to wish us happy holidays. He was fishing for details about the "downtime" on my schedule tomorrow. The man actually asked whether we were planning on going to church! Apparently there have been some press inquiries. He said, "You should think about hitting the pews. We could use a photo op of the First Family dressed in their Christmas best." This got me thinking—I haven't been in a church since Easter (which is fine by me). I get my spiritual highs on Sundays with a cigar in my mouth and a nine-iron in my hands. I always tell Reggie, "If the weather is good, and there's a ball on a tee—brother, I'm in heaven!"

I mean, I used to love going to church at Trinity. They had great singing, a hell of a rhythm section, and Reverend Jeremiah preaching truth to power. Where am I going to find that in Hawaii? The best I'm going to get here is a Joel Osteen wannabe with a ukulele.

On the other hand, maybe I do need a time-out, a moment to reconnect in silence with my deepest thoughts. There is something moving about being among like-minded believers in prayer—like my visit to the Blue Mosque in Turkey. That was powerful. And I do love the old black church hymns. Some of my best ideas came sitting in a pew, swaying to that music: The title for The Audacity of Hope, a clear understanding of the deep-seated racism in America, and the confirmation that there was something uniquely divine in me. Hallelujah!

Yeah, it'd be good to get back to church. Why not give the congregants a little excitement? They'd enjoy seeing us—and Michelle can get all dolled up for the press. I'll have to tell Secret Service to back off a little bit should the people start waving those palm branches at me as I enter. (Is that what they do at Christmas?) Maybe they'll just come forward with frankincense and holly, or whatever the Hawaiian Christians do these days. I'd better bone up on the Christmas story in the Bible in case they want me to say a few words. I'm a natural in the pulpit. It would be good for them to hear the Chicago-style spark that Reverend Jeremiah gave me.

Hmmm . . . on second thought, my abs are looking a little soft. I think I'll just go to the gym with Michelle in the morning. Sorry, Axe, there's more than one way to worship.

---

Barack Obama never seems entirely comfortable with religion or religious people. He seemingly holds the entire enterprise at a distance, the way a museum curator might appraise a collection of Nazi art or medieval torture devices. Religion is an interesting curiosity to Obama, even a nice indulgence once in a while—but not something that should get in the way of livin' large.

There is no denying that the religious views of our elected leaders profoundly affect our country's domestic and even foreign policy agendas. Think of George Washington's reliance on the "all-powerful Providence" of God during the War for Independence and throughout his presidency. Think of Ronald Reagan's almost spiritual attachment to Pope John Paul II and their mutual commitment to bring down communism. Think of Barack Obama's speech to the 2009 graduates of the University of Notre Dame.

His literal and metaphoric road to the venerable Blue & Gold was lined with protests. More than seventy bishops and tens of thousands of Catholics signed their names to petitions urging not that he be disinvited, but rather that he not be given an honorary degree. This, after all, is a school dedicated to the Virgin Mary. The U.S. bishops had a policy in place that forbade Catholic institutions from honoring or even granting a platform to individuals who dissent from Church teaching—particularly on essential matters such as the right to life or the sanctity of marriage. Given his radically pro-abortion stance and the anti-life policies advanced by his administration, it is clear that Notre Dame had made a terrible mistake.

Yet there he was, invited and encouraged to attend by members of the Catholic left, who consider the Church's life teachings to be optional, repressive, and outdated. The numerous pro-Obama clerics and officials who engineered this moment could not publicly dissent from the Church for fear of punishment, but they were more than willing to have Obama do the dissenting for them.

This image of the president striding onto one of the most important Catholic platforms in America represented a pivotal turning point in the relationship between faith and government. In the course of his address, Obama would seek to establish himself not only as a secular spiritual authority, but as the last word on the role of faith in America.

The president began by listing a host of challenges facing the world, from "global recession" to "violent extremism," to "the spread of nuclear weapons or pandemic disease." He then offered these telling lines:

". . . No one person, or religion, or nation can meet these challenges alone. Our very survival has never required greater cooperation and greater understanding among all people from all places than at this moment in history."

It all sounds very reasonable. "No one person or religion . . . can meet these challenges alone." But this was an odd assertion coming from someone who claims to be a Christian, since Christians, in fact, believe that Christ *is* the answer to every question. Christianity makes the bold pronouncement that the King of Kings and the Lord of the Universe possesses the answer to all our challenges. He is the Way, the Truth, and the Life. Indeed, Christians hold that their religion—their Christian faith—is exclusively capable of moving mountains. So yes, Mr. President, there is a "religion" that can meet these challenges alone—it is the one you profess.

He went on to plead for some sort of "common ground" on contentious moral issues. Speaking of embryonic stem cell research, Obama said:

"Those who speak out against stem cell research may be rooted in an admirable conviction about the sacredness of life, but so are the parents of a child with juvenile diabetes, who are convinced that their son's or daughter's hardships can be relieved. . . ."

This false moral equivalency is typical of the left, and illustrates why faithful Catholics objected to the president's appearance at Notre Dame. He used the platform to confuse and distort elementary Catholic teaching. As any first-year theology student can tell you, our desire to extend life cannot come at the cost of another human life, period. Surely the president can understand this basic ethical reasoning. Though it is doubtful that he does.

With abandon, he rhetorically cast the Church teaching on abortion as some narrow special interest, beneath the dignity of the enlightened. He told the Notre Dame graduates:

> When we open our hearts and our minds to those who may not think like we do or believe what we do—that's when we discover at least the possibility of common ground. That's when we begin to say, "Maybe we won't agree on abortion, but we can still agree that this is a heart-wrenching decision for any woman to make, with both moral and spiritual dimensions." I do not suggest that the debate surrounding abortion can or should go away. . . . [T]he fact is that at some level, the views of the two camps are irreconcilable. Each side will continue to make its case to the public with passion and conviction. But surely we can do so without reducing those with differing views to caricature. Open hearts. Open minds. Fair-minded words.

This gibberish would be uproariously amusing if it were not human life he was talking about. Of course, he really *does* think this debate "should go away." Anyone who holds *Roe v. Wade* as sacrosanct hoped that the Supreme Court would have ended the argument once and for all. Notice also, how the president says that the views of the two sides of the abortion struggle are "irreconcilable," but then insists that everyone should have "open hearts" and "open minds." Like so much of what he says, this is meaningless fluff. Obviously, since pro-lifers believe abortion involves the taking of an innocent human life, they can have no "open mind" to finding "common ground." No more than the abolitionists could have had "open hearts" when it came to ending the scourge of slavery in America.

For all his years of schooling at elite institutions, one gets the feeling that the president has not thought deeply about these moral and ethical issues—or perhaps he is just not that interested. Faith is a hurdle that has to be cleared rather than a rock to lean on. The most telling part of the Notre Dame speech was when he spoke about the nature of faith:

"The ultimate irony of faith is that it necessarily admits doubt. It's the belief in things not seen. It's beyond our capacity as human beings to know with certainty what God has planned for us or what He asks of us."

Actually, it is not beyond our capacity to know what God asks of us, particularly for Christians. God asks us to follow His teachings, His word, and His example. While it is true that to doubt is human, the president seems to be encouraging these young people to follow their own lights and toss aside the "worn-out dogmas" that he referenced at his inauguration. Doubt appears to be the spine of Obama's faith; he has muddled notions of what faith demands and no concept of what Christians believe is our final destination.

If he had his druthers, President Obama would never have to speak publicly about his faith or the demands of Christianity again. Of the many attempts to describe his faith, Barack Obama was perhaps most candid in a 2004 interview with *Chicago Sun-Times* columnist Cathleen Falsani. He told her:

> I retain from my childhood and my experiences growing up, a suspicion of dogma. And I'm not somebody who is always comfortable with language that implies I've got a monopoly on the truth, or that my faith is automatically transferable to others. . . . I think that religion at its best comes with a big dose of doubt. I'm suspicious of too much certainty in the pursuit of understanding, just because I think people are limited in their understanding.
>
> I think that, particularly as somebody who's now in the public realm and is a student of what brings people together and what drives them apart, there's an enormous amount of damage done around the world in the name of religion and certainty.

Hallelujah! I cannot believe I did not think of this sooner. You see, only the enlightened, those who doubt and strut about the world with an unfixed morality, are capable of uniting us and bringing "people together." It is religion that divides and "damages" the world. These comments are key to understanding this president's predisposition toward people of faith.

Examining Obama's past and present, it is clear that he has evolved beyond belief to a state of enlightenment that we churchgoing simpletons could not possibly understand. At least he is true to his dogma of doubt. Just listen to him commenting on his Lord and Savior:

FALSANI   Who's Jesus to you?

OBAMA   *(He laughs nervously.)* Right. Jesus is an historical figure for me, and he's also a bridge between God and man, in the Christian faith, and one that I think is powerful precisely because he serves as that means of us reaching something higher. And he's also a wonderful teacher. I think it's important for all of us, of whatever faith, to have teachers in the flesh and also teachers in history.

Finally, clarity! No wonder the apostles died to follow Christ—to reach "something higher"! What is that *something*? Of course he knows what heaven is, you critics! It starts with an O and ends with an o . . . Oslo, where he accepted the Nobel Peace Prize and wowed the crowd with banalities about the global community. Peter and Paul had Jesus to teach them "in the flesh"; Obama had Jeremiah Wright. You can compare and contrast the outcomes on your own.

## THE CHURCH SEARCH

When most families who take their faith seriously move to a new town, one of the first things they consider is where they will worship. For some, the decision about which church or synagogue to attend comes first, and determines the neighborhood where they choose to live. But the Obamas are different. When they moved from Chicago to take up residence in the White House, the whole church thing seemed like an afterthought. In fact, since he tossed Reverend Jeremiah Wright overboard, Obama has been a pilgrim adrift—a man without a spiritual home.

Shortly before moving into the White House, Barack and Michelle Obama indicated that they wanted to find a permanent place to worship among a community of believers in D.C., a place where they could feel at home. Suddenly the *Washington Post* was filled with stories of pastors and congregations urging Obama to grace their respective sanctuaries with the First Presence.

The day before the Inauguration, the Obamas started to audition D.C.-area churches with a huge caravan that included everybody except Simon Cowell and Ryan Seacrest. Their first stop was one of the oldest black churches in the District, the 19th Street Baptist Church. On the day of their visit, the two-hundred-year-old structure was filled to capacity and even regular church members were turned away at the door. The Obamas arrived five minutes before the start of the service and pandemonium ensued. Once the Reverend Derrick Hawkins restored order, he launched into a sermon about Barack Obama's favorite subject: Barack Obama. If the reverend wanted to make an impression on the soon-to-be president, he was certainly starting on the right foot.

The sermon, titled "For Such a Time As This," likened the biblical characters of Mordecai and Esther to the journey of Barack Obama. According to the *Washington Post*, Hawkins advised the president-elect "to remember two things when times grow difficult. First, look to your wife as an encourager," he said. And second, "God is in the transformation business." (Maybe he was trying to say that after a transformation, Michelle could be an encouragement to her husband!)

The *Post* reported that the church enshrined Obama within the long line of civil rights heroes who had sacrificed for equality. A child rose during the service to offer his own bit of worship: "Rosa Parks sat so that Martin Luther King, Jr., could walk. Martin Luther King walked so that Barack Obama could run. Barack Obama ran so that all children can fly." But all the shameless pandering didn't merit the 19th Street Baptist Church a return presidential visit. Citing security concerns and shock over the attention being paid to him (as if), Obama opted against joining the 19th Street Baptist Church.

—⁓—

# The Diary of President-elect Barack Obama

Blair House

January 18, 2009

This church thing in D.C. is not going to go well. It's Sunday, and with the inauguration tomorrow, Miche thought it would look good to take the girls to church. The staff got some recommendations and decided on the 19th Street Baptist Church. They met all our requirements: they're progressive, have a rockin' band, and they ordain women. We were all looking forward to it—even Mother Robinson, who I don't think has been to church since the original Easter Sunday.

The music was okay, but the preaching was a snore-o-rama. This reverend stands up and starts comparing me to the biblical character Esther! Reggie thought that was cold. Now of all the figures in the Bible, couldn't he have compared me to a more appropriate one? Somebody like Moses or Spartacus or Jesus, maybe—but Esther?! What is that supposed to mean? Once I heard that Esther jazz, I thought, <u>He can forget about ever having the president darken the door of this crappy church again!</u>

Nothing about this place made sense. It's called the 19th Street Baptist Church, but it's on 16th Street! Now how is that possible? These people can't even get their church on the right street and they're supposed to get me to heaven—come on! Thank God we have the inaugural concert at the Lincoln

Memorial tonight. That's the kind of worship I can really throw myself into. And I know damn well that Bruce Springsteen and will.i.am won't be comparing me to a dead Jewish queen.

---

On Easter Sunday 2009, the First Family ventured across Lafayette Park to St. John's Episcopal Church. Just steps from the White House, this worship space was ideally situated, but apparently not what the Obamas were seeking. After sitting in the pews of Trinity United Church of Christ, the formal liturgy of St. John's must have seemed foreign to the Obamas. A *Time* magazine piece by Amy Sullivan suggested that they were disturbed by worshippers "snapping photos of Obama on their camera phones as they walked down the aisle past him to take communion." Whatever the case, they haven't returned since.

---

## THE DIARY OF FIRST LADY MICHELLE OBAMA

### THE WHITE HOUSE

*Easter 2009*

*Stiff and lily white — that's the only way to describe the horrendous service we just suffered through at St. John's Episcopal Church, "the Church of the presidents." I know it's just a block from the White House, but there is no way I can go back there. The girls fell asleep. As for me, I was just aching to hear some preaching like Reverend Jeremiah's. That man knew*

how to spice up a Sunday. Listening to this pastor today drone
on about Jesus rising and the power of the resurrection just wasn't
interesting at all. We're used to hearing about contemporary issues
at church — like climate change and how Israel is screwing over
the Palestinians.

I'll never forget when Reverend Jeremiah taught us that
the women who went to Jesus's tomb were the first community
organizers. They were "looking for life among the dead just like
our people here on the South Side," he said. "We're standing
in the tomb with an America that is rotted and diseased — worm
ridden! The maggots are eating her whole. The maggots, who
are the rich, the white, the middle class, and the Jews. Like those
women in the Gospel, we have to come out of the tomb and take
our message to the streets. Scream to the whole world: We are
risen! We ain't going back! You get in the tomb! It's your turn!
You get in the tomb, America!" What an uplifting message.
I used to listen to the recording of it almost every day on my
way to work.

Anyway, I told Smokey that if he wants to cross the park to
watch Mr. Rogers host this boring wine tasting each week, that's
OK with me, but I'm not going again. Let him take Reggie with
him. Mama had no use for St. John's, either. On the walk back,
she was her usual insightful self, saying, "That is the reason I
haven't been to church in years. It's always Jesus this and Jesus

*that. Can't they talk about somebody else for a change?" Mama's analysis is always spot-on.*

---

I am not suggesting that presidential churchgoing alone is a guarantee of virtue. Bill Clinton was a regular churchgoer, and we know how that ended up. In fairness, Ronald Reagan and George W. Bush didn't attend church regularly either, nor were they members of a congregation in D.C. But unlike Obama, Reagan and Bush were spiritually grounded and spoke about their faith and Christianity in a way that tracked with the beliefs of the overwhelming majority of Americans. They didn't enact policies that defied the precepts of classic Christianity, and neither Reagan nor Bush degraded religious people or practices in the way that the Obama administration has.

Reports have surfaced that members of the Obamas' staff have been screening sermons and visiting churches on the First Family's behalf. The church search continues. The Obamas have found time to tour the world, enjoy romantic dinners in exotic locales, host lavish parties, and plant a garden of untold powers, but they still have yet to find a spiritual home for their worship on Sunday.

---

## THE DIARY OF PRESIDENT BARACK OBAMA

### THE WHITE HOUSE

March 14, 2009

Picking a church is harder than coming up with an Afghanistan policy. I've been reviewing literally hundreds of sermons. Once a week, over lunch, Axe, Gibbs, Valerie, and

I meet to review the church question. Here's the problem: Politically, it's wise to be a member of a church. (That way if any questions about my affiliation come up later, I've got a place to send the press.) But we've got to find a church with a pastor who doesn't make inflammatory statements—otherwise they'll have him all over Fox News and I'll have to resign from another congregation.

On the other hand, I _need_ the inflammatory statements! I hear diplomatic talk all week. On Sundays, I want to hear some kick-ass, burn-the-house-down social justice, the-capitalists-need-to-fry oratory. This is what I am used to, and what my soul craves. Valerie snuck Reverend Jeremiah into the East Room for a few secret prayer services, but we can't do that every week. Otherwise the press will catch on, since his name will show up on the guest rolls. If somebody questions it, Gibbs says we'll just tell them that it's a different Jeremiah Wright.

I've got to go to some church tomorrow. We haven't been to church in a while and I need to prove that the Democratic Party is not hostile to religion. The picture of me going into a house of worship is reassuring to the masses—makes them think I'm turning to God during this economic crisis. It could even stabilize the world markets. And for a president, quiet time is a good thing. Maybe we'll head over to the Metropolitan AME Church. It's close by and Frederick Douglass used to go there from time to time. But is it worth wasting a morning?

Nahh. My backswing needs work. And Reggie and Jay-Z would be disappointed if I canceled our golf plans.

# THEY'RE NOT THAT INTO HIM

Of all the startling admissions to slip from the mouth of former White House social secretary Desiree Rogers, there was one that really stood out. It came during a luncheon with former social secretaries. Desiree was unveiling the administration's plans for "Obama-tizing" the White House when she let fly a most Grinch-like vision of Christmas. According to the *New York Times*, Rogers said the Obamas were "planning a non-religious Christmas." She later confided that the First Family would not display the traditional crèche scene in the East Room. Who needs all that Jesus statuary around at Christmas time anyway? It only distracts from the important things of the season: Michelle's clothes and the subversive Christmas ornaments.

The reported nativity omission at the White House drew outrage from all quarters, not the least of which was expressed by Bill Donohue, president of the Catholic League: "Unlike almost all Americans—including atheists—the Obamas do not give their children Christmas gifts. We know this because Barack bragged about this last year to *People* magazine. . . . If the Obamas want to deprive their children of celebrating Christmas, that is their business. It is the business of the public to hold them accountable for the way they celebrate Christmas in the White House. We know one thing for sure: no other administration ever entertained internal discussions on whether to display a nativity scene in the White House."

Eventually tradition and sustained disapproval from the citizenry prompted the White House to display the nativity scene in its normal spot. The president even made reference to the crèche during the lighting of the National (Don't Call It Christmas) Tree in December 2009. Though it was tinged with his particular brand of faithful doubt:

"Tonight, we celebrate . . . the story of a child born far from home to parents guided only by faith, but who would ultimately spread a message that has endured for more than 2,000 years—that no matter who we are or where we are from, we are each called to love one another as brother and sister. While this story may be a Christian one, its lesson is universal. It speaks to the hope we share as a people. And it represents a tradition that we celebrate as a country—a tradition that has come to represent more than any one holiday or religion, but a season of brotherhood and generosity to our fellow citizens."

In one fell swoop Barack Obama succeeded in turning Christmas to 'mas—stripping the holy day of Christ and its religious foundation. With his "We Are the World" verbiage, he drained Christmas of its Christ-centric emphasis. There is no mention of the coming of the Savior or the Messiah; no talk of Christ's birth being the hope of mankind. Brotherhood and generosity based on "a tradition" is the hope we share. As muddled and secular as Obama's Christmas discourse was, none of it was surprising.

Obviously, Christmas is not a big deal for the Obamas. They barely celebrate the day at all. The president told *People* magazine that the First Daughters get no presents at Christmas because Michelle and Barack are trying "to teach limits" to their children. They must also be trying to teach limits to each other. On Christmas Day 2009, Anne E. Kornblut reported that the Obamas did not go to church, did not exchange gifts, but like the wise men and the shepherds before them, hit the gym on Christmas morn. They capped the day with a special meal of "roast beef and potatoes."

---

## THE DIARY OF PRESIDENT BARACK OBAMA

### THE WHITE HOUSE

Sunday, January 24, 2010

Reggie and I took the girls to a worship service this morning. We left the White House around 10:30. They were all excited. It's important that they have some alone time with their father. It also gives Miche and Mother Robinson a break.

Secret Service made sure the place was all ready for us.

When we got inside, those girls didn't know what hit them. Yeah, the old man's still got it. I landed jump shot after jump shot. If she can pick up a few of my moves, Malia could be a fine player— she's got the height. Reggie and I played a little one-on-one (I kicked his butt), then I helped the girls with their technique. When we were done, the girls had that starry look in their eyes—like Alexrod after I give a speech. "Daddy, nobody can play basketball better than you," Sasha said. Now that's the best kind of Sunday worship there is.

---

Obama's aversion to public displays of religion was particularly in evidence on April 14, 2009, when the president appeared at Georgetown University's Gaston Hall to speak about the economy. Though the administration wanted to use the backdrop of a Catholic university to lend some spiritual heft to the president's address, the symbols of faith displayed in the hall made someone at the White House very uncomfortable. The *Washington Times* reported that Obama officials asked Georgetown to cover all Catholic signage and symbols, and specifically that a pediment on the stage bearing the carved gold letters *IHS* (an abbreviation for Jesus's name) be obscured. So black painted plywood was shoved in front of the pediment and—voilà!—no more Jesus. I suppose the stage was big enough for only one Messiah.

The president's religious indifference is so pronounced, he routinely attempts to downplay the obvious religious majority in America. During a visit to Turkey on April 6, 2009, he proclaimed, "One of the great strengths of the United States is—although as I mentioned, we have a very large Christian population, we do not consider ourselves a Christian nation or a Jewish nation or a Muslim nation; we consider ourselves a nation of citizens who are bound by ideals and a set of values."

I'd like to know exactly what "values" the president believes binds us as a people. Open hearts, open minds? The fact is, numerically speaking, this *is* a Christian nation. Upward of 76 percent of the population is Christian. Even the Supreme Court in 1892 referred to America as a "Christian nation." Obviously the United States allows all her citizens to freely practice the faith of their choice, but to downplay America's Christian majority and its Christian heritage is ludicrous.

Not that Obama cares. In fact, he attempted to make the case that we are a Muslim country. During an interview on Canal Plus, a French TV outlet, in June 2009, before a trip to Cairo, the president told Laura Haim: "One of the points I want to make is that if you actually took the number of Muslim Americans, we'd be one of the largest Muslim countries in the world. And so there's got to be a better dialogue and a better understanding between the two peoples."

This is, of course, nonsense. The *CIA World Factbook* reports that there are roughly 1.8 million Muslims in the United States, representing 0.6 percent of the population. The *St. Petersburg Times'* Politifact.com did a rundown of the top sixty Muslim countries in the world. The United States came in at number fifty-eight. Hard as it might be for the president to accept, the United States is virtually tied with Israel as being the largest Jewish country in the world—and we *are* the largest Christian country based on population.

In February 2009, the president went out of his way to appoint a special envoy to the Organization of the Islamic Conference. With member nations including Saudi Arabia, Syria, Iran, and Libya, the group is committed to spreading sharia law around the world, and according to its website, has "the singular honor to galvanize the Ummah [Muslims around the globe] into a unified body." Just the kind of group the United States needs to send an envoy to engage, right? The president didn't choose just anybody for the job. He chose a thirty-one-year-old attorney already working in the White House: Rashad Hussain. Hussain's only real qualifications were that he was a Muslim and "a hafiz of the Qur'an," someone who has committed the whole Koran to memory. Hussain, a graduate of Yale Law School, participated in a Muslim Student Association meeting in 2004, where he said that the case against Sami Al-Arian (the North American head of Palestinian

Islamic Jihad) was one of many "politically motivated persecutions," according to the Washington Report on Middle East Affairs. This is just the sort of individual who—in between Koran recitations—will no doubt vigorously argue the American perspective before the Organization of the Islamic Conference.

While the president went out of his way to reach out to Muslims, Israeli prime minister Benjamin Netanyahu got the cold shoulder during a visit to the United States in March 2010. Obama wanted written assurances from Netanyahu that he would cease building settlements in East Jerusalem, which the president viewed as an obstacle to peace talks. Netanyahu refused. According to some reports, the meeting was cut short and the White House withheld any photographs of the two leaders. In what was seen as another snub, the president did not dine with Netanyahu. This offended Israelis and many prominent American Jews.

Presumably to blunt the fallout, the always reliable *New York Times* featured a front-page story the following Sunday titled "Next Year in the White House: A Seder Tradition." It explored the Obama Seder, a tradition coined by the president and some of his Jewish staff on the campaign trail. The first dinner took place in 2008, during a dark time in the campaign—the days leading up to the Pennsylvania primary, when the Reverend Wright controversy was dominating headlines.

At the end of a seder, it is traditional to cry, "Next year in Jerusalem." But Obama had to add his own spiritual capper: "Next year in the White House," he said. And the tradition has since continued in the executive manse.

"The Obama Seder seems to take on new meaning each year, depending on what is happening in the world," the *Times* reported. Susan Sher, Michelle Obama's chief of staff, suggested that the 2010 seder would focus on "taking care of people who can't take care of themselves and health-care reform." On the surface this seems like a nice gesture to the Jewish community, until you read the fine print. "No one considered inviting prominent rabbis or other Jewish leaders; it is a private event," according to the *Times*. This makes perfect sense. Why ruin Obama's secularized version of a religious ritual by inviting religious people?

The president has truly made history with his religious outreach. In addition to hosting the first seder in the White House, his administration is also the first to invite atheists in for a sit-down. That's right; on February 26, 2010, several high-ranking Obama officials attended a special meeting at the White House with a group of some of the most rabid antireligious bigots in America. The Secular Coalition for America, including groups like American Atheists and the Council for Secular Humanism, attended the meeting. According to ABC News these "nontheists" came to express their opinions on "faith healing on children, which the coalition describes as a form of 'child abuse'; the 'pervasive' religious atmosphere in the US military; and faith-based initiatives."

Clearly, the most dogmatic thinkers in America—activist atheists—had found a friend in Barack Obama.

---

## THE DIARY OF PRESIDENT BARACK OBAMA

### AIR FORCE ONE, EN ROUTE TO GHANA

July 10, 2009

Went to the Vatican today. Frankly, I wasn't impressed. I brought the pope some kind of liturgical shawl from Philadelphia. They tell me that this religious accessory was part of some saint's wardrobe. In return, I thought he'd give me something I could use: Vatican cuff links or a piece of furniture or something. But for all our trouble, all I got was a mosaic of the Vatican. I told Reggie in the car after the meeting, had I known I'd be given some souvenir from the Vatican gift shop, I would have brought the German shepherd (I came up with that nickname—pretty good, huh?) a picture of the White House with Bo and me in the foreground.

While I was meeting with His Holiness Colonel Klink, Miche, Mother Robinson, and the girls went on a tour of the Sistine Chapel. After the meeting, Reggie and I were taken underground to see St. Peter's Crypt. This archbishop kept going on and on about the history of the Church and how "this is the rock of the faith" . . . To be honest, I don't care much about history. I'm a man of the here and now. What I do becomes history. Who cares where St. Peter's bones are? Where will St. Barack's bones be?—that's what I'm worried about.

This German pope just didn't do it for me. He kept blathering about "the sanctity of human life" and "protecting human life." As a throwaway, I told him that I would work to "reduce the number of abortions." (What I didn't share with him was that I'll reduce them by distributing free contraceptives!) You can tell this guy was a professor. On the way out, he actually gave me homework: a Vatican pamphlet titled "An Instruction on Certain Bioethical Questions." I'm sorry, but I don't need schooling in ethics from a man in a dress.

Though I will say one thing for Catholicism: I didn't realize that the pope is a monarch. He rules without a popular election. I'm friendly with a couple of the progressive cardinals in the U.S.—most of them even supported me during the campaign. If I can ingratiate myself with a few more of these red hats, the pope thing might not be a bad follow-up to the presidency. Of course, I'd have to convert to Catholicism to pave the way. But this wouldn't be the first time that I joined a church for political reasons. I'll also have to figure out what to do with Michelle. I'll make Reggie a cardinal, and Gibbs is already Catholic so he can come along. But before I move in, I'd have to get Desiree to redecorate those private quarters. The pope's crib is a little plain for my taste.

---

## POLITICIZING GOD

In a 2006 speech to the liberal Christian group Called to Renewal, Obama disparaged the use of the Bible as a tool to weigh or direct public policy.

"Which passages of scripture should guide our public policy?" Obama asked in the speech. "Should we go with Leviticus, which suggests slavery is okay and that eating shellfish is an abomination? Or we could go with Deuteronomy, which suggests stoning your child if he strays from the faith? Or should we just stick to the Sermon on the Mount? . . . So before we get carried away, let's read our Bible now. Folks haven't been reading their Bible."

Jim Dobson, the founder of Focus on the Family, reacted quickly to Obama's theology lesson: "I think he's deliberately distorting the traditional understanding of the Bible to fit his own worldview, his own confused theology . . . dragging biblical understanding through the gutter."

Obama falls back on the oldest trick in the liberal playbook when it comes to religion, one usually deployed by atheists. In this talk, he attempted to create disparity between the Old and New Testaments as a way to undermine the authority of the Holy Scripture and the faith of those who hold it dear. By casting general aspersions on the Bible itself, Obama seeks to discredit his critics, particularly those concerned about the taking of innocent human life and the sanctity of marriage. Interestingly enough, the president never dares to stand before a Muslim audience to point out conflicting passages in the Koran.

In June 2008, Obama shot back at Dobson with a familiar refrain: "Democracy demands that the religiously motivated translate their concerns into universal rather than religion-specific values," Obama said. "It requires their proposals be subject to argument and amenable to reason."

He reflexively tries to portray faith and the faithful as being opposed to reason: wild-eyed lunatics flipping through the Scriptures for their every thought or political conviction. But if you listen closely to Obama as he tries to explain his own position on certain issues, he begins to buckle under the weight of reason and retreats to his purportedly religious convictions for cover.

For instance, when asked by Rick Warren at the Saddleback Forum in August 2008 to "define marriage," Obama said: "I believe that marriage is the union between a man and a woman. Now, for me as a Christian—for me—for me as a Christian, it is a sacred union. God's in the mix." He then added that he would not support a constitutional amendment defining marriage, but would support same-sex civil unions: "I can afford those civil rights to others even if I don't have . . . that view." Translation: I believe as a Christian that marriage is restricted to one man and one woman, but other people take another view and that's fine, too.

Faith is something entirely private in Barack Obama's mind, a thing to be sealed off from public policy concerns—except when it can be used to further his own political ends.

---

## The Diary of President Barack Obama

### The White House

March 15, 2010

We're going to pass this health-care bill yet. Kathleen Sebelius came up with a great idea to break the Catholic bishops' hold on Stupak and that gang of "pro-life" Democrats.

Without their votes, we're sunk. Kathleen suggested that I invite Sister Carol Keehan, the president of the Catholic Health Association, in for a private meeting. She's been a cheerleader from the start and is a sucker for a little attention. Sister Carol's also not hung up on this abortion thing—she's got an open heart and an open mind.

To be honest, I didn't even know she was a nun. I was expecting more of a Sally Field playing Sister Bertrel look. When she walked into the Oval, I thought, "She could pass for Rachel Maddow's grandmama." From the polyester blazer she was wearing, it looked like she'd just won the Masters. They don't make nuns like they used to . . . But right off the bat, I knew she'd be an easy touch. The woman just wanted to touch the hem of my garment.

The moment we sat down in the Roosevelt Room, I got real solemn and told her that her bishops were getting in the way of reform. "Sister Carol, you can't serve two masters," I said. She got real quiet, closed her eyes, and then looked over at me. "Mr. President, speak. Your servant listens," she said. Together we came up with a plan: she's going to endorse the bill and say that no federal funds go toward abortions; then later in the week, a group of more sisters who wear blazers are going to issue a letter backing her up. It will appear that there's a split in the Catholic Church and that'll give Stupak and his gang of pious Annies enough cover to vote for the reform package.

On the way out, Sister Carol asked for my blessing. I'd never done anything like that, but I had seen my friend Father Pfleger trace a cross on people's foreheads. So I leaned down, traced an

"O" on Sister Carol's head with my thumb, and sent her on her way. She slobbered all over my hand and practically genuflected as we parted (she needs to work on her bowing). If she pulls this thing off, I'm giving her one of the pens I use at the signing ceremony—along with a few million dollars for her hospitals, and thirty pieces of silver for all her trouble.

---

When in early 2010, it became obvious that health-care reform would not pass without the Democrats getting some serious religious cover, President Obama and Speaker Nancy Pelosi pulled out all the stops to find any Catholic with name recognition and a title to support the bill. The Catholic bishops, generally supportive of universal coverage, were not going to budge on opposing the final bill because of its abortion funding provisions. In fact, a number of prominent bishops were personally telephoning "pro-life" Democrats in Congress, urging them to stand by their principles and vote against the bill. Nevertheless, in the end, a group of vocal left-wing nuns came out of the woodwork to express their support for the bill, and checkmated the bishops. Game over. After all, who could argue with a flock of selfless, sweet nuns? Now that Nancy Pelosi had a sisterhood supporting her, there was no stopping her massive new entitlement program.

## THE DIARY OF SPEAKER OF THE HOUSE
## THE HONORABLE NANCY PELOSI

### THE U.S. CAPITOL

*March 19, 2010*

At my press conference, I marched right up to the microphone and proudly announced that today was the feast of St. Joseph the Worker. Then, just to smear it in the faces of those smug bishops and the right-wingers, I said, "We're praying to St. Joseph to benefit the workers of America. And that's exactly what our health-care bill will do." Take that, you holier-than-thou SOBs! And abortion funding <u>will</u> be in the bill!!

I'm just as good a Catholic as any other. That dear Sister Carol and her other women friends in drab clothing encouraged me to stand firm. How dare that pope lecture me about the sanctity of life? Back in February of last year, in the Vatican itself, after I saluted his leadership on global warming and reducing poverty, he had the gall to lecture me in front of Paul and the entire delegation. I'll never forget the way he put it: "You have a moral obligation as a legislator to create a just system of laws capable of protecting human life at all stages of its development." Some nights I wake up hearing that wispy, German voice and I just want to scream . . .

As an ardent, practicing Catholic, I can vote my conscience and my conscience says it is perfectly fine to offer women choice! And they will have that choice, so help me God! Once I flip a few more pro-life holdouts, we're home free. It looks like Stupak will go for a meaningless executive order, but there are others who will need more attention.

I just got off the phone with dear Father Hesburgh at Notre Dame. He's promised to call Joe Donnelly, a Notre Dame grad and the congressman in South Bend. I know Father Hesburgh can get him to drop his anti-choice position and support our bill. I told Father to just keep telling Joe to "vote his conscience." He'll know what to do.

This bill will "protect human life"—at least the lives of those who are already with us and in relatively good health.

For Barack Obama, faith and talk of faith is not so much rooted in personal conviction as in political necessity. On January 4, 2008, he told the *Concord Monitor,* "We know that ninety percent of Americans believe in a higher power, we know that huge chunks of voters in swing states consider religion a really important part of their lives. If we aren't speaking to those issues, then I think we're missing a huge part of the electorate . . ."

He would use his campaign to build bridges to religious-minded voters who had long been estranged from the Democratic Party. At least Obama was a Democrat willing to acknowledge that faith was central to the American character and had a role in shaping the destiny of the country—even if he did twist that faith to accommodate his own policies.

In a speech to a national meeting of the United Church of Christ on June 22, 2007, Obama explained his vision of faith and politics. "People are coming together around a simple truth—that we are all connected, that I am my brother's keeper; I am my sister's keeper," he said. "And that it's not enough to just believe this—we have to do our part to make it a reality. My faith teaches me that I can sit in church and pray all I want, but I won't be fulfilling God's will unless I go out and do the Lord's work."

Can we get a definition of "the Lord's work" on aisle 666, please?

It is true that Christianity has long taught that faith without works is dead. But similarly, works without faith are sterile. Obama believes that we have an obligation to help our fellow man—so long as we do so via a government agency or program or maybe a left-wing NGO. This is not the charity that God demands of us, nor does it qualify as faith-based. It is little more than social work in religious drag. But try explaining that to Joshua Dubois.

Dubois heard the Messiah's call and followed. After watching Obama's convention speech, Dubois, an evangelical minister and grad student at Princeton, drove to Washington and offered his services to the senator from Illinois. He would eventually become Obama's director of the White House Office of Faith-Based and Neighborhood Partnerships. But during the campaign, the twenty-five-year-old was in charge of religious outreach, trying to convince pastors, rabbis, imams, and priests to support his man.

The "reverend" initiated a series of faith-based "home parties" in battleground states. At these religious Tupperware-style gatherings, Dubois tried to sell voters on Obama's religiosity and dodge his problematic stances on abortion and embryonic stem cell research. He simultaneously launched "the Joshua Generation Project," an outreach to young evangelical voters. Poverty, Darfur, and climate change were stressed as moral issues, while those secondary moral concerns like life and the future of the family were set aside.

It worked like a charm. Obama racked up huge gains in the 2008 race among religious voters. Forty-three percent of regular churchgoers supported him and 57 percent of occasional pew sitters went his way. Fifty-four percent of the crucial Catholic swing vote also went for Obama, besting George W. Bush's Catholic support by two percentage points. Once Obama seized victory, he promised to turn Bush's Office of Faith-Based Initiatives into the moral center of his administration. He changed its name to the White House Office of Faith-Based and Neighborhood Partnerships and quickly changed its focus.

In a speech on July 1, 2008, Obama laid out his vision for the office that was originally founded to make it easier for religious groups to compete for federal contracts without forfeiting their identities. Obama said, "Religious organizations that receive federal dollars cannot discriminate with respect to hiring for government-funded social service programs." This one line completely gutted the reason for having a faith-based initiative office in the first place. It essentially forces all faith groups into the shadows and out of the public square. They can either suppress their religious values or go out and raise money to do "the Lord's work" in the private sector. And Obama quickly made that more difficult by reducing the tax deduction for charitable giving.

The president had other plans for his faith-based office. It would now be entirely devoted to policy matters with four main priorities: working to reduce poverty, promoting fatherhood, reducing the need for abortion by preventing unintended pregnancies, and reaching out to Muslims while encouraging interreligious dialogue.

When I first read this list of priorities, I found it stunning that the government and this administration, which has been so deaf to the concerns of believers, would take it upon themselves to instigate "interreligious dialogue." This type of religious dialogue is usually initiated by spiritual leaders: the ecumenical patriarch, the pope, the archbishop of Canterbury— people who represent sizable numbers of religious believers. But for his fervently devoted followers, Barack Obama does almost rise to the level of religious guru.

Twenty-five spiritual advisors were chosen by Obama to serve as his religious sounding board. The Faith-Based Advisory Council included everyone from the president of the Southern Baptist convention to Harry Knox, director of the Human Rights Campaign's Religion and Faith program. (Knox famously called the pope a "discredited leader" for refusing to distribute condoms in Africa as a way to combat AIDS. According to Harvard researcher Dr. Edward Green, however, the pope was right, as condom distribution may have contributed to the spread of the disease.)

It didn't take long for the faith-based council to abandon any discussion of how to reduce abortions. Too many disputes arose. They might have actually come up with a plan to reduce abortions, but liberals feared that the entire approach demonized "the procedure." A year after they began their work, in February 2010, the council finally issued its recommendations to the president. Whether Obama acts on any of their suggestions or has even read the report is anyone's guess. What is clear is that a few of the Faith-Based Advisory Council members did not like what they saw.

Frank Page, the president of the Southern Baptist Convention and a member of the council, told the *Washington Post*, "It's been a mixed experience. For example, I serve on the fatherhood task force. That's pretty low-hanging fruit. Who's not going to want more responsible fathers? But even within that, you have to leave your faith at the door in a lot of these discussions. You can't say here's why fathers ought to do better, this is what encouragement comes from the Bible, how being a better father is a godly right and biblical thing to do. When you have twenty-five people from such a wide range, you're virtually reduced to a neighborhood group of folk. . . . When the president launched his office, he talked about abortion reduction as one of his four priorities. That was very quickly taken off the table as something we'd deal with."

At least the Muslim outreach has been successful . . . that is, once you discount the Iranian nuke buildup, the rise in Somalian Islamism, and a growing Islamic homegrown threat.

---

## THE DIARY OF PRESIDENT BARACK OBAMA

### THE WHITE HOUSE

February 12, 2010

Valerie told me that Auntie Zeituni was evicted from another apartment today. That must have been why she was trying to reach me through the White House switchboard. I really wanted to give her a pep talk, maybe a few signed copies of Audacity and a couple of boxes of those presidential Jelly Bellies, but Giblet told me it wouldn't be a good idea PR-wise.

She will surely be deported now. But how would that look? The aunt of the most historic president of the United States being shipped back to her home country like a common criminal! When Rahm and I were having a smoke this evening, sitting at the picnic table, it came to me—why not turn lemonade into lemons? This is the mother (or aunt) of all immigration sob stories! When the time is right, we could arrange for her to be sent to an immigration holding center—those God-awful places where they keep aliens until they are deported. I know I could get someone like Anderson Cooper or Ann Curry to do a sympathetic story. We'd feed them all the details about what a sweet, lovely woman she is, how she loves America, and how it was all that confusing government paperwork that led to her problems. By the time my friends in the press get through with this story, immigration officials will end up looking like the heartless bastards that they are, while auntie is seen as the neighbor next-door (if you happen to live in a trailer park or subsidized housing, that is).

This one sad tale can help me with the real goal—finding fifteen million more Obama voters before 2012! Amnesty, "a path to citizenship," "comprehensive immigration reform" . . . it doesn't matter to me what we call it. As long as these undocumented citizens get to the polls and vote for me, they can call it the Mexican line dance for all I care!

In the meantime, I knew I had to get auntie some help. Like it says in the Book of Exorcist: "The power of my faith compels me." So I placed a few calls to that immigration judge up in Boston and told him to grant her asylum—but to take his time doing it.

Last week I sent Reggie to Boston to place auntie with one of the charity groups until the ruling is handed down. The first place they visited was an immigrant center run by the Catholic Church. They do all the paperwork for the immigrants, help them get jobs and housing—the whole shebang. Since the government gives that outfit $150 million a year in contracts, they'd better offer the whole shebang! The only problem is, Reggie said, they have crucifixes in the hallways of this place. And he saw a picture of the pope hanging in one of the offices! That is simply unacceptable. Where is a portrait of their president?! The Catholics always use their social services to proselytize. But it didn't work this time. Auntie and Reggie walked right out of there. (Soon as we get immigration reform passed, I'm going to make sure that we do something to get the Catholic Church in line—like remove its tax-exempt status!)

Later Auntie and Reg went down to an evangelical church that provides aid and shelter to immigrants. The minute they sat down, Pastor Bob began quoting the Bible and asked if they were "saved." Reggie answered, "If she was saved, she wouldn't need your help." (Reggie's honesty is one of the many attractive things about the man.) He called me on his cell from the evangelical agency and asked how to proceed. I told him, "Forget it and hurry home. Take Auntie down to the YWCA and let her stay there. Better to be a little uncomfortable than to be harassed by those religious zealots."

---

## THE FAITH OF HIS FATHERS (AND MOTHER)

Barack Obama's awkwardness with faith, his ambivalence, can be traced back to his upbringing. As I noted earlier in the book, if you want to know what a man believes, find out what his family believes.

"I was not raised in a religious household," Obama wrote in *Time* magazine in October 2006. "My maternal grandparents, who hailed from Kansas, had been steeped in Baptist and Methodist teachings as children, but religious faith never really took root in their hearts." But in *Dreams from My Father*, he is even more blunt. Speaking of his grandfather, he writes: "In his only skirmish into organized religion, he would enroll the family in the local Unitarian Universalist congregation. . . .

"For my mother, organized religion too often dressed up closed-mindedness in the garb of piety, cruelty, and oppression in the cloak of righteousness," Obama wrote in *Time*.

This isn't to say that she provided me with no religious instruction. In her mind, a working knowledge of the world's great religions was a necessary part of any well-rounded education. In our household, the Bible, the Koran, and the Bhagavad Gita sat on the shelf alongside books of Greek and Norse and African mythology . . . I was made to understand that such religious samplings required *no sustained commitment on my part* [emphasis added]—no introspective exertion or self-flagellation. Religion was an expression of human culture, she would explain, not its wellspring, just one of the many ways—and not necessarily the best way—that man attempted to control the unknowable and understand the deeper truths about our lives. In sum, my mother viewed religion through the eyes of the anthropologist that she would become; *it was a phenomenon to be treated with a suitable respect, but with a suitable detachment as well* [emphasis added].

This is probably the best way to describe Barack Obama's approach to religion. He treats it with a "suitable respect, but a suitable detachment as well."

High school friends of Stanley Ann Dunham, Obama's mother, told the *Chicago Tribune*, "She touted herself as an atheist, and it was something she'd read about and could argue. She was always challenging and arguing and comparing." Barack Obama, Sr., was also a confirmed atheist by the time he met Barry's mother. Here, in his mother and father, are the roots of the doubt that Barack Obama always references when speaking of faith.

Stanley Ann Dunham exposed her son Barack to religion the way one would expose a child to poisonous snakes—as a distant curiosity.

## THE DIARY OF PRESIDENT BARACK OBAMA

### THE WHITE HOUSE

April 4, 2010

On Friday, when I was busy campaigning for the health-care bill I already signed into law, Gibbopotomus told me that Easter was in two days and we really needed to hit a church given where I am in the polls. Since we were still getting grief for not going on Christmas, I reluctantly agreed.

Awesome decision. Rahm and Susan Sher picked the Allen Chapel AME Church in Southeast Washington because it was a guaranteed friendly congregation and the area had suffered recently from terrible crime and high unemployment (the latter being Bush's fault). Without a doubt, my presence was the beginning of the resurrection of this struggling community. The highlight of the service wasn't the same old "He rose from the dead to cleanse us from our sins" claptrap. It came when the senior pastor, the Reverend Michael Bell, wrapped up his sermon by describing me as "the most debonair, the most suave president of this United States of America." The congregation went nuts. The cheering went on so long that I felt like I was back in Grant Park on election night . . . or backstage with the folks at SNL.

I see that the AP and the Washington Post already published great pieces on the Web about my hero's welcome

at Allen Chapel. Soon, like St. John the Baptist, I'll be rising
again . . . in the polls! I can feel it. Take that, Sean Hannity!
  Maybe this church thing isn't such a time-suck after all.

---

After college, Obama relocated to Chicago, where he took up community organizing: mobilizing people to boycott and strike against "power,"
à la Saul Alinsky. Obama has often said, "It was a Catholic group called The
Campaign for Human Development that helped fund the work I did many
years ago in Chicago to help lift up neighborhoods that were devastated by
the closure of a local steel plant."

Obama, the community organizer, was to bring black churches together
to pressure business and government entities for change "in the community." Many of the ministers he approached suggested that the young activist
join a church. But as Obama (or more likely his unacknowledged co-author
Bill Ayers) wrote in *Dreams from My Father*, "I remained a reluctant skep-
tic, doubtful of my own motives, wary of expedient conversion, having too
many quarrels with God to accept a salvation too easily won."

Still, he was attracted to being a part of a community with historic roots
and a strong sense of its own identity. "I was drawn to the power of the African American religious tradition to spur social change . . . it understood in
an intimate way the biblical call to feed the hungry and clothe the naked and
challenge powers and principalities. In the history of these struggles, I was
able to see faith as more than just a comfort to the weary or a hedge against
death; rather, it was an active, palpable agent in the world."

For Obama, social activism became a sort of sacrament. The principal
role of the church was not to reform or redeem the individual, but to deliver
the community to some secular utopia in the here and now.

"The historically black church offered me a second insight: that faith
doesn't mean that you don't have doubts, or that you relinquish your hold
on this world," Obama wrote in *Time* magazine. "It was because of these
newfound understandings—that religious commitment did not require me

to suspend critical thinking, disengage from the battle for economic and social justice, or otherwise retreat from the world that I knew and loved—that
I was finally able to walk down the aisle of Trinity United Church of Christ
one day and be baptized."

Obama's choice of church and his decision to be baptized can best
be described as an exercise in religious political opportunism. Jeremiah
Wright's Trinity United Church was located just outside Obama's organizing district, so he could join the church and avoid offending any of the
pastors he dealt with each day. Trinity United also had one of the most politically connected black congregations in Chicago—even Oprah had been
a member. But without the zeal and fiery social justice proselytizing of its
pastor the Reverend Jeremiah Wright, Trinity United would be just another
predominantly black church in Chicago.

Wright was the spiritual leader of choice for Chicago's elite black community. Dressed in his glittery dashiki, he would rail against white power,
the military, and the Jews, while supporting gay rights. Obama's biographer,
Christopher Anderson, writes that Wright promulgated an "Afrocentric,
black liberation theology . . . Barack was intrigued by Wright's message of
black empowerment; the pastor's rantings against the 'white power' structure in Washington and the state of Israel—not to mention his defense of
Communists in Nicaragua and the Castro regime in Cuba—were met with
a chorus of amens every week, and fellow churchgoers remember that
Barack chimed in with the rest."

It is safe to say that Jeremiah Wright, the man that Barack Obama identified as his "spiritual father," had more influence over the future president
and his thinking than anyone in his life. Once Obama determined that he
needed a law degree to realize his political ambitions, Wright, and an array
of radical Muslims and Alinsky acolytes, lobbied to get him into Harvard
Law School. But even at Harvard, the guiding hand of Jeremiah Wright was
never far away.

For twenty years, Barack Obama not only bathed in the thought and
perverse theology of Jeremiah Wright, but the cadence, the sound, the
pulse of his oratory became part of Obama's DNA. As the *New York Times*

reported: "When Mr. Obama arrived at Harvard Law School . . . where he fortified himself with recordings of Mr. Wright's sermons, he was delivering stirring speeches as a student leader in the classic oratorical style of the black church."

When you hear Obama on the stump, when he goes into campaign mode, a strange metamorphosis occurs. The measured, staccato Obama of the exclusive interviews vanishes, and out pops Obama the pastor. What you are hearing is the ghost of Jeremiah Wright.

After Harvard, Barack Obama returned to Chicago. He was married by Reverend Wright, and later the pastor baptized his two daughters. Though Obama was forced to distance himself from his spiritual mentor in 2008 and repudiate his message for political reasons, the influence of Wright remains.

As president, Barack Obama can easily identify with the social face of Christianity—its care for the community and the good works it can do in the world. Divorced from fixed moral requirements, Obama sees religion as a force to enact social change. What the president seems to lack is a transcendent faith. There is no heaven and hell in his conception, no final judgment, no destination beyond this fleeting life:

"I thought of Sasha asking me once what happened when we die— 'I don't want to die, Daddy,' she had added matter-of-factly—and I had hugged her and said, 'You've got a long, long way before you have to worry about that,' which had seemed to satisfy her," Obama wrote in *Time* magazine. "I wondered whether I should have told her the truth, that I wasn't sure what happens when we die, any more than I was sure of where the soul resides or what existed before the Big Bang."

⟐∾∾∾⟐

## THE DIARY OF FIRST LADY MICHELLE OBAMA

### THE WHITE HOUSE

*April 6, 2010*

I may call him Smokey, but I'll never have to call him Holy Smokey. Barack and I held an Easter breakfast for Christian leaders here at the house this morning. (Don't ask me why we are having an Easter breakfast two days after Easter — it's another one of those Christian mysteries, I guess.) Anyway, this being an election year, Axe wants us to build bridges to the religious types. So we had to go to church last weekend (boring!) and Barack has been working on this Christian breakfast speech for weeks. All these ministers and pastors have been traipsing through the house, adding Bible quotes and prayers to the talk. It's just too long, if you ask me. Last night, Barack even tried to act out parts of his speech at dinner. I could see that all that talk of blood and dying on the cross was making Mama sick to her stomach. She finally threw her napkin down and stormed out of the dining room in frustration. I wish I could have joined her.

So this morning we go down to the East Room, and Smokey gets up to welcome the religious fanatics. The teleprompters slide in and he's about to launch into his big speech when one of the pastors asks, "Excuse me, Mr. President, could you lead us in grace?" I had to put my coffee cup in front of my mouth so they wouldn't see me laughing. The only time I've ever heard Barack say grace is when it was preceded by "Will &. . . ." He mumbled and stuttered and ummmed for at least two minutes. In desperation, I got up and said, "Pastor, Barack and I are so moved by your request. But you really should say grace. We're not worthy. Can I get an amen?" The whole room said "Amen" and the Pastor happily said grace. Smokey owes me big-time.

I told him when we got upstairs: this is what happens when you let the holy rollers get too close. He agreed, and out of the blue, promised that we won't be putting that Jerusalem Barbie Nativity display up in the East Room this Christmas. It gives the girls and the public weird ideas about the holidays. "Why don't we set out those snowmen you bought last Christmas instead?" Barack suggested. "We really won't have to worry about religious displays again until at least 2011. And then 2012 will be 'O come let us adore him' time!"

---

Incidentally, the president did finally decide on a place of worship in June 2009: the Evergreen Chapel at Camp David. In a carefully worded statement, the White House said, "The President and First Family continue to look for a church home. They have enjoyed worshipping at Camp David and several other congregations over the months, and will choose a church at the time that is best for their family." According to *Time* magazine,

Robert Gibbs made sure to add that the First Family was not "joining" the Evergreen Chapel, as it was not open to membership. That's a good thing because one doesn't get the feeling that the president is all that interested anyway.

Nine months later, in March 2010, NBC's Matt Lauer asked President Obama why the First Family still had not selected a hometown church. The president's excuse put them, of course, in the best possible light:

> Michelle and I have realized we are very disruptive to services. . . . And in the meantime, what we've done, there was a prayer circle of pastors from across the country who, during the campaign, would say a prayer for me or send a devotional. And we've kept that habit up and, and it's a wonderful group because it's a mix of some very conservative pastors, some very liberal pastors, but all who, you know, pray for me and Michelle and, and the girls and, and I get a daily devotional on my BlackBerry which is a, is a wonderful thing.

Let us take his points in chronological order. First, his reason for not choosing a church had nothing to do with concern for fellow parishioners, and everything to do with politics. Choosing any individual black church in the District of Columbia would immediately upset the other black congregations and possibly cause hard feelings. This is the same sort of political calculation that drove Obama to choose Trinity all those years ago: his membership offended no one in his orbit and helped propel him into politics.

Second, the fact that other people are praying for him is nice but fails to answer the question. Indeed, millions of Americans pray for their president regardless of political party, every night. And how exactly is it relevant that a daily devotional is sent to his BlackBerry? One can only imagine the type of liberation theology action items landing in his inbox. "Thou shalt stick it to the rich until the rich actually bleed money from their pores!" "Thou shalt not praise the United States too often if doing so obscures the great sins America has committed across the globe!"

THE U.S. NAVAL OBSERVATORY

March 31, 2010

An entire day has gone by and not a single gaffe from me.
Of course, I wasn't let out of the compound all day, either. Not
a lot going on here, so I caught up on my DVR'd TV shows. For
some reason, it automatically records all the "Hair Club for Men"
infomercials.

Yowza, that <u>Today</u> show interview POTUS did this morning
was a home run. "Hey, Matt, I don't need to go to any particular
church," Barack said. "I get regular blast e-mails from some pastor
friends, dude!" Why didn't I think of that?! Maybe there's some
website number I can visit to sign up for meditations or fortunes
specifically tailored to me! If they came from a Catholic-focused
World Wide Web domain structure resource thing, and I read
them every day, I wonder if that would count for going to Mass?
The homilies about all that "respecting human life" baloney are just
too much to take. Plus, if I never see a collection basket again,
it'll be too soon . . . Wait . . . Damn it! That doesn't work because I
would still need to take communion. Well, I've gotten around that

one before. I know—why not get some priest to set up a special home delivery service for the wafers and wine? (You know, sort of the way that other Sunday sacrament—the New York Times—is delivered right to my door!)

I know—I'll call Cardinal Ted McCarrick and see what he thinks. Since he's retired he might even be willing to make the dropoffs himself. If he won't go for it, I'll give Archbishop Wuerl a call. Worse comes to worse, Giblet can get the Washington Post to dig up some old abuse case—that's always a good way to soften these guys up. Enough negative publicity and they'll give you the vestments right off their backs. I mean, all I'm looking for is a drive-by cracker, for God's sake. I've got a lot on my plate, man.

---

## THE WINNING WAY

We are called neither by God nor America to hide our faith or secularize it. Rather, Christians are commanded in the Gospels to let our faith shine in all aspects of our lives.

> You are the salt of the earth. But if salt loses its taste, with what can it be seasoned? It is no longer good for anything but to be thrown out and trampled underfoot. You are the light of the world. A city set on a mountain cannot be hidden. Nor do they light a lamp and then put it under a bushel basket; it is set on a lampstand, where it gives light to all in the house. Just so, your light must shine before others, that they may see your good deeds and glorify your heavenly Father. (Matthew 5:13–16)

Religious faith speaks to what is central to us as human beings. It speaks to our deepest convictions about this world and the next. The beauty of America is the freedom we have not only to express our religious faith, but also to practice it and to allow that practice to seep into our everyday life. Religion has a role to play in the health of the republic. As John Adams, our second president, wrote, "It is religion and morality alone which can establish the principles upon which freedom can securely stand. The only foundation of a free constitution is pure virtue."

There is no shame in permitting our religious convictions to shape our politics, particularly when considering issues that touch on human life, ethics, and morality. In fact, it is a civic responsibility. The challenge in this ever more secular culture is finding ways to express our religious viewpoints so that they have maximum impact. Obama is partly right when he says that quoting the scripture in a public policy dispute is not enough. We must confront the Obamaites on their own terms. The stirrings of our faith must be translated into coherent, well-reasoned arguments that will persuade others and truly advance the "common good" that Obama often invokes, but rarely assists.

With faith as our guide, we can truly help our fellow man to reach his potential today, and to reach that faraway eternal shore that is our shared destination—whether the president knows it or not.

# CHAPTER 7

# PLAYING BASKETBALL
# WITH DICTATORS

I t certainly felt like something important was happening.

On April 12 and 13, 2010, a fourteen-square-block area of down-town Washington was closed to all but official traffic. Barricades were positioned everywhere. Military vehicles parked at key intersections. Security officers from around the world rubbed shoulders in the big hotels. International reporters crowded into press briefings. Words like *historic* and *ambitious* were used to describe the Nuclear Security Summit. The White House created another nifty logo for the occasion, but this time "the Obama magic" did not work. This nonproliferation gathering was a non-starter.

At the end of the multiday extravaganza, the forty-seven countries in attendance promised to pursue *voluntary* efforts to secure nuclear materials within four years, presumably to keep them out of terrorists' hands. Attendees also agreed to the obligatory follow-up meeting later in the year, and another summit in two years. Six countries did agree to dispose of some highly enriched uranium used in civilian facilities—Ukraine, Mexico, Chile, Kazakhstan, Vietnam, and Canada. Americans can rest peacefully in their beds tonight now that we have reduced the risk of Ottawa providing al Qaeda with nukes. Whew!

Meanwhile, Iran, which is racing to get a nuclear weapon, was not even on the official agenda. The only progress that Obama could cite on the Iran issue was when the Chinese leader Hu Jintao actually used the word *sanctions*. Maybe Obama thought he had softened him up by doing that weird half-bow thing. Full bows were reserved for Saudi Arabia's King Abdullah (April 2009) and the Emperor Akihito of Japan (November 2009).

There was nothing worthwhile accomplished regarding North Korea, either. And completing the trifecta of failure, the impressive stagecraft yielded nothing meaningful vis-à-vis Pakistan, which continues to produce weapons-grade plutonium.

For all the pomp and pageantry, the "Nuclear Security Summit" did virtually nothing to limit the spread of nuclear weapons or to make Americans more secure. Nevertheless, it was invaluable in demonstrating how President Obama deals with foreign policy. As part of its summit coverage, the *Washington Post* described Obama's role at the summit as that of a "seminar leader": "For four hours Tuesday, Obama led a pair of planning sessions to iron out the final details of the communiqué that was the culmination of the summit. He sat at the center of the gathering, calling on leaders to speak, embellish, oppose, and offer alternatives to the plan taking shape." One European diplomat was quoted as saying of President Obama: "He's never better than when he's the teacher."

In some ways, you can't blame him. After all, President Obama comes from the Ivy League, and there is nothing that Ivy League professors (and students) like better than a nice, friendly seminar, where everyone sits around and puts forward his views in a careful, pleasant manner. Good times. I used to take seminars myself back at Dartmouth—it was an easy way to pad my schedule with additional credits without having to do a lot of work. Of course, the problem was that by the end of the term you realized that you had wasted a lot of Thursday nights and had not actually learned much.

And that pretty much sums up President Obama's foreign policy—lots of talk, lots of "breakout sessions," lots of "my good friend President X" references . . . with very few results. The hard truth is that great nations—or even small nations—don't change their foreign policy because they had a good time chatting with our president. In the real world, nations change their ways only if they believe that doing so is in their best interest. Diplomacy is a great tool—and one that every president should master—but there's more to diplomacy than pleasantries and friendly gestures. Diplomatic efforts must fit into a coherent view of how the world works, and must be backed by hard power. President Obama's view of the world is incredibly naïve, and under his leadership America is growing weaker rather than stronger.

## SOME OF MY BEST FRIENDS ARE DICTATORS

Obama's boosters love to point out how popular their guy is with foreign leaders. For example, just before the big summit, on April 9, 2010, President Dmitry Medvedev of Russia (Vladimir Putin's handpicked successor) told ABC's George Stephanopoulos that Obama is "a thinker, he thinks when he speaks." This statement was widely seen as a compliment for President Obama and an implied criticism of President George W. Bush (who, presumably, was not viewed by the Russian regime as a "thinker"). But look at it from an American perspective. Putin has created a new type of soft dictatorship in Russia. Medvedev is, therefore, for all intents and purposes, merely his mouthpiece. Why would we respect *his* views regarding *our* president? Is there any reason to believe that Russia wants the United States to have a strong and effective leader? The fact that men like Medvedev say nice things about President Obama should be seen as a warning, not an endorsement.

Of course, we could see that President Obama would be friendly with dictators even before he was elected. On February 11, 2007, he complained to *60 Minutes'* Steve Kroft that the Bush administration had not done enough to reach out to Iran: "The fact of the matter is that Iran currently is governed by an oppressive regime, one that I think is a threat to the region and to our allies, but there are a lot of people in Iran who potentially would like to be part of this broader community of nations. For us not to be in a conversation with them doesn't make sense."

In response to a specific question about whether he would use military force to prevent Iran from acquiring nuclear weapons, Obama said that while he would keep all options on the table, "our first step should be a much more aggressive approach to diplomacy than we've displayed thus far."

Obama's comments sparked significant controversy—and claims that he advocated negotiating with terrorists. But he did not back down, and he has never wavered from the basic notion that the rest of the world holds an immense reservoir of goodwill toward the United States, and that even dictatorial states like Iran will rally to our cause if we simply show them some kindness. Like any good seminar leader, he seems to believe that the highest accolade for an American president is "plays well with others."

## OUR "SORRY" STATE OF AFFAIRS

In accordance with his vision of a more humble America, Obama opened with a blizzard of apologies to the rest of the world for our many sins.

---

### THE DIARY OF PRESIDENT BARACK OBAMA

#### THE WHITE HOUSE

January 30, 2009

My national security advisor, Jim Jones, and his staff gave me a briefing today. Hillary sat in, too. What a bunch of Debbie Downers. Everything they said was preceded by "Mr. President, we have a problem with . . ." "Mr. President, you need to be careful about . . ." "Mr. President, you'll want to keep an eye on . . ." Blah, blah, blah, national interest. Blah, blah, blah, danger. Blah, blah, blah, terrorism. It was like listening to one of McCain's campaign commercials.

I explained to them that I do know something about foreign policy—didn't I deliver that speech in Germany during the campaign? Don't the Euros all love me? Weren't they all pulling for me last year? How hard can it be to cut deals with people who love you?

So I told them: "Guys, I hear what you're saying, but calm down. That cowboy 'my way or the highway' stuff, that's all finished. I'm gonna charm these folks. Have you ever seen me work a room? I'll go to these foreign countries, treat them with respect, and speak their language—anti-American." (No one laughed.) "Talk about regrets for what we did in the past, how that's all behind us now, and how we all need to work together. They'll love it. What W didn't understand is that, deep down, everybody wants to be our friend. We've got Hollywood, we've got rock 'n' roll; we're like the cool exchange students at school."

They seemed to like the part about using more diplomacy, although it was obvious they wanted to get into a bunch of specifics about Russian politics and Pakistan. Geez! Can't I have a breather to enjoy the historic nature of my presidency? The world community likes me and I like them.

The meeting was starting to drag so I pushed the button I use to summon Biden whenever I need him to interrupt me and clear the room. I may have finally found a job that Biden can do well.

---

The Obama apologies were not mere diplomatic niceties. They were part of his plan to convince the world that he was unusually decent and humane—for an American. Even before he was elected, Senator Obama used a July 2008 speech in Berlin to tell a European audience that "we've made our share of mistakes, and there are times when our actions around the world have not lived up to our best intentions."

But that was only the beginning. Soon after he was inaugurated, President Obama made so many "sorry" statements about U.S. foreign policy, many of us began to wonder whether Michael Moore had joined his speech-writing staff:

- April 2, 2009: President Obama, speaking at a press conference in London after the G-20, described the negotiations that led to the Bretton Woods system that stabilized global finance after World War II as "just Roosevelt and Churchill sitting in a room with a brandy." He went on to say, "That's not the world we live in, and *it shouldn't be the world we live in* [emphasis added]"—thus clearly indicating that the United States and the United Kingdom should not be trusted with so much power.
- April 3, 2009: At a town hall in Strasbourg, France, Obama stated, "In America, there's a failure to appreciate Europe's leading role in the world. Instead of celebrating your dynamic union and seeking to partner with you to meet common challenges, there have been times where America has shown arrogance and been dismissive, even derisive."
- April 5, 2009: Speaking to two hundred thousand people in Prague, Czech Republic, Obama said, "As the only nuclear power to have used a nuclear weapon, we [the United States] have a moral responsibility to act" in limiting nuclear weapons.
- April 6, 2009: "Our country still struggles with the legacies of slavery

and segregation, the past treatment of Native Americans," he told the Turkish parliament.

- May 21, 2009: At this point, President Obama's "apology tour" was coming under severe criticism at home. (I remember this well, because I was one of the chief critics.) But he wasn't finished. Our actions at the Guantanamo base in Cuba "set back the moral authority that is America's strongest currency in the world."

- July 7, 2009: President Obama traveled to Russia, where he met with President Dmitry Medvedev and former KGB chief and President Vladimir Putin. President Obama later explained to Russian opposition leaders: "I think it's very important that I come before you with some humility. I think in the past there's been a tendency for the United States to lecture rather than listen." A few months earlier, Secretary of State Hillary Clinton had famously presented Russian leaders with a button that she thought read "reset" in Russian (as in resetting our relationship with Moscow). Instead, the Russian word stamped on the button meant "overcharge." If President Bush's team had found themselves similarly lost in translation, they would still be hearing about it.

- July 18, 2009: Secretary of State Clinton told India: "We acknowledge now with President Obama that we have made mistakes in the United States, and we along with other developed countries have contributed most significantly to the problem that we face with climate change."

- November 13, 2009: Obama spoke in Japan of the importance of multilateral organizations in building security and prosperity throughout the Asia-Pacific region. Referring to himself as America's "first Pacific president" (Isn't California on the Pacific? Wasn't Ronald Reagan governor of California?), President Obama said, "I know that the United States has been disengaged from these organizations in recent years," but promised to do better if given a chance.

---

The Diary of ~~President~~ Secretary of State
Hillary Clinton

Washington, D.C.

January 31, 2009

Hello, America! It's 3 a.m. Do you know who's answering the phone? An overinflated egomaniac who doesn't know the first thing about foreign policy, that's who.

Yesterday, a team of us tried to educate the former senator from Illinois about the dangers we face in the world. He had that same deer-in-the-headlights look I remember so well from the debates—his eyes would glaze over whenever I would point out how his stance on foreign policy was going to weaken America. I thought it was important for him to understand that there are bad people out there who do bad things.

Of course, I know he won't listen to me. Bill once told me that no politician ever takes advice from someone he defeated. And he's probably right.

So Jim Jones and I summoned some of the "best and the brightest" types from NSA to brief him on the key crisis points. I told them to keep it as simple as possible. They wanted to know whether the kinds of briefings they give me would suffice. Ha! I told them to imagine briefing someone who reaches for his BlackBerry during your introduction and will be halfway through a game of Tetris by the time you've made your second point.

Sure enough, almost as soon as we started, he glanced at his watch and pulled out the BlackBerry, feet up on the table. I was signaling to the NSA guys to speed things up and to simplify the data, but it was too late. Professor Gandhi cut us off with a predictable routine: "Calm down, Hillary. Remember, we've got to drop the combative language and build bridges. There are no enemy states, just world leaders who haven't met us yet. Let's all locate our inner peace and commit to spread that peace to all those we meet. Politics is about people and I have a way with people."

We tried to stay on track and get the message across to him, but he pushed that stupid button on the desk he uses to call Biden in to break up meetings. (He thinks this is a big state secret, which shows how well he understands Washington. Bill used that same button to call Podesta in to break up his meetings.) So we had to leave.

Anyway, the whole thing was embarrassing, and there is no doubt that the man is in over his head. Does he really think the Europeans like him any more than they liked Bill? Fat chance. And as for Michelle (his "secret diplomatic weapon"), it's only a matter of time before she and Carla Bruni get into a diva smackdown <u>Dynasty</u>-style! It's so obvious that Michelle is jealous of me. She's probably already started picking her campaign staff for an Illinois Senate run. Copy cat.

These other countries are going to roll her husband every chance they get. And I just know the right-wingers will go nuts, and we'll get hammered in the elections.

Oh, well. Stupid Democrats. I tried to warn them.

---

By the end of his first year in office, President Obama had gone out of his way to criticize former U.S. foreign policy in Western Europe, the

Middle East, the Americas, Russia, and Asia. That pretty much covers the entire world. Fortunately for President Obama, we are not in contact with life on other planets, or he would have had to apologize to them as well. (I can hear him addressing the United Federation of Planets right now: "Too often, we have viewed your precious and invaluable habitations as nothing more than a wasteland to be 'explored.' ")

---

## THE DIARY OF FIRST LADY MICHELLE OBAMA

### THE WHITE HOUSE

*April 20, 2009*

So I've been reading the press accounts of Barack's foreign tour—what a bunch of nonsense! All this stuff about how he's been "apologizing" to everyone! That's so wrong. In every speech, he includes a whole paragraph about the greatness of America, and how we've helped the world, and so forth. That's an apology?

I told him: You haven't apologized <u>enough</u>! This country <u>needs</u> a president who will apologize. We have a lot to atone for. Makes you wonder if he was listening when Reverend Jeremiah was preaching. What a prophetic voice. "U.S. of KKK" . . . "God damn America" . . . Amen, amen.

Being the supportive wife that I am, I shared with him some of the things I learned about American history while I was at

Princeton — things that aren't normally taught in America . . .
well, they're taught at good schools like Princeton, but they're
not taught to enough regular Americans. But he didn't seem all
that interested — he acted as though he had heard it all before.
Whatever. He's never been serious about his studies.

But I wouldn't let him off that easily. I explained that we
should use our high office to tell the truth about all the bad
things this country has done. He started giving me a list of excuses
about domestic politics, and whining about how the Republicans
would criticize him. I said, "Barack, you need to be asking
yourself what's the right thing to do." He started to say something
about polling, parroting Axelrod's advice, and how Hillary wasn't
on board with his apology strategy. But I wasn't going to let him
turn a moral argument into a discussion about political tactics.
Plus, Hillary is just jealous of me anyway. Just when I had Barack
cornered, Biden crashed in and said they had to run off to
another meeting. Who does that old fool think he is, waltzing into
the Oval uninvited when a wife is talking to her husband? When
I'm ~~president~~ a senator, I won't put up with such nonsense.

---

The apologies continued in 2010. Most recently, President Obama held
an embarrassing summit with President Felipe Calderón of Mexico in which
he and other Democrats cheered Calderón's attacks on Arizona's new
immigration law—a law that is overwhelmingly popular in the United States.
Now leaders from other countries feel free to come here and denounce our

laws. But why shouldn't they denounce us? They are merely following the president's example.

## A SORRY EXCUSE FOR LEADERSHIP

Contrary to what the dinosaur media would have you believe, President Obama's apologies have not led to a stronger or more secure America. There are (at least) three critical problems with his approach.

### We're Not the Bad Guys

Our seminar-leader-in-chief accepts and promotes the simplistic version of American history promoted by anti-American left-wingers in university history departments nationwide. They believe the United States achieved power and prosperity by exploiting everyone and everything—destroying the environment, abusing "indigenous peoples," and using its military to intimidate and kill its enemies. This warped view of history teaches that Americans are generally cold and indifferent toward foreigners, and that we often reject efforts to work in partnership with other nations.

But foreign policy is not checkers. The game of nations is played for keeps, and the losers are often killed. For centuries, prudent American statesmen have realized these facts, and they have not hesitated to act forcefully to defend American interests—even if doing so brought protests from abroad. By such actions, they were simply fulfilling the primary obligation of any national government—the obligation to protect its citizens from harm.

Consider, for example, President Obama's statement that the United States has a special responsibility to restrain the spread of nuclear weapons because we are "the only nuclear power to have used a nuclear weapon." Such a phrase leaves the impression that President Truman dropped a couple of A-bombs on Hiroshima and Nagasaki just because he could— that Americans were indifferent to the massive destruction of life resulting from nuclear weapons. You wouldn't know that U.S. policymakers were trying to end a devastating war that we did not start, one that had already resulted in the deaths of more than four hundred thousand Americans, and that threatened to continue for years if we were forced to invade Japan.

You would never know that ever since 1945, Americans have had a robust debate over the proper use of nuclear weapons, and that generations of Americans grew up in the shadow of a potential nuclear holocaust. In other words, you would not know that U.S. policymakers prior to Obama were dedicated and earnest men and women trying to do their best in a dangerous world—not a bunch of trigger-happy cowboys. By leaving such an impression, President Obama not only insults the memories of men like Harry Truman and George C. Marshall, he invites other countries to do so as well.

---

## THE DIARY OF RUSSIAN PREMIER VLADIMIR PUTIN

### MOSCOW, RUSSIA

### July 4, 2009

Given the date, I thought this was an appropriate day to talk to ~~Comrade~~ "President" Medvedev of Russia about final preparations for our upcoming meeting with the new American president.

I hate dealing with a puppet president! It would be so much easier to do everything myself. I always have to explain things to Dmitry—simple things that even a lowly ~~KGB~~ security agent should be able to understand.

Today, for example, he tried to be clever about Obama. He said to me, "Mr. Premier, what sort of scheme is this Obama up to? I know he appears to be weak, but isn't he hiding something? What is he really up to?"

I replied, "Dmitry, do you not remember President Carter?" He reminded me that he was still in school during

that glorious era. I always forget how young he is. So I
had to explain: "Dmitry, let me tell you about American
liberals. They are not clever. They are not complex. They
are very simple people, who live by one basic rule: So long
as America is nice to the world, the world will be nice to her
in return."

He said, "I thought that had to be a ruse."

I explained, "It is no ruse. I have sat through meetings
with them ~~and listened to tapes of their telephone
conversations~~ for years, and I know how they think. They
feel great guilt over the wealth and power of their country,
and they seek ways to make it up to the rest of the world.
They feel great loneliness, so they always look for friends in
other countries."

He then asked: "What should we do?"

I said, "Prey on their guilty feelings. Talk about their
favorite issues—like climate change, or helping the poor.
Make them believe that all we ~~Soviets~~ Russians have ever
wanted was brotherhood among the nations. And at the
same time, keep making demands. Whenever they yield on
one point, simply ask for something else. Never let them
feel that their guilt has been expiated."

"Don't they ever push back?" he asked.

I said, "Of course not. They'll love you for it. Remember,
they want you to forgive them. The tougher you are, the
more they'll respect you."

I hope he understood it all. But even if he fails, I have
my own meeting with the new president, and I can take care
of this myself—as usual.

Americans have no reason to go hat in hand to the rest of the world, begging for forgiveness as though we're some sort of rogue nation. By the standards of other great nations in history, our power has been used with a remarkable spirit of generosity. One would expect that our own president would know this fact, and would use his bully pulpit—and his great eloquence—to defend our reputation on the world stage. The last thing we need is a president who uses his own speeches to peddle anti-American stereotypes.

## Where's My Apology?

Have you noticed how President Obama apologizes only to *foreign* audiences? Where are the apologies for the liberal welfare programs in this country that have wasted enormous sums of taxpayer money? Where are the apologies for the criminals who went free because of excessive liberal concerns about legal technicalities? Where are the apologies for the countless American schools run into the ground by incompetent liberal administrators? Where are the apologies for the "arrogant" liberal justices on the Supreme Court who imposed their opinions about abortion and other social issues on the rest of us? Where are the apologies for the "dismissive" attitudes many American liberals have shown toward the millions of fellow citizens who listen to talk radio, attend tea parties, and watch Fox?

President Obama's defenders justify his apologies abroad by saying that they were necessary to rebuild relationships after the Bush administration. In other words, the apologies are merely a tactic to win popular support for President Obama's pro-American ideas. But if this were the case, why not use apologies at home? If apologies are so effective in winning over hostile foreigners, why doesn't Obama use them to win over hostile Republicans— or even hostile talk-show hosts?

The answer is simple: President Obama knows a lot more about American politics—and American audiences—than he knows about his foreign listeners. He remembers what happened when President Clinton said, "The era of big government is over." For years, Republicans used that concession to bash liberal efforts to create new government programs. President Obama understands (and I think understands correctly) that if he were to publicly admit the many mistakes made by liberals—even if he did so as part of an effort to promote liberalism—conservatives would use such an admission to convince their fellow Americans to reject liberalism altogether. President Obama is far too talented a politician—and far too realistic about the American political process—to give Republicans such a compelling propaganda victory.

When it comes to American politics, President Obama properly recognizes that some differences are lasting and cannot be smoothed over with an apology. Or maybe he simply believes that foreigners are somehow more "reasonable" than American conservatives—that it's easier to reach a meeting of the minds with Vladimir Putin or angry left-wingers in Western Europe than with the GOP. Perhaps—and this strikes me as the most likely explanation of all—he's never thought about these issues in a rigorous manner. For decades, American liberals have divided their time between ruthlessly attacking American conservatives and shamelessly apologizing to foreigners. President Obama is just following that same ignoble tradition.

Liberals cry foul whenever anyone criticizes their patriotism, but this behavior cries out for such criticism. I find it simply incredible that an American president would repeat simplistic anti-American stereotypes as though they were true—knowing that he would thereby give ammunition to people who hate us. I would think that feelings of national pride and honor alone would be sufficient to restrain Obama from being so critical, in both word and gesture, of his own nation—*the same nation that elected him president.*

---
≈≈≈
---

## The Diary of Vice President Joe Biden

U.S. Naval Observatory

April 12, 2010

I'm trying to wrap my mind around Barack's newfound penchant for bowing. Today at the nuclear summit he reached a new low, and I mean that physically and figuratively. Lord Almighty, is there anyone he hasn't gone ninety degrees for?!

Barack is something else. In front of the press, he bent right over for the Chinese president Hu Jintao. Granted, I was a little red-faced myself when they introduced me to the Chinese dictator. The staff told me his name rhymes with that tasty chicken dish, Kung Pow. So when the time came I said, "Great to meet you President Kung Pow [sic], uh, Pow Wow. Aw, s*#t." It's hard keeping all these names straight. But at least I didn't make a "Hu's on first?" joke. And I certainly didn't bow to the little guy!

Barack's "bowing movement" has become a nasty habit that I have to clean up afterward. He's curtsied to everybody from Japanese royals to Stevie Wonder to that Middle Eastern sheik wearing the bathrobe! (What the hell was his name—King Abraca-labra or something?) If I were the clean, articulate

African-American that Barack is, the last thing I would do is prostate [*sic*] myself to a fella who looks like he just delivered a bowl of egg drop soup to the table—hold the MSG. But all joking aside, bowing like that makes him look weak. And I don't consider it a diplomatic victory that the Chinese actually used the word sanctions for the first time. What the f#@k is this—Wheel of Fortune? Where's Vanna White when you need her to turn the tiles that spell: DIPLOMATIC DISASTER!

For Chrissakes, he's supposed to be for "change"! Why doesn't he stand upright for a change. He should just let me run this foreign policy thing. Truthfully, how much foreign experience could he have possibly picked up between his leafleting career and hanging around the Ivy League? I'm the guy who got in Milosevic's face and called him a "damn war criminal." I'm the guy who tried to stop the Bush adventure in Iraq. I was even chairman of the Senate Foreign Relations Committee, for Pete's sake. Barack's got the heavyweight champion of foreign policy standing right next to him, and I'm spending my days giving pep talks at girls' basketball games. My only official duty is barging into the Oval when he wants to end a meeting. I'll tell you one thing, if old Joe were the top man, he wouldn't be bowing to nobody. Aw, s*@t, the car is here. I'm speaking at a Girl Scout pin ceremony in Southeast tonight. I need a drink—a double.

# Bashing Our Friends

President Obama doesn't merely apologize for prior American policies—he also distances himself from those who seek to be our friends.

Israel has long been our most important ally in the Middle East—a haven of pro-American sentiment in one of the most anti-American regions of the globe. In May 2009, President Obama repaid this support by denouncing Israeli settlements in the West Bank—placing Israel in the humiliating position of being publicly criticized by the country that is supposed to be its closest friend. Israelis quickly got the message. In a March 2010 poll, Smith Research found that 48 percent of Israeli Jews viewed President Obama as pro-Palestinian, while only 9 percent saw him as pro-Israel.

Israel ignored President Obama's demands—leading to more criticism from the Obama administration. By the spring of 2010, the rift over the settlements had led to a serious deterioration in U.S.-Israeli relations. When Prime Minister Benjamin Netanyahu met with President Obama on March 23, 2010, the *Washington Post*'s Glen Kessler described the two-hour exchange as occurring "under a virtual news blackout." The president was clearly sending a message to the Muslim world that Israel, our friend, does not always get what it wants. Yet to many Jews here and abroad, this episode was insulting. Most political observers could not remember a time when an Israeli leader was treated in such a rude fashion.

In June 2009, the Honduran Supreme Court ruled that President Manuel Zelaya had taken unconstitutional efforts to abolish term limits so that he could remain in power, and the Honduran military subsequently forced Zelaya from office. This move was supported by the Honduran Congress. These developments were good for the United States—Zelaya was backed by Venezuelan strongman Hugo Chavez, who has devoted himself to spreading anti-Americanism throughout Latin America. But the Obama administration condemned Zelaya's ouster, and actually pressured the Hondurans to reinstate their law-breaking president. Fortunately for us, they didn't listen.

For years, leaders in Poland and the Czech Republic resisted pressure from Russia and cooperated with the United States on missile defense. These countries, like many others in Eastern Europe, understand all too well what it is like to be ordered around by Moscow. But as part of his effort to reach out to Putin & Co., President Obama threw the Poles and Czechs under the bus, announcing that he would scrap long-standing plans for missile interceptors in Poland and a radar station in the Czech Republic. In another masterstroke of Obama diplomacy, this announcement was made on September 17, 2009—the seventieth anniversary of the Soviet invasion of Poland.

And who can forget April 18, 2010, when the president cancelled his trip to attend the funeral of Polish president Lech Kaczynski and his wife because of a volcanic ash cloud and decided to go golfing instead? Nice image of concern and solidarity with the Poles, who were in mourning after a horrific plane crash near Smolensk, Russia, that wiped out nearly the entire Polish leadership.

What is striking about these examples is how often they embody exactly the type of arrogant, dismissive attitude for which President Obama likes to apologize. If he's so sensitive to the feelings of other nations, then why did we embarrass Poland by pulling the missile defense program on the seventieth anniversary of the Soviet invasion? Why were we so indifferent to the feelings of the Honduran people in their efforts to defend their constitution?

# IT'S NOT WORKING

For the sake of argument, let's grant the liberal assumption that we should never criticize anyone's patriotism. Let's further assume that President Obama's apologies to our enemies (and insults to our allies) were not motivated by hostility toward American power, and that he actually viewed such tactics as a Machiavellian way to *advance* U.S. power by convincing the rest of the world to trust us and work with us. If we look at President Obama's actions in that light, how effective has his approach been? Have other countries stepped up to the plate to help us out? Are we seen as stronger now than when President Obama took office?

President Obama has certainly *asked* for help. On September 23, 2009, for example, he gave a major address to the United Nations General Assembly. After telling his audience: "I took office at a time when many around the world had come to view America with skepticism and distrust"—a mild apology by his standards. He assured them that there was a new sheriff in town and called upon the nations of the world to work with us going forward: "Those who used to chastise America for acting alone in the world cannot now stand by and wait for America to solve the world's problems alone. We have sought—in word and deed—a new era of engagement with the world. And now is the time for all of us to take our share of responsibility for a global response to global challenges."

So, what happened? Is the United States now safer or more prosperous because of our new humility?

Well, it's worked out pretty well for President Obama *personally*. On October 9, 2009, the Norwegian bureaucrats who give out the Nobel Peace Prize announced they would award it to none other than Barack Hussein Obama "for his extraordinary efforts to strengthen international diplomacy and cooperation between peoples."

---

## The Diary of President Barack Obama

### The White House

October 9, 2009

Oh, so Mr. Senator from Illinois can only do domestic policy, huh? He's in over his head, is he? I've got three words for you, Diary: NOBEL PEACE PRIZE. How do you like them apples?

Here's a complete list of all the American presidents who won the Nobel Peace Prize while in office (I'm not going to count Carter's award for building houses): Theodore Roosevelt, Woodrow Wilson, and me—Barack Hussein Obama. Pretty good company, if I do say so myself.

I thought I would have a little fun, so I told the White House switchboard to call Clinton. "Hey, Bill," I said. "I want your advice. I just won the Nobel Peace Prize. What do you think I should say?" I could hear him seething over the telephone. Priceless! If those Norwegians only knew how badly Bill and Hillary wanted that award. Just to rub it in, I should host a dinner for Carter and Gore, and then tell Clinton, "I'm sorry, Bill, only Nobel Peace Prize winners allowed."

I told you this foreign policy stuff isn't that hard.

—◦◦◦—

## THE DIARY OF ~~PRESIDENT~~ SECRETARY OF STATE HILLARY CLINTON

WASHINGTON, D.C.

October 9, 2009

The Nobel Prize! <u>The Nobel Prize!</u> He just got here ten months ago and they give him the <u>Nobel Prize!</u> How is that possible? What did Bill and I ever do to deserve this? All those years of cultivating relationships with those nitwits in Europe, and this is what we get? Gore and Obama? Hell, why not give one to Tipper—she's done as much for America as those two. For that matter, that yappy dog Bo is really a force for international peace and harmony . . . give him one, too!

Bill's been calling me all day, and I know he wants to vent, but I just cannot deal with it right now. Let him grouse to one of his "friends."

Come on, Hillary—find your happy place . . . calm down, take it easy, relax . . .

<u>The Nobel Prize?!</u>

For the rest of us Americans, the benefits of the president's new style of "leadership" are few and far between. Indeed, on issue after issue, President Obama's pleas for cooperation have gone unheeded.

Winning the war in Afghanistan was a focal point of President Obama's 2008 campaign, and the president has made success in Afghanistan a major priority of his administration. But a call for 3,200 additional NATO soldiers to help train the Afghan army was answered with commitments for only half that number. Indeed, by February 2010, Secretary of Defense Robert Gates was complaining that the dearth of helicopters, cargo planes, and spy aircraft caused by low military budgets in Europe was "directly impacting operations in Afghanistan."

In his speech to the United Nations, President Obama said, "If the governments of Iran and North Korea . . . put the pursuit of nuclear weapons ahead of regional stability and the security and opportunity of their own people . . . then they must be held accountable. The world must stand together to demonstrate that international law is not an empty promise, and that treaties will be enforced." But key countries (including Turkey and Brazil) refuse to support significant sanctions on Iran, even though that country is clearly moving closer to developing nuclear weapons. For all his charm, Barack Obama has had great difficulty in galvanizing his newfound "friends" in the world community—so much so that now Cold War–style containment of the belligerent mullahs may be the only option. While the administration took credit for getting Russia and China to agree to "sanctions" on Iran, it should be noted that Charles Krauthammer described the proposed Security Council resolution as "laughably weak." Ralph Peters warned that China and Russia were actually working with Turkey, Brazil, and Iran to undermine U.S. influence around the world. And the administration admitted that the "sanctions" deal would not prevent Russia from selling Iran missiles to defend its nuclear facilities. Some deal. North Korea, meanwhile, continues to proceed with its own nuclear program—and the White House now fears that it may be providing nuclear-weapons-related technology to another rogue nation, Burma. In short, the world has not "stood together," and Iran and North Korea have not been "held accountable."

One of the centerpieces of President Obama's efforts to "reset" relations between the United States and Russia was his decision to scrap plans for missile defense facilities in Poland and the Czech Republic. But in December 2009, Vladimir Putin complained that President Obama's alternative plan—putting sea-based interceptors in southern Europe—would fundamentally disrupt the balance of power in Europe and force Russia to develop new offensive weapons in response. So naturally, our president decided to reward Russia by signing a new START Treaty—how 1975! The treaty called for the reduction of the number of warheads in the former Soviet Union's decrepit nuclear cache. Going into the signing ceremony, the Russians claimed that the treaty would constrain America's missile defense efforts in Europe. No wonder Medvedev was smiling. Serious Russian analysts understand that the elites who actually run the former Soviet Union remain extremely suspicious of the United States, and see us as adversaries. So much for the reset button.

---

## THE DIARY OF RUSSIAN PREMIER VLADIMIR PUTIN

### Moscow, Russia

### July 20, 2009

Dmitry called me after his meeting with Obama. "Oh, he's a real charmer, this one," he insisted. "We should keep an eye on him."

Dolt. With geniuses like him running amok, it's no wonder the Soviet Union collapsed.

I had my own meeting with Obama and I thought it went very well. He is not the cowboy type, that one. He is just as I expected: a nice, pleasant American liberal who wants to do what he can to help his fellow neighbors. So naturally

I berated him about the many injustices my great country has suffered. And he lapped it up. I had him eating out of my hand. He even said that he was impressed at the density and definition of my pectoral muscles. A very promising encounter, indeed.

Afterward, I called up Merkel in Germany and teased her a bit. "Angela," I said, "if we could have had this president back in the 1980s, the Warsaw Pact would still be going strong." She laughed that nervous German laugh, but I knew she agreed.

I can hardly wait to see the reaction of our former comrades in Eastern Europe when they realize that their fate lies in the hands of a man who cares more about pleasing me than about pleasing them.

---

THE DIARY OF PRESIDENT BARACK OBAMA

THE WHITE HOUSE

July 20, 2009

Met with Putin today. I am now convinced that he's totally misunderstood in the West. He seemed sincere in his desire for friendship and cooperation between our two countries. Even though he didn't exactly say that Russia wouldn't sell missiles to Iran, I could tell by the way he commented on my rippled forearms and upright posture that it's only a matter of time.

---

President Obama hoped to win support from China on a number of key issues, including significant curbs on greenhouse gas emissions. But China has proved largely immune to his charm. (Maybe those speeches lose something in translation.) At a major climate change summit in Copenhagen in December 2009, China rejected calls from the West that it do more to restrain carbon emissions going forward—thereby causing those talks to fail.

In addition, since President Obama was inaugurated, China has protested U.S. weapons sales to Taiwan, gotten into a feud with Google, attacked President Obama for his meeting with the Dalai Lama, and refused to help U.S. companies by allowing its currency to rise in accordance with market forces. By March 2010, it was clear that Sino-American relations were in trouble. President Obama was forced to send two high-ranking envoys to Beijing in an effort to repair a damaged relationship. But those efforts apparently failed, as China's foreign minister announced further complaints about Taiwan and the Dalai Lama, blaming the United States for increased tensions.

Soon afterward, on March 15, 2009, the *Washington Post*'s John Pomfret reported that "China's government has embraced an increasingly anti-Western tone in recent months and is adopting policies across a wide spectrum that reflect a heightened fear of foreign influence." One Chinese expert was quoted as saying that "[Chinese] people are now looking down on the West, from leadership circles to academia to everyday folk."

So how exactly has groveling on the world stage significantly improved America's security? The notion that our foreign policy dilemmas were significantly affected by President Bush's personal popularity (or un-popularity) is incredibly naïve. Many Europeans were certainly angry with Bush over the Iraq War, but they were also furious with Reagan for refer-ring to the U.S.S.R. as the "Evil Empire," and for pursuing an aggressive policy to win the Cold War. But because Reagan's policies were obviously successful—and because the United States clearly grew in stature under his administration—European opposition to President Reagan has been largely forgotten. On the other hand, President Carter constantly talked about the importance of human rights, treated international organizations with great respect, and worked hard to bring peace to the Middle East. Like his friends Barack Obama and Al Gore, he also has a Nobel Peace Prize. And look at his sterling foreign policy record.

## YOU CAN'T TEACH THE WORLD TO SING IN PERFECT HARMONY

The hard truth—a truth that President Obama is either unwilling or unable to understand—is this: foreign countries do not generally allow their personal feelings toward the president of the United States to drive their policies toward the United States. Indeed, they would be foolish to do so. No foreign leader can afford to take actions favorable to the United States solely because he thinks President Obama is a nice guy. The job of a national leader is to adopt policies that improve his country's standing in the world.

Believe it or not, most world leaders are remarkably talented and successful politicians—that's how they became world leaders in the first place. So they understand, for the most part, that their primary obligation is to satisfy their constituents—not to worry about their personal ties to President Obama. When European politicians are deciding whether to send troops to Afghanistan, or the Chinese are deciding whether to work with us on Iran, or the Russians are deciding whether to enter a new treaty on nuclear weapons, they are not going to be motivated by their personal opinions of Barack Obama, any more than they will be motivated by their feelings about bluegrass music, or Mark Twain, or any other aspect of American life. Instead they will examine the facts of the situation, and determine whether cooperating with the United States will make their countries stronger or weaker. If they will benefit from cooperation, they will cooperate. If not, they won't; it's that simple.

We have so much wealth and power, and play such a huge role in global affairs, that almost anyone with an instinctive desire to support the under-dog enjoys seeing the United States get its comeuppance. As long as the United States remains the world's superpower, we will find it hard to win the world's sympathy. This isn't anyone's fault; it's simply human nature. The only way to solve this problem would be for the United States to lose its power—a situation in which the cure is far worse than the disease.

---

## THE DIARY OF FIRST LADY MICHELLE OBAMA

### THE WHITE HOUSE

*March 20, 2010*

I've really got to talk to Mama about the influence she's having on the girls. Today was supposed to be an electronics-free day—a day for the girls to play with toys that make them use their imagination instead of just pushing buttons.

So I go upstairs, and I hear this yelling from Sasha's bedroom. I go in there, and the girls are playing that old board game, Risk. It's a terrible game, all about one country trying to conquer others. They claimed they got it from Grandma. I don't know where she got it—she must have smuggled it in from Chicago.

Anyway, when I got there, Malia had conquered most of the "world," and Sasha was crying because she only had a few spaces left in Australia. So I told them: "Girls, this is why we don't believe in conflicts of this kind. I've got an idea. Instead of playing Risk, let's play a new game called 'Take a Risk.' In this game, Malia, you will reach out to Sasha and ask her to be your friend. And then some of her armies can come into your territory and some of your armies can go into her territory and you guys will just share everything."

Malia said something about how that sounded "boring," but I said, "No, it will be fun." And so we moved the armies all over the board and talked about how the nations should work together to bring about sustainable agriculture and new policies to stop climate change, and discussed other socially constructive ideas. We would roll the dice to see how much money the rich countries should send to help the poor countries.

We played for about fifteen minutes, until I won. I think they had a good time and learned a lot about making peace internationally. That reminds me, Smokey needs to send Vladimir a thank-you note and some White House memorabilia for agreeing to sign that big START treaty. Lord knows, if we leave these diplomatic gestures to Hillary, the whole thing will go down in flames. Or maybe I should just add Russia to my international "speak to young people" tour. Those Russians don't know the first thing about talking to the young. Mama Michelle will show Vladimir how it's done. And what could possibly say "thank you" better than a solo visit by the First Lady?

# POWER MATTERS

History shows that if President Obama really wants to persuade other countries to work with the United States, he should quit trying to convince them that we are soft and start showing them that we are strong. We need to convince other countries that the United States has so much power that they will benefit from cooperating with us—and will suffer if they do not.

Unfortunately, President Obama's approach, instead of convincing the rest of the world that we are getting stronger, has done much to persuade others that the United States is growing less powerful. The *Times* of London reported on April 17, 2009, that President Nicolas Sarkozy of France came away from his initial meeting with Barack Obama with the impression that the United States had a weak president, whom he described as "incredibly naïve and grossly egotistical."

---

## The Diary of President Barack Obama

### The White House

September 25, 2009

So Pepe Le Pew is dissing me? Calling me "naïve"? "Egotistical"?! That I'm "obsessed with disarmament"? Well, it's better than being obsessed with height the way he is! The man is obviously wracked with jealousy. Maybe he noticed that Carla lingered just a few seconds too long when we first hugged. Maybe he's ticked off because I didn't bow down to him. Truth is, I would have, but he's so damned diminutive that I don't think I could have gotten down that low.

You know, the more I think about this the more offended I get. The next time we're in the same city, I'm going to ask him to play hoops with me. LOL!!! We'll see if he's still trash-talking me when I slam-dunk his French-fry ass.

---

There is a growing consensus at home and abroad that America's best days are behind her, that she is in decline.

If the United States is perceived as losing power relative to the rest of the world, then no apology will persuade other countries to follow our lead. But if the United States is seen as a rising power, we will find it much easier to persuade other countries to go along with us.

Unfortunately, President Obama's muddled performance on the world stage has done little to boost confidence in the United States. As is painfully obvious, foreign countries regularly defy him with impunity—while countries that have long been friendly to the United States, such as Great Britain and Israel, find themselves shunted aside. Under these circumstances, the smartest course of action for any foreign leader is to oppose the United States. You certainly won't lose anything by it, and you might even get your own personal apology.

The American people have already figured out that President Obama's foreign policy is not working. Fifty-one percent of likely voters believed that the United States is *less respected* than it was two years ago, while only 41 percent believed we were more respected. The American people are smart enough to distinguish between policies that cause foreigners to like President Obama and policies that would cause them to respect the United States.

Unfortunately, as talk of American decline has become more common, some, like the *Economist* magazine on March 9, 2010, have suggested that losing our place at the top is no big deal:

If America loses its position as the world's largest and most powerful economy, does it really matter? The country's national pride would take a blow. And perhaps there are geopolitical reasons for wanting to hang on to the top spot. But, economically speaking, it probably wouldn't be so bad. Often when it comes to growth and globalization, a high tide raises all boats. For example, the quality of life today is far better for most Britons than it was a century ago, when it was the world's leading empire. Britain's economy still grew even as America's topped it.

So long as growth continues and successive generations of Americans live better than the last, does it really matter that someone else is getting even richer?

The answer to that last question is "Yes." Of course it matters. As the commentator himself states: "Perhaps there are geopolitical reasons for wanting to hang on to the top spot." That is one of the great understatements of all time.

---

## THE DIARY OF PRESIDENT BARACK OBAMA

### THE WHITE HOUSE

April 22, 2010

So this afternoon I get a call from Geithner saying he needs to talk about our credit rating. There were some stories in the press about how the rating agencies are concerned that our AAA bond rating could drop due to the growing national debt. Well, you gotta spend money to make money, right? I told Geithner, "Look, the main thing is to make sure that China keeps buying our debt. They'll have to do that—if the U.S. falters, they falter, too." He went into this tiresome explanation about how Larry thinks they may be willing to let us suffer financially for their own long-term advantage.

Now that is yesterday's thinking if I ever heard it. The leaders in China understand that we all have to work together. I know they do. I've met the folks in China, and that's what they all told me.

I told Geithner I'd call Hu and see if we can't get him to issue a statement to calm the markets. We're very close—I had a great chat with him on his home turf, and we had a moment earlier this month here in D.C. So I called him. Left a message. I'm sure he'll get back to me.

Then this afternoon, Hillary jumps on my case about China's reeducation camps, "gendercide," and forced abortions. If you haven't lived abroad you don't understand. They have 1.3 billion people in one place. You can't keep punishing the country with babies. This story that the Chinese government has targeted girls causing a "gendercide" is overstated. The government only limits each family to one kid—it's up to the Chinese women to decide which gender they are going to keep. That seems fair to me. In fact, I instructed John Holden, my science czar, to connect with the Chinese authorities to see how they implemented their one-child policy. This could be the reason their economy is doing so well.

As far as the reeducation camps, as I said to Hillary, this is the way the Chinese teach patriotism and pass along love of their leaders. Hell, we have our own reeducation camps right here—only we call it the public school system.

Then tonight Gates calls up complaining that the Chinese

are one of the largest exporters of oil to Iran and recently
opened their own missile plant in the country—providing the
Islamic Republic with arms. But the Chinese have to make a
living, too. And those missiles can't reach farther than say, Tel
Aviv, so there is nothing to worry about. Once I talk with Hu, we'll
resolve all of this. These people need to relax and stop worrying
so much.

---

# THE WINNING WAY

Under the American system, foreign policy is dominated by the president.
His powers here are greater than in any other area. For this reason, it is absolutely essential that we elect only presidents who show a determination
to preserve U.S. power and independence. In recent years, we have spent
too much time talking about how to bring the nations of the world together.
We need to spend more time thinking about what we're going to do if that
doesn't happen. What if China does decide to challenge us? What if Russia
wants to replay the Cold War? What if anti-Americanism in Europe makes
it more and more difficult for other Western nations to work with us? Contrary to what some have suggested, history has not come to an end. The
world is still a very dangerous place. And we need a president who understands this and has the will to deal with it.

As we get closer to the 2012 presidential election, we should be asking
potential GOP candidates, Do you believe America is getting weaker relative
to the other great powers of the world? If so, what *practical* steps will you
take to change that trend? Who do you see as trustworthy allies? Who do
you see as potential adversaries? I don't pretend to have all the solutions to
these questions—and indeed, conservatives are divided on many of them.
Some insist that capitalism will cause China to remain friendly toward us.
Others disagree. President Bush obviously believed he could work with

Vladimir Putin. Does that still seem correct? Can a huge debtor nation like the United States remain a great power? The GOP hasn't had a true wide-ranging debate over the United States and its role in the world since 9/11. That was almost ten years ago, and a lot has changed since then. Just as the Tea Parties are pressing members of Congress to get more serious about fiscal issues, all of us need to press our leaders to take issues of American power and prestige more seriously.

# CHAPTER 8

# THE AUDACITY OF NARCISSISM

*There's a vanity aspect to politics, and then there's a substantive part of politics. Now you need some sizzle with the steak to be effective, but I think it's easy to get swept up in the vanity side of it, the desire to be liked and recognized and important.*
—BARACK OBAMA, *CHICAGO SUN-TIMES*, MARCH 27, 2004

It was June 3, 2008, the night Senator Barack Obama sewed up the Democratic nomination. The St. Paul, Minnesota, audience was in awe. Lifting his chin to the heavens, he belted out a stunner of a self-tribute: "I am absolutely certain that generations from now, we will be able to look back and tell our children that this was the moment when we began to provide care for the sick and good jobs for the jobless; this was the moment when the rise of the oceans began to slow and our planet began to heal. This was the moment—this was the time—when we came together to remake this great nation."

Not even Jesus spoke about Himself like this. For a politician to imagine that he has the power to slow "the rise of the oceans" and "heal" the planet takes real brass ones. And to so boldly predict what the next generation will say about his candidacy is the sort of narcissistic grandiosity that cries out for professional help. (Dr. Drew, if you have an opening on next season's *Celebrity Rehab*, I think we have a guest for you.)

—⟨⟨⟩⟩—

## THE DIARY OF PRESIDENTIAL CANDIDATE BARACK OBAMA

### SPRINGFIELD, ILLINOIS

August 24, 2008

The man has been my running mate for less than twenty-four hours and we're already having problems. I told Axelrod that I don't need Senator Foot-in-Mouth jeopardizing my historic moment. I give him the chance of a lifetime, and he has a thirty-minute argument with me about whether we should wear jackets at the announcement ceremony. This has got to be some kind of joke . . .

Then, after thirty-five years of sitting his ass in the Senate, Biden gets up there and says, "These politicians in Washington are the problem today!" The last time I saw a someone morph so quickly into something else, I was watching The Crying Game.

"You need Biden to give you foreign policy cred, Barack," they kept telling me. "You need him to help you push legislation on Capitol Hill, Barack." Help on Capitol Hill? Sending him up there would undercut my commitment to end our policy of torture! But hell, maybe we could deploy him to Afghanistan for secret talks with the Taliban. He could bore the enemy to death.

Leadership on the world stage is about tone, posture, magnetism—and I've got that down all by my lonesome. Once the world gets a taste of me, half the diplomats at the State Department can probably take early retirement. The world is hungering for an intelligent, cosmopolitan American leader—and he is coming.

Following our big running mate announcement, Plouffe brought me the new campaign bumper stickers with Biden's name on them. The "Biden" was nearly as big as the "Obama"! Plouffe said: "This is the way it's done." Well, not this time. I ordered the press office to make his name gray, put it in the smallest font size they can render, and leave mine at forty-eight points. Like anybody will notice. Plouffe's going to give the Bidens the mock-up stickers to pass out to their family and friends—they'll be nice collector's items.

---

## DIAGNOSING OBAMA

The *Diagnostic and Statistical Manual of Mental Disorders*, published by the American Psychiatric Association, is the bible of mental disorders. It describes Narcissistic Personality Disorder (NPD) this way: "an all-pervasive pattern of grandiosity (in fantasy or behavior), need for admiration or adulation and lack of empathy, usually beginning in early adulthood and present in a variety of contexts . . ." Sound like anyone we know?

There are certain traits of the narcissistic personality that help physicians identify the condition. To be diagnosed with Narcissistic Personality Disorder, the patient must show signs of at least five of the eight criteria. Some mental health experts have suggested that Barack Obama may suffer from NPD.

## TRAITS OF NARCISSISTIC PERSONALITY DISORDER

- [The narcissist] has a grandiose sense of self-importance (e.g., exaggerates achievements and talents, expects to be recognized as superior without commensurate achievements)
- [The narcissist] is preoccupied with fantasies of unlimited success, power, brilliance, beauty, or ideal love

*—DIAGNOSTIC AND STATISTICAL MANUAL OF MENTAL DISORDERS*

Here's a rule of thumb: if you want to identify a narcissist, find the guy who writes his memoirs before the age of thirty and you're probably getting warm. As Charles Krauthammer wrote: "[Obama's] most memorable work is a biography of his favorite subject: himself."

Obama's *Dreams from My Father* is one of those elegant, self-indulgent exercises in navel-gazing that elevates the mundane to the epic. In *Dreams*, it becomes evident early on that Obama is on a quest to reinvent himself. He struggles to construct an enlightened personality, an image befitting the mythic figure he imagines himself to be. The assumption that anyone would or should care about the internal noodlings of an unknown community agitator and Harvard Law School student is itself an act of supreme arrogance. But then to summon the chutzpah to actually release the thing takes a special pathology. This initial expression of public self-love was but a precursor of the narcissism that would follow.

In Obama's mind, there are no limits to what he can accomplish or what he represents. As he said throughout the 2008 campaign: "We are the ones that we've been waiting for." That would be the "royal we," of course. By the end of an Obama speech, one might think that God gets His divine rights from Obama, and not the other way around.

Several months before the election, so sure was Obama of his ultimate winning destiny, that he had a pseudo-presidential seal attached to the front of his lectern when he addressed the Democratic governors. On the outer periphery "The President of the United States" was replaced with "Obama for America." The real presidential seal features an eagle with a shield bearing the stars and stripes on its breast. The Obama shield is also emblazoned with an eagle, but this eagle wears the iconic O logo. (Who needs Old Glory when you have the glorified "O"?!) And the Latin "E Pluribus Unum" was replaced with "Vero Possumus" ("Yes We Can"). But "No We Can't" assume any semblance of humility.

From his earliest stirrings in politics, there is little evidence that the press did anything to challenge his delusions of grandeur. In fact, to this day, the old media machine merely enables this shameless narcissism. Take, for example, this journalistic gift masquerading as a front-page *Washington Post* news story on Christmas Day 2008. It came courtesy of Eli Saslow, a sportswriter turned "serious" journalist:

> Obama has gone to the gym for about 90 minutes a day, for at least 48 days in a row. He has always treated exercise less as recreation than requirement, but his devotion has intensified during the last few months. Between workouts during his Hawaii vacation this week, he was photographed looking like the paradigm of a new kind of presidential fitness, one geared less toward preventing heart attacks than winning swimsuit competitions. *The sun glinted off his chiseled pectorals* [emphasis added] sculpted during four weightlifting sessions each week, and a body toned by regular treadmill runs and basketball games.

"The sun glinted off his chiseled pectorals . . ." If Saslow ever finds himself out of work, he may have a second career writing Harlequin romances—or porn scripts.

## THE DIARY OF PRESIDENT-ELECT BARACK OBAMA

### KAILUA BEACH, HAWAII

December 25, 2008

I'm reading the <u>Washington Post</u> this morning and there on the front page is a piece titled "As Duties Weigh Obama Down, His Faith in Fitness Only Increases." Come on now. With everything I'm doing, with everything I am, it's insulting that the <u>Post</u> would publish this kind of trash—and right on the front page of all places. I'm not "weighed down" by anything! I'm doing fine. I haven't altered my routine in the least. Whether I'm president, Supreme Court justice, General Secretary of the UN, or EU High Commissioner—no matter what life doles out—my workout routine is unalterable. I will never be "weighed down"! But this reporter will be before we're finished with him.

In the second paragraph of the article, this pipsqueak Eli Saslow writes: "the sun glistened off his chiseled pectorals." I'm having Gobbler send Ben Bradlee a letter of complaint today. What kind of crap is that? What about my carved abs? What about my bulging biceps? What about these latissimi dorsi? No mention of them. I'm killing myself each day to perfect this bod for the people of the world and this scribbler ignores half the story! My physique has more definition than Merriam-Webster! I want a published correction in tomorrow's edition—and that better be on the front page, too! I'm the damn president-elect of the United States. If you're going to talk about my body, cover the whole story, not just a fraction of it! Journalism in America is truly dead.

---

## TRAITS OF NARCISSISTIC PERSONALITY DISORDER

- [The narcissist] believes that he or she is "special" and unique and can only be understood by, or should associate with, other special or high-status people (or institutions)
- [The narcissist] requires excessive admiration

—*Diagnostic and Statistical Manual of Mental Disorders*

Obama and his ego are ably abetted by an intimate group of worshippers, who are constantly there to prop him up at every turn. Oprah Winfrey was one of his earliest boosters. At a December 11, 2007 rally in South Carolina, the talk-show queen referred to Obama as "the One." She said the country needed politicians who could do more than speak the truth, but could in fact "know how to be the truth." She finally attested: "The reason I love Barack Obama is because he is an evolved leader who can bring evolved leadership to our country." Look out, Michelle: "Oprah Obama" has an interesting ring to it.

But it is not only Hollywood elites who fan the flames of Obama's narcissism. There is also a cadre of close advisors who can be relied upon to feed the beast known as the president's ego. "Obama's problem is that his . . . confidantes—particularly Valerie Jarrett and Robert Gibbs, and, to a lesser extent, David Axelrod—are part of the Cult of Obama," Dana Milbank explained in the *Washington Post* on February 21, 2010. "In love with the president, they believe he is a transformational figure who needn't dirty his hands in politics."

The Iranian-born Valerie Jarrett was Mayor Richard Daley's chief of staff in 1991, when she hired Michelle Robinson as a political staffer. It was through Jarrett that the young Ms. Robinson was introduced to the upper echelon of the Chicago political machine. Later, Michelle's husband began to turn to Jarrett for advice, political connections, and counsel. She now serves as senior advisor to the president and perpetual suck-up. "I mean, he's really by far smarter than anybody I know. . . . Not just smart-intelligent, but he's perceptive; he watches body language," she told the *New York Times* in a July 26, 2009, story.

In the varsity sport that is Obama adulation, the president's rumpled strategic adviser David Axelrod is a champion. In a profile of Axelrod, *New York Times* writer Mark Leibovich quotes him in full-blown Obama adoration: " 'I love the guy' . . . [and] in the space of five minutes, [he] repeated the sentiment twice."

Psychoanalysts refer to this sort of outside reinforcement as "narcissistic supply." The obsequiousness, nonstop compliments, and endless lionization are all part of the external nutrition craved by the narcissist. Without it, he cannot really survive. Luckily for Barack Obama, there is no shortage of the "supply."

---

## THE DIARY OF SENIOR ADVISOR TO THE PRESIDENT DAVID AXELROD

### THE WEST WING

March 3, 2010

11:30 p.m. I love Barack. I <u>really</u> love the guy, or I wouldn't be able to endure all of this—but I don't think he realizes how much he hurts me. Granted, Barack is still an amazing man. The breadth of his knowledge, his eloquence, his abilities as a communicator, remain unmatched. Who knows, maybe I am to blame for the low poll numbers and the legislative constipation. Maybe I should go home to Chicago and make some real money...God, I hate this city.

Today I was in the middle of an interview with a New York Times reporter, Mark Leibovich, (trying to tamp down the idea that I am the cause of the administration's failings and the communications gaffes). I had a mouthful of beef on rye, a turkey leg on the desk, and I was in full schmooze mode with the reporter. We were sharing a great moment, and he was buying my every line. That's when Barack strode in. He looked down at the turkey leg and said, "What is this, King Arthur's Court?" The reporter laughed that sycophantic laugh that I have heard a million times whenever Barack is in the room. I just know he'll print that comment. Ungrateful bastard. Barack actually winked at him and smiled. Before I knew what was happening, he took Leibovich out in the hall and said, "Let me introduce you to a few of the more fit members of my crew. Hey, Rahm, come over here..." Wow, there are times I wish I didn't love him as much as I do.

Tonight I did something that I haven't done in three months—I looked at myself naked in a full-length mirror. Jesus! I have gained at least twenty pounds worrying about this man. My hair is falling out so fast the shower drain looks like Janet Napolitano's back! And yet Barack laughs at me—in front of a New York Times reporter...and I mean a real self-satisfied laugh! It was probably just his way of blowing off steam. He is easily one of the most compassionate, outgoing, brilliant men of our

generation. I'm sure it was my fault for having the
turkey leg on the desk in the first place. Stupid!

---

## TRAITS OF NARCISSISTIC PERSONALITY DISORDER

- [The narcissist] is interpersonally exploitative, i.e., takes advantage of others
  to achieve his or her own ends
- [The narcissist] lacks empathy: is unwilling to recognize or identify with the
  feelings and needs of others

  —*Diagnostic and Statistical Manual of Mental Disorders*

---

## THE DIARY OF PRESIDENT BARACK OBAMA

### THE OVAL OFFICE

March 7, 2010

Every morning, Valerie and I spend a couple of hours going
through the press clippings of the day. The staff knows we're
not to be disturbed. They think we're discussing nuclear policy
or health-care revisions. Ha! The laugh's on them. We actually
spend most of the time reading through press material
referencing me. It's one of the few chances I have during the
day to kind of kick back and have a good laugh. Valerie found the
howler of all howlers today.

The <u>New York Times</u> featured a story that was obviously Axe's attempt to garner some positive press. When Valerie read me the title of the story, "Message Maven Finds Fingers Pointed at Him," I said, "Is that a reference to Rahm's middle fingers?" We laughed so hard we had tears in our eyes. Then she started reading the story and I thought Val was going to wet her pants.

Smack-dab in the middle of the piece, I walk in and ridicule Axe's supersize lunch! It was classic. He did have half a turkey sitting on his desk. The man has no self-control. This is where the example set by the First Lady could be instructive for him. You can eat whatever you want, just don't do it in front of the press. I mean, that woman I'm married to always has a burger in her mouth and an order of buffalo wings in her purse. But when <u>Ladies' Home Journal</u> shows up, it's apple bowls and fennel as far as the eye can see!

After she finished reading the article, Valerie made the observation that the message maven's message was stopped dead in its tracks by one person: <u>me</u>! Poor Axe. I'll have Reggie fly in some Chicago pizza for him or something. He needs to calm down. He seems to be getting bigger and balder by the day. Conversely, I have noticed that Valerie is shrinking. She's a little itty-bitty thing. Or maybe I'm just getting taller. As she was leaving this morning, I told her, "You better start wearing higher heels or you're going to sink into the pile of the carpet one of these days." She looked sore for a few seconds, but then she smiled and scooted out the door. What else is she going to *do? These are the best days of her life and I don't see too many other presidents interested in her advice.*

---

Dr. Sam Vaknin, an expert on Narcissistic Personality Disorder and author of the book *Malignant Self-Love*, raises the possibility that Barack Obama is, indeed, a narcissist. On the website Global Politician, in 2008, Dr. Vaknin wrote: "The malignant narcissist invents and then projects a false, fictitious, self for the world to fear, or to admire. He maintains a tenuous grasp on reality to start with, and this is further exacerbated by the trappings of power. The narcissist's grandiose self-delusions and fantasies of omnipotence and omniscience are supported by real-life authority and the narcissist's predilection to surround himself with obsequious sycophants."

Despite evidence to the contrary, Obama and his courtiers believe that he possesses an almost mystical power to alter the future and transcend politics. They believe that if the public is exposed to the wonder of his presence, if they just hear the voice of "the One," hearts and minds will move and history will be transformed forever. For Team Obama, the outcome of the gubernatorial elections of 2009 must have been sobering.

In Virginia, only weeks before the election, Creigh Deeds, the Democratic candidate for governor, was ten points down in the polls. His Republican challenger Bob McDonnell, was riding a wave of anti-Democrat fever spreading through the swing state. He seemed unstoppable. On October 15, 2009, TalkingPointsMemo reported that Obama's grassroots organization, Organizing for America, was using its might to furnish Deeds with door-to-door volunteers to resuscitate his campaign in its waning days. Then they brought in the big gun.

On October 27, President Obama appeared at a Norfolk rally with Deeds. This was to be the turning point in the campaign, the moment when the Virginia swing voters would wake from their slumber and do what the man they elected asked: cast their votes for Creigh Deeds.

## THE DIARY OF PRESIDENT BARACK OBAMA

### AIR FORCE ONE

*October 27, 2009*

On a mission of mercy here. Creigh Deeds finally admitted he needed my help in Virginia. Rahm and Tim Kaine told this fool months ago that it was time to go nuclear on Bob McDonnell, time to unleash the election monster, time to summon the Kraken—time to bring in the president! All along Deeds kept saying he could do it without me. Look at him now, ten points down and the internal polls look even worse.

But I'll turn it around for him. When I walk in, I'll do a few "Yes We Can" shout-outs to help Virginia recall the glory days of my campaign and we'll take it from there. Once they get into the spirit of "O," they won't be able to resist. I'll pull Deeds back from the brink.

Axe thinks it's a lost cause and I should sit this one out. I, myself, realize the daunting challenges. First, the man's name is Creigh Deeds, which sounds like a colon disorder. And when you see him, he looks like a disorder that just slipped out of a colon! His hair's a mess. He's got that receding comb-over thing on top, terrible posture, and clothes that look like they were purchased at a Newt Gingrich yard sale.

Despite all that, Barack will still triumph. I've never met a voter I couldn't turn around, and I'll be damned if this white turd is going to break my winning streak.

Before a hand-picked crowd of thousands, Obama turned on the charm in Norfolk. Dismissing the depressing poll numbers, the president compared Deeds' struggle to his own campaign, and recalled those who doubted his ability to win. Then Obama went in for the kill: "You know, you've got the chance to elect somebody whose got a good heart and a good head and a commitment to work hard on your behalf. He may not be perfect—my wife reminds me I'm not. . . . You know, Creigh, sometimes his tie gets a little askew, and you know, his hair is a little—but here's the question is [*sic*]—here's the question is [*sic*]; is that what the people of Virginia are looking for?"

Creigh Deeds was decidedly *not* what they were looking for. Days after Obama's visit, Virginia voters elected Republican Bob McDonnell governor by a margin of 59 percent to 41 percent. The same independents who swept Obama to victory a year before, now swung to the Republican candidate. The Obama surge never happened—or perhaps it did.

In New Jersey, the incumbent governor, Jon Corzine, faced a tough challenge from the former U.S. attorney Republican Chris Christie. At the top of November, a Quinnipiac poll found the men in a dead heat: 40 percent of likely voters were leaning toward Corzine and 42 percent were leaning toward Christie. Enter Obama.

The president headlined repeated rallies in New Jersey for Corzine, culminating in a final pair of events on November 1. Before 6,500 people in Camden and 11,000 in Newark, the president attempted, in the words of *Time* magazine, "to rub his political magic off on Corzine." The unions even got in on the act. Service Employees International Union (SEIU) sent out a hundred thousand glossy mailers on behalf of the governor, featuring a photo of Obama. The mailer read: "One man will work with the president. The other will fight him." Inside was a photo of Corzine standing in the shadow of Obama at a lectern. The Corzine campaign bet everything on its connection to Obama.

—⟨ℓ⟩—

## THE DIARY OF PRESIDENT BARACK OBAMA

### AIR FORCE ONE

November 1, 2009

On yet another mercy mission. Headed to Jersey to lock it up for Jon Corzine. He's been a huge supporter of mine. I've got one objective for both the rallies today: when the voters think of Corzine, they have to see me! That's the only way this man will win. My charisma and charm will ensure victory for him.

I just got off the phone with Jon and briefed him on my plan. As I climb up the stairs of the stage, I'm going to dramatically throw both my arms back and let my jacket slide off. He'll catch it and hang it on the guardrail. Then I'll rise to greet my people. It's going to be special.

Valerie had a great idea: tie Corzine to health reform. Make this election a referendum on my health care plan. Between my persuasive powers and the promise of free health care, Jon can't lose!

---

In his trademark move, Obama shed his jacket at the first rally and tied Corzine to his administration. "He's one of the best partners I have in the White House. We work together," the president said. From the sound of it, you'd swear that Corzine was a West Wing staffer.

Obama then launched into a ten-minute health-care pitch. The message was clear: a vote for Corzine is a vote for health-care reform. For his part, Corzine recalled that a year earlier voters followed Obama with cries of "Yes We Can." "I'm here to ask a simple question: are you ready to keep it going?" the governor asked. "Today I am standing with President Obama. That tells you everything you need to know."

Apparently. Voters got the message. They threw Corzine from office and made Chris Christie governor of New Jersey by a four-point margin.

Of all the races Obama inserted himself into, none had the emotional power or political significance of the fight for Ted Kennedy's U.S. Senate seat in Massachusetts. Loss of that seat would cause the Democrats to lose their filibuster-proof majority in the Senate and potentially spell doom for the health-care reform bill. In the first week of January 2010, mine was the first radio show to give Republican challenger Scott Brown a national platform. At the time, Brown was gaining on Democrat Martha Coakley. He was nine points within striking distance of his opponent. Peter Baker reported in the *New York Times Magazine* that Rahm Emanuel, Obama's chief of staff, was furious over the Massachusetts situation. " 'We've got to get up there and take it over,' Emanuel told (his White House) colleagues." Here again we see the prevailing narrative: there are politicians and then there is Obama. He had to get "up there and take it over."

The Savior descended on Massachusetts in the eleventh hour to campaign alongside Coakley. Having won Massachusetts with 68 percent of the vote in 2008, Obama had star power to spare. At the Boston rally on January 17, 2009, the president would eclipse the politics of the moment, saving Martha Coakley and his health-care reform plans.

—∽∾∾∾—

## The Diary of President Barack Obama

### Air Force One

January 17, 2010

I can only pull off so many of these mercy missions. I'm sacrificing precious time on the BB court as it is. But when I tried to get out of this trip, Rahm jumped on my case. "If you want to be responsible for the death of f*#@ing health care, if you want to f#@& up everything we have been working for, then go play your f@#*ing ball game," he said. I told him to go ahead and book the flight to Boston.

Trying to resurrect Martha Coakley politically will be heavy lifting. I look at her and I think Cathy Rigby in Peter Pan . . . that is, if the wire snapped in one of the flying scenes and she landed face first in the orchestra pit. At the rally, we're going to try to just mention her in passing and focus on her opponent. I'll hit that Cosmo Boy, Burt Reynolds Wannabe, Scott Brown hard. Anybody who drives a big gas-guzzling truck is obviously out of touch with the American people—particularly people in Massachusetts! I'll just keep reminding voters of his environmentally hostile transportation choice. Though it'll hardly matter; once I start shouting, "Fired up, ready to go!" Coakley will be home free.

I've got to protect my family's Senate seat. Remember, our dog, Bo, belonged to Ted Kennedy—so there's a familial stake in this for us. As I headed for the plane, Michelle whispered in my ear, "Barack, kick some butt. We need you to protect Bo's seat. Who knows, if we buy that house on Martha's Vineyard, Mama may need it in a few years!"

---

At the penultimate moment, Obama offered this rationale for supporting Coakley:

> Now I've heard about some of the ads that Martha's opponent is running. He's driving his truck around the commonwealth—and he says that he gets you, that he fights for you, that he'll be an independent voice. And I don't know him; he may be a perfectly nice guy. I don't know his record, but I don't know whether he's been fighting for you up until now. . . . Everybody can run slick ads. Forget the truck. Everybody can buy a truck. . . . If you were fired up in the last election, I need you more fired up in this election.

Notwithstanding this inspiring oratory, Scott Brown pulled off a stunning victory, besting Coakley, in the liberal stronghold of Massachusetts, by a margin of 51 percent to 47 percent. The conventional wisdom was that Obama's health-care dream was dead. But that didn't stop Obama or his team.

After a string of crushing political defeats, in clear defiance of the American people, the president took to the road. He believed that his personal power could somehow reverse public opinion and summon a majority of Americans to support his massive health-care takeover. But the polls never moved. In the end, it was Nancy Pelosi and Harry Reid, using every parliamentary tactic and sleazy backroom deal imaginable, who secured the votes needed to pass health-care reform.

Still, the president clings to the myth that his words and presence can work miracles. Once again, Dr. Sam Vaknin's perspective is illuminating: "The narcissistic leader prefers the sparkle and glamour of well-orchestrated illusions to the tedium and method of real accomplishments.

His reign is all smoke and mirrors, devoid of substances, consisting of mere appearances and mass delusions."

## TRAITS OF NARCISSISTIC PERSONALITY DISORDER

- [The narcissist] has a sense of entitlement, i.e., unreasonable expectations of especially favorable treatment or automatic compliance with his or her expectations

  —*Diagnostic and Statistical Manual of Mental Disorders*

# MISSED MANNERS AND PITCHED PROTOCOL

When you are perfect, or imagine yourself to be, the old rules simply don't apply. In the case of the Obamas, it isn't that they don't understand protocol and basic etiquette. They simply assume that the "old ways" do not apply to them. They are special, set apart, historic, groundbreaking, and above the rules. In their minds, they aren't flouting protocol or displaying horrendous manners; they are simply putting their own unique stamp on traditional practices. In a word, courtesy of Desiree Rogers, it's all being "Obamatized."

Few realized that in April 2009, when Barack Obama said that America had "shown arrogance and been dismissive," he was talking about himself.

When a head of state visits the United States, it is appropriate to exchange gifts as a sign of respect and gratitude. It is, of course, also a way for world leaders to connect on a personal level. Such was the case when former British prime minister Gordon Brown and his wife visited the United States in March 2009; they brought along gifts for the president and his children. Mrs. Brown purchased a pair of handmade dresses from a trendy British store and a collection of books by English authors for the Obama girls. This was thoughtful and appropriate. Michelle Obama presented the

Brown children with cheap toy models of Marine One available from any Washington tourist kiosk. This was thoughtless and inappropriate.

The prime minister presented Obama with two gifts: a seven-volume biography of Winston Churchill and a pen holder carved from the timbers of the H.M.S. *President,* the British antislave warship that was sister to the H.M.S. *Resolute.* Wood from the *Resolute* was used to make the massive desk that sits in the Oval Office. This was also a well-considered gift and entirely proper. When it came time for Obama to present his gift to Gordon Brown, the prime minister's jaw must have hit the floor. Out came a collection of twenty-five DVDs of American movie classics. Aside from the cheapness of the gift, the American disks do not play on British DVD players and Gordon Brown is blind in one eye! This made Obama—and thus America—look cheap and stupid.

---

## THE DIARY OF PRESIDENT BARACK OBAMA

### THE WHITE HOUSE

March 7, 2009

First of all, for the sake of posterity, it was Miche's idea to give the DVDs to Gordon Brown. I knew it was a mistake when I asked her to pick something out. Unless it's for herself, Miche is incapable of picking an appropriate gift. (I still don't know how to operate that smokeless ashtray she gave me for my birthday last year.) I should have had Desiree select something for the Browns. At least it would have been expensive and covered in designer labels. If I let her, Michelle would run over to Target and pick up a couple of Sham-Wows and a Snuggy for the Sarkozys when they come for their state visit.

Still the <u>Daily Mail</u> was downright cold. They said our gifts were "about as exciting as a pair of socks." What makes a pen holder made from a rotted old ship any better? Everybody's writing about how thoughtful and generous Brown's gifts were. That pen holder was old junk he had lying around 10 Downing Street—probably something Margaret Thatcher kept her teeth in. Who do these Brits think they are, turning our White House into their personal flea market? He was insulted by my gifts?! I am insulted by his! That pen holder sucks. I gave it to Mother Robinson to use when she plays craps with her girlfriends.

Naturally, we had to issue a press release, scraping and bowing to the United Kingdom to smooth over their hard feelings. Gibbopotamus told them that the pen holder would have a prominent place in the Oval and that the first-edition Winston Churchill biography was "in the president's personal study." It remained there for all of fifteen minutes! That's where I told Reggie to get that old racist's biography out of my sight and get whatever he could for it on eBay.

That's the last time we make "gift-giving" mistakes in this White House. Reggie and I will be doing the buying for our global peers from now on. We've got to get something nice for the Queen—something that she'll remember, something that's American, enjoyable, and lasting. I'm thinking maybe show tunes, and some of my selected speeches—basically anything that calls <u>me</u> to mind.

On April Fool's Day 2009, the Obamas were in London for the G-20 summit. As part of the visit, they had an audience with Queen Elizabeth at Buckingham Palace. Now, it is protocol at Buckingham Palace to never touch the person of the Queen. But to Michelle Obama, she was just another old lady with an ugly purse. Michelle took it upon herself to embrace the Queen, physically sparking international headlines. So much ink was spilled over the rank breach of protocol that Buckingham Palace had to do damage control. A palace spokesperson (who asked not to be identified) told the Associated Press that the royal mauling was a mutual gesture of affection. Uh-huh. The Obamas can thank God that the Queen possesses more class than they do.

Just moments before the embrace, the Obamas gifted Her Highness with a coffee table book containing Rodgers and Hart lyrics and an iPod. The iPod was loaded with Broadway show tunes and, according to the Canadian Broadcasting Company, also had "photos and video of the Queen's 2007 visit to Virginia, photos of Obama's January 20 inauguration, and audio of his inauguration address." Just what the Queen always wanted for those long sessions on the treadmill.

The president and First Lady's violations of protocol and absent etiquette are now legendary. They run like bulls through the world's china shop and expect to be treated like royalty no matter what they do. Whether it's inappropriate bowing to kings in Japan and Saudi Arabia or sloppy dress when on official business, Obama and his intimates have a knack for always sending the wrong message.

President Bush made it a policy never to enter the Oval Office without a coat and tie. It was a sign of respect for the office and respect for the country he served. Not so with Obama. He and his slovenly team treat the West Wing like a frat house. Visit the White House website and you will find numerous candid pictures of the president lounging around the Oval Office in golf shirts, propping his feet up on the furniture as he rifles through documents, and hardly ever wearing a tie.

For all of their celebrity and self-importance, the Obamas habitually fail to maintain the decorum of the "People's House." They feel perfectly justified doing whatever they like at any moment because they are so significant and special.

On December 29, 2009, the president addressed the press in Hawaii about the attempted Christmas Day airplane bombing. Though this was a major press conference, carried all over the world, Obama appeared in a jacket with an open-collar shirt. On March 7, 2010, when the president reacted to the Iraqi elections, he was joined by the vice president in the Rose Garden: Biden wore a tie, Obama did not.

For those who think that I am being overly fussy, here is an e-mail I recently received from a listener, Kevin, that says it all:

> . . . the fact that our president doesn't wear a necktie at all times . . . [is] just one more sign of the cavalier attitude he has toward the office. There is no respect. He represents the US 24/7/365. Is it too much to ask him to dress with the reverence and respect the highest office in the land deserves? If he's trying to look "cool" and casual, he's failing. I'm sure I'm not alone in this. Please, Mr. President—dress the part. We may totally disagree with your agenda, but we could at least respect you a tiny bit if you wore a tie.

Ditto for me.

The president, whoever he is, sets a tone of decorum and respect that will inevitably trickle down to his entire staff. If he observes the traditions of the office and maintains a modicum of social etiquette, it will be reflected clear down the line. President Obama has chosen a different path. His own personal lapses have given those around him permission to replicate his bad behavior with no regard for the feelings of others.

Whether we are talking about Hillary Clinton giving the Russian foreign minister what she imagined was a button that read "reset" in Russian (owing to a translation problem, it actually read "overcharged"), Desiree Rogers seating herself at a State Dinner while uninvited guests crashed the White House doors, or chief of staff Rahm Emanuel's endless lapses of civility—these people feel empowered to act according to their whims, blind to their own stupidity and arrogance.

In August 2009, at a private health-care strategy session, Rahm Emanuel admonished liberal groups threatening to run ads against conservative Democrats opposed to the president's health-care bill. "F---ing retarded," he told the assembled liberals, according to the *Wall Street Journal*'s Peter Wallsten. "F---ing stupid."

The negative reactions to Emanuel's comments were immediate. Sarah Palin wrote in a Facebook post: "Just as we'd be appalled if any public figure of Rahm's stature ever used the 'N-word' or other such inappropriate language, Rahm's slur on all God's children with cognitive and developmental disabilities—and the people who love them—is unacceptable, and it's heartbreaking." Within days, Emanuel was on the phone with Tim Shriver, the CEO of Special Olympics, making apologies. The White House said, "The apology was accepted."

But on February 3, 2010, Politico reported that a Special Olympics spokesman claimed: "Tim did not accept (Emanuel's) apology . . . he can't accept an apology on behalf of all people with disabilities." This White House can't even issue an apology without lies and misrepresentations. Later, at a meeting with several advocates of those with disabilities, Emanuel issued a second apology (which was accepted) and signed a petition to end the use of the word *retarded*. (No word on whether Emanuel has carved out a "Biden exception" to his pledge.)

Those with long memories will recall that Emanuel is not the first White House official to offend people with disabilities. Obama, himself, on *The Tonight Show*, told Jay Leno in March 2009 that he had bowled a pathetic score of 129. Leno laughingly said, "That's very good, Mr. President." "It's like Special Olympics or something," Obama replied. Although I'm no fan of the PC word police, imagine if Mitt Romney had said such a thing on the campaign trail. It would have been his "macaca" moment.

One is not even safe from the crudeness of the Obama camp in the shower. Disgraced Democratic congressman Eric Massa revealed that Rahm Emanuel made it a habit to bully legislators in the shower at the House Gym. From the March 10, 2010, *Washington Post*: "I am sitting there showering, naked as a jaybird, and here comes Rahm Emanuel, not even with a towel . . . his finger in my chest, yelling at me because I wasn't going to vote for the president's budget," Massa said. "You know how awkward it is to have a political argument with a naked man?" If you really want to know how the Obama agenda moves through Congress, check the drains of the House Gym. If Rahm Emanuel crawls up, you have your answer.

------

## THE DIARY OF WHITE HOUSE CHIEF OF STAFF RAHM EMANUEL

### THE WEST WING

March 8, 2010

That fat f@#king f&*k! I knew that Eric Massa was poison the first time I laid eyes on his retarded ass. He was always talking about the veterans, and trying to strike this middle-of-the-road bullsh#% posture. For him to publicly reveal one of the most successful Emanuel strategies for whipping votes is un-f$#@king-forgivable! I'm glad I leaked tidbits about that groping thing to drive him from office. And f*#k anyone who thinks I should feel a shred of guilt over this! We need the health-care bill to pass for the good of this presidency, and I am not going to stand by and let some sweaty walrus from upstate New York obstruct our success and dictate terms.

"I will not support this bill, Rahm," he told me again and again. Now you won't be able to support your family, you fat f$#k! Like I always say: if you can't beat 'em, destroy 'em.

I won't forget what Massa did to me. For years I have used that shower technique. I had it down to a science. When you've got a lean dancer's body like mine, that alone usually intimidates the hell out of these slobs. I'd walk in, real quiet, with the towel tied around the jewels, start a conversation from just outside the shower, and slowly walk toward the congressmen. That's when I would demand that they support whatever bill I was pushing. My voice would start to escalate. Then when I was about three yards away from them, I'd rip the towel off and <u>whammo</u>. The Member met my member. Most of them were struck speechless. That's when I'd ask, "Are you with us or not?" Nine times out of ten I got the vote I needed. One time, I even got Sheila Jackson Lee to vote against a bill she had sponsored.

The only time the technique failed was when I tried it on Barney Frank. I yanked the towel off, he looked down and said, "Is that your final offer?"

Now this piece of s@*t from the sticks has blown it for

me. That shower technique was going to be my path to the Speakership someday. The key is, to attack these people when they are at their most vulnerable—shock them so their reason is crippled. I'm thinking of developing a new approach in the men's room, a Larry Craig kind of thing. Imagine a congressman sitting on the john, when all of sudden from under the wall of the adjoining stall, <u>whoosh</u>. I slide in and demand their vote on cap-and-trade. This could be a real f%o#+ing winner.

---

For all the breathless commentary about Michelle Obama as fashion icon, she horrified even her most ardent admirers when, in August 2009, she descended from Air Force One wearing gray cotton shorts and a button-down shirt, opened to reveal a ratty ribbed tank top. These were not long shorts (like the ones she wore earlier that summer to walk Bo on the South Lawn of the White House); these were the kind of thigh-revealing shorts that one would wear to wash the car or hose down the trash cans. Some in the media defended the First Lady, claiming that she was going to hike in the Grand Canyon, so what else was she supposed to wear? Tell that to the fully uniformed servicemen standing at attention at the bottom of Air Force One's stairway. If those military officers had showed up in flip-flops and Hawaiian shirts, the same people would be denouncing the military's disrespect for the Obamas. I suppose respect runs in only one direction where Michelle and Barack Obama are concerned.

Even the *Washington Post*'s columnist Robin Givhan, a woman who has spent years celebrating Michelle Obama's every fashion choice, could not resist commenting on the shorts fiasco on August 23, 2009.

The noteworthy aspect of Obama's ensemble is that in recent history, first ladies have rarely dressed so informally in public, particularly as they are emerging from Air Force One while a phalanx of photographers stands ready to record the moment. This exclusive group of women might have dressed in a relaxed manner—khakis or jeans, for instance—but it was always in a way that suggested that they were keenly aware of the ever-present cameras. None of them revealed as much leg as the current first lady. . . . No matter that so many other women of her generation choose travel clothes that mimic pajamas. When the first couple disembarks from Air Force One, military personnel stand at attention, shutters click and minions scurry. It's not as though they are climbing out of their own personal RV with their backpacks—like celebrities caught unawares by the paparazzi.

Ultimately, the first lady can't be—nor should she be—just like every-one else. Hers is a life of responsibilities and privileges. She gets the fancy jet. She has to dress for the ride. . . . Avoiding the appearance of queenly behavior is politically wise. But it does American culture no favors if a first lady tries so hard to be average that she winds up looking common.

For once, Robin Givhan and I are in total agreement. I would make only one additional point. This episode gives us a window into the thinking of the Obamas. They don't consider the trappings of power to be privileges, but rather an entitlement. The presidential perks—security details, motor-cades, Air Force One—exist more to support their personal stardom than the office of the presidency. Most professional athletes are expected to look presentable when traveling with their teams because coaches and owners want to project a positive image. The good news is the because of the up-roar, Michelle's dingy short shorts seem to have been permanently retired.

## TRAITS OF NARCISSISTIC PERSONALITY DISORDER

- [The narcissist] is often envious of others or believes that others are envious of him or her
- [The narcissist] shows arrogant, haughty behaviors or attitudes
  —*Diagnostic and Statistical Manual of Mental Disorders*

# THE NEVER-ENDING VACATION

Officially, the Obamas had only two vacations in 2009: a weeklong stay at a $20 million estate on Martha's Vineyard and their Christmas vacation in Hawaii. But the truth is the Obamas have been very generous to themselves with vacation time.

The weekend before the Obamas' trip to Martha's Vineyard, the whole clan visited the Grand Canyon and Yellowstone National Park. The "official justification" for the jaunt? According to *USA Today*, the Obamas were there to "spotlight the National Park Service's fee-free weekends, and to encourage park visitation." If only the cost of Air Force One and the entire presidential detail were "fee-free" for the American taxpayers.

According to the *Chicago Tribune*, a Government Accountability Office report in 2000 revealed that it costs $67,000 dollars to operate Air Force One domestically, for each hour in flight. That means that the family hike through the national parks probably cost taxpayers nearly a million dollars.

Immediately following the summer vacation on Martha's Vineyard, the Obama family headed to the presidential retreat, Camp David, for five more days of fun in the sun. The president was "looking to get a break from his vacation," Deputy Press Secretary Bill Burton told Politico on August 28, 2009.

Considering the economic condition of the country, one would imagine the president would scale back any extraneous travel and jet-set only when necessary. He certainly has no problem calling for restraint from heads of private industry.

On February 9, 2009 in Elkhart, Indiana, the president had a message for those banking CEOs who had accepted his federal bailout:

"You can't get corporate jets. You can't go take a trip to Las Vegas or go down to the Super Bowl on the taxpayers' dime. There's got to be some accountability and some responsibility, and that's something that I intend to impose as president of the United States." He obviously meant to impose this standard on everyone but himself!

Never once does Obama question the lavish expenditures racked up by him and his family as they crisscross the globe to do little more than sightsee and enjoy themselves. It is fantastic that the president wants to expose his daughters to the wonders of the world and wine and dine his glamorous wife in far-flung ports—but he should stop using taxpayer dollars to do it.

Obama traveled to more foreign destinations in his first year in office than any president in history (with less to show for it than any president in history). And when the president makes an international visit, his family rarely misses a chance to tag along and extend the itinerary to suit their own interests.

---

## THE DIARY OF FIRST LADY MICHELLE OBAMA

### ROME, ITALY

*July 8, 2009*

*I am so damn tired of the media criticizing our "working trips." Yes, that is what this is: a working trip! Every member of this family works damn hard on these international voyages. I've spent half the day in hair and makeup — which is much more draining than it sounds. Looking beautiful is tough work. When I saw that* poor fireplug of a German chancellor, Merkel, the other day at a G-8 event, for a moment I thought: it might be nice to kind of let myself go the way she has, and never have to worry about makeup or how my hair looks again. Then she came over to say hello and I banished those thoughts immediately. <u>That woman is butt ugly up close . . .</u>

The European media is complaining about the cost of Barack traveling with the family. Well, he's a family man! He loves his family and why shouldn't we travel with him? Why should Reggie have all the fun?

No one even considers the economic stimulus we provide when we visit one of these foreign countries—and I'm not talking about Barack. Just look at our girls' trip to London last month. Taking the children to see <u>The Lion King</u> on the West End will probably keep that show running for another year. The little people want to do whatever we do. When I think of all the actors and singers, waiters and maids that we alone have kept in business, it makes my head spin. Our just walking into an establishment can revive its fortunes for years to come.

Look what happened today—Mama and I took the girls to the Colosseum. The Secret Service made sure that we had it all to ourselves—but I don't think many people go there. Who but history buffs like us would want to go see a drafty, old stone arena in the middle of Rome? But after we appeared there today, tour buses from all over the world began lining up! I made Malia wear another peace sign T-shirt today. People want to know how we work? This is how we work. My own child was sending a subtle disarmament message to the G-8. Axelrod and Desiree conspired on this one. Who else could pull off that kind of artistic, global messaging? Us — that's who!

I want to do something special for the girls while we're here. Last month we went to tea at the prime minister's house in London and had a birthday celebration at the Sarkozys' in Paris. Now that we're in Rome, I'm trying to get Hillary to arrange some kind of concert in our honor at St. Peter's Square. It's the least the pope can do. And getting photographed with us could help raise his international profile. Standing next to me, he might actually get his picture in <u>Vogue</u>.

---

On June 5, 2009, the entire Obama family arrived in Paris. The official business was to commemorate the sixty-fifth anniversary of the D-day invasion in France, but Michelle seemed more interested in plotting the Obama invasion. She and the girls toured the Eiffel Tower, visited Notre Dame, hit a museum, and made time for shopping. Why dwell on the Allied landing on Omaha Beach when you can land yourself a swell holiday on the taxpayers' dime?

The First Couple snubbed their French hosts by refusing a dinner invitation by President Sarkozy and his wife, Carla Bruni. This was reported to be payback after news reports that Sarkozy was less than impressed with Obama's grasp of the issues. President Obama's conceit once again got the best of him, and made him appear petty and vindictive, not to mention supremely thin-skinned. Shoving their rebuke in the faces of the French, the First Lovebirds hit the town, and lingered over dinner alone at the Jules Verne Restaurant. Despite the Obamas' insult, the Sarkozys opened their residence to the Obama family for brunch on Sunday, June 7. Nicolas Sarkozy led everyone in singing "Happy Birthday" to Sasha Obama, who was only days away from her eighth birthday. Naturally, they presented her with a cake. Yet this was only the beginning of what would be a multiday international celebration.

On Monday, June 8, Dad flew home to Washington, but the rest of his family stayed behind to jet-set off to London to continue celebrating Sasha's birthday. Michelle, her girls, and Marian Robinson dropped by a pub to have fish and chips (Michelle had a sirloin steak, according to the *Washington Post*). They visited the Tower of London and Westminster Abbey, had tea with the prime minister's wife, and even found time to catch a performance of *The Lion King*. On the big day, Sasha's birthday, Michelle had something really grand planned: a visit to the active set of the last Harry Potter movie. The Obama girls got to tromp through Hogwarts and party with the film's stars. This would all make for an adorable story, if it weren't so expensive, and if you weren't paying for security and the government plane.

The *Guardian* reports that the president regularly travels abroad with a staff of five hundred people—two hundred Secret Service personnel, chefs, a team of doctors, up to thirty-five vehicles (including the presidential limo, Marine One, and several decoys), Michelle's eight-member staff, and the president's valet, Reggie Love. On October 7, 2009, McClatchy News Service reported that a Clinton trip to Asia in 2000 cost taxpayers $50 million. The White House refuses to comment on what these family vacations are costing us today.

Regardless of the expense, the family piled into Air Force One for a second European vacation only a month later, in July 2009. This time it was off to Moscow and then to Rome for the G-8 Summit. While Dad conversed with world leaders, the Obama girls visited the big tourist sites and had a great time sampling gelato with the First Grandmother.

In March 2010, they had another family vacation planned: a trip to Indonesia to acquaint the girls with one of the places their father had spent his youth (clearly, a pressing national priority). It was scheduled to coincide with the Obama girls' spring break in late March (natch). Robert Gibbs offered the lamest of justifications for the taxpayer-funded jaunt: "This trip is an important part of the president's continued effort to broaden and strengthen the partnerships that are necessary to advance our security and prosperity. Indonesia is the world's fourth most populous country, the third largest democracy, is home to the largest Muslim population in the world. . . ." In other words: the president wants his girls to see where he grew up.

The dramatic House vote on his health-care overhaul would frustrate the travel plans, forcing a delay. Politics may have required the president to remain behind, but Michelle Obama and her girls were going on a vacation come hell or high water.

---

## THE DIARY OF FIRST LADY MICHELLE OBAMA

### THE WHITE HOUSE

*March 19, 2010*

There is no way I am going to sit around this house watching C-SPAN all weekend as these fools on the Hill dither over this obvious vote. I told Barack earlier this week, "Nancy and Harry bought all the votes we need. Forget about it. Whether you're here or not won't make a bit of difference. We need to get away. We need some time away as a family." But he didn't pay me any *mind. The girls were so looking forward to seeing Indonesia and Australia. We even had a trip to that koala reserve and a visit with Bindi Irwin planned!*

*It's those damn Republicans. If they'd helped out instead of stirring up those tea-baggers, health-care reform would have been signed last Thanksgiving. Now they've ruined our Spring Break trip. But I'm going to fix them. They were worried about us spending money on a trip to the East. I can spend federal money traveling to the East right here at home. I told Susan (my chief of staff) to schedule a trip to New York City for a few days. I'm taking my girls to see some Broadway shows and Mama's never been to the Russian Tea Room. I'll lock down that city and create so much havoc, the taxpayers will beg us to travel abroad.*

---

There is a certain tone-deaf arrogance that must have overcome the First Lady when she told the high-end magazine *Condé Nast Traveler* in May 2010, "I felt that my kids learned so much more about the history in Europe than they did here," referring to eleven-year-old Malia and eight-year-old Sasha. "And I thought, 'Well, the only way we're going to do that is to show them, right?' And you can't read about it, you have to go to see it. So this summer, I really felt like, instead of putting them in camp, we would have what I called Camp Obama."

Camp Obama apparently never shuts down. In place of their Indonesian trip, Michelle took her mother and daughters to New York City for several days. They saw the Broadway shows *Memphis* and *Wicked*, and visited the Empire State Building and the Russian Tea Room. At least ten Secret Service agents and untold numbers of New York City police were needed to pull off each of their stops.

The First Lady was not in the least bit contrite when she spoke of the logistics of her culinary outings with *Condé Nast Traveler*. "It's like, 'Okay, we're going to that restaurant, and everyone's going to get mad, 'cause I'm there eating my hamburger.' People are excited but . . ."

This is just the sort of thoughtless response one expects from people who are so narcissistic that they think only of their own happiness and discount the feelings, schedules, and everyday lives of the thousands of people they inconvenience to keep Camp Obama up and running.

Without a doubt the most offensive example of the Obamas' self-indulgent vacationing was when the White House announced that the First Family would head home to Chicago, on May 27, 2010, for the long Memorial Day weekend. This meant the president would skip the traditional wreath-laying ceremony at Arlington National Cemetery—which many military personnel and veterans considered an insult. As this incident unfolded the President was coming under intense criticism for his handling of a catastrophic oil spill off the Gulf Coast. For a president to advertise vacation plans while a major region of the country was under a withering environmental assault was abominable and typically self-centered. The White House felt the ferocious blowback and hastily added a presidential drop-by in Louisiana to his vacation itinerary.

## RACIAL MISSED MANNERS

For a country that had long struggled with the sin of slavery and the many wounds it created, President Obama's election represented a historic milestone. He was to be a uniter, a postracial president. Yet during a televised White House press conference on July 22, 2009, he waded into a controversy that he had no business engaging and, in the process, enflamed racial sensitivities.

Obama was asked about the arrest of the African-American Harvard professor Henry Louis Gates by the Cambridge, Massachusetts, Police

Department. The police were called by a neighbor who thought someone was breaking into Gates's home. When Sergeant James Crowley, a white officer, arrived on the scene, he was verbally assaulted by Henry Louis Gates (an Obama friend), who was trying to enter his own home at the time. Gates, according to reports, made threats and yelled profanities at the officer before being arrested for disorderly conduct.

Rather than staying out of what was obviously a local law enforcement issue, Obama read the situation through his own personal prism and threw kerosene on the racially charged story:

> I think it's fair to say, number one, any of us would be pretty angry; number two, that the Cambridge police acted stupidly in arresting somebody when there was already proof that they were in their own home. And number three, what I think we know, separate and apart from this incident, is that there is a long history in this country of African-Americans and Latinos being stopped by law enforcement disproportionately. That's just a fact.

Police unions derided the president's comments and came to the defense of their fellow officer, Sergeant Crowley. James Preston of the Fraternal Order of Police Florida State Lodge said, "To make such an off-handed comment about a subject without benefit of the facts, in such a public forum, hurts police-community relations" . . . "By reducing all contact between law enforcement and the public to the color of their skin or ethnicity is, in fact, counter-productive."

The president did not for a moment consider the outstanding record of Sergeant Crowley or even pause to give the officer the benefit of the doubt. Instead, our president, who considers himself an expert on all things race-related, shot from the hip and outraged Americans coast to coast. The post-racial president had become the most racial president. Crowley had, in fact, taught classes warning police about profiling suspects based on their race. According to the *Boston Globe*, he also tried to save the life of Celtics basketball star Reggie Lewis by performing CPR, in 1993.

Obama quickly realized he had stepped in it and issued repeated clarifications and pseudo-apologies for his comments. To put the issue to rest, the president hosted a "beer summit" at the White House, bringing Gates and Crowley together over suds, as if he were brokering a Middle East peace deal. For Obama to try to portray himself as the healer in this situation was ludicrous, but entirely consistent with his audacious track record.

Obama's vice president has his own checkered past with racial utterances. In 2006, Joe Biden said, "In Delaware, the largest growth in population is Indian Americans moving from India. You cannot go to a 7-Eleven or a Dunkin' Donuts unless you have a slight Indian accent. I'm not joking."

In 2007, then-senator Biden botched it again when he told the *New York Observer* during the Democratic primaries that Obama was "the first mainstream African-American who is articulate and bright and clean and a nice-looking guy." The amazing thing is Biden actually gets away with this stuff—and he's not alone.

In their 2010 bestselling book *Game Change*, Mark Halperin and John Heilemann wrote of Senate majority leader Harry Reid: "He was wowed by Obama's oratorical gifts and believed that the country was ready to embrace a black presidential candidate, especially one such as Obama—a 'light-skinned' African-American 'with no Negro dialect, unless he wanted to have one,' as he said privately."

Had these same words been uttered by a conservative politician or talk-show host, the media condemnation would have been ferocious. But in the case of Harry Reid, liberal Democrats rushed to his defense. The president issued a statement in January 2010: "Harry Reid called me today and apologized for an unfortunate comment reported today. I accepted Harry's apology without question because I've known him for years, I've seen the passionate leadership he's shown on issues of social justice, and I know what's in his heart. As far as I am concerned, the book is closed." The Cambridge Police Department and Sergeant Crowley might have appreciated this kind of racial understanding a few months earlier.

Even Michelle Obama felt compelled to defend Reid's racial stupidity on January 13, 2010: "Harry Reid has no need to apologize to me because

I know Harry Reid. I measure people more so on what they do rather than the things they say."

"There is this standard where Democrats feel they can say these things and apologize, as long as it comes from one of their own," the black Republican National Committee Chairman Michael Steele told the media. "And if it comes from somebody else, it's racism."

---

## The Diary of Senate Majority Leader Harry Reid

### The United States Capitol

*January 9, 2010*

These *Game Change* reporters have taken my comments totally out of context. They were meant as a compliment to Barack. I thought it was an accurate and true description of why the president won the election. The American people *were* in fact ready to embrace a light-skinned, darker fellow—that's all there is to it. His amazing rhetorical gifts, free of that Negro, George Jefferson jive talk made him more appealing to white voters. That is all 100 percent true. Having shared so many hours with Barack, I've heard him turn that Negro accent on and off like a light switch. He does it at will, and it's a great talent—that's what I was trying to tell those reporters.

Honestly, I wish I could sound like a Negro when I appear at some of these black churches. It would make them more receptive to my message, and God knows I could use their votes right about now . . .

The staff has been all over me since those <u>Game Change</u> quotes hit. They're very agitated that I used the word <u>Negro</u>. Truth is: I didn't realize that the term had fallen out of fashion. There are so few dark-skinned Mormons, and I just don't socialize with those people. I mean, don't get me wrong, I've got nothing against the blacks. I promoted them to political office, I listen to Johnny Mathis in the car, and I think Oprah is a much better talk-show host than Mike Douglas. All of that is 100 percent true; I'd repeat it to anyone.

I called Barack to apologize earlier today. He was very strange on the phone. I said, "Mr. President, I want to apologize if I caused any harm . . ." He cut me off. "Brutha Harry," he said using his ~~Negro~~ nonwhite dialect, "I got cho back. Ain't no thang!" It was very curious indeed, and at that point we shared an awkward pause. (I didn't know if he was joking or not, so I just kept quiet.) He then reverted to his preppy, Caucasian dialect: "I've already got members of the Congressional Black Caucus drafting letters of support, and Michelle and I are going to make a statement. But Harry, you better get that health-care bill through the Senate. Do you understand me?" I told him I did, and he hung up.

I've sure learned my lesson. I've got to be more careful with my choice of words. It's not the analysis, it's the words that offend. If anyone asks me about the vernacular of the president again, I will say, "He is brilliant at reaching all voters with both his normal and his colored dialects."

---

By allowing Harry Reid to escape all responsibility for his comments, the Democrats have lost credibility on this issue and weakened the norms of what is acceptable racial speech in the country. It is either always wrong to use the n-word and antiquated terminology like *Negro*, or it isn't. And since it is wrong, let's condemn it always and everywhere and not just when it falls from the mouths of conservatives.

---

## THE DIARY OF VICE PRESIDENT JOE BIDEN

### U.S. NAVAL OBSERVATORY

November 10, 2009

We were at Andrews Air Force Base today, and when that chopper landed, my hair looked like the grasses parting on the Serengeti. Jesus, when I saw the footage on MSNBC, I looked like

Mr. Clean! All kidding aside, I should have waited to relocate the hair until after they perfected the procedure.

After getting the teeth caps and the hair plugs, I thought I'd be leading the American people, not playing second fiddle to the Prince Charming of Honolulu. I've scheduled another procedure to add some volume to the old crown over the Christmas holiday. The doc says I barely have enough donor hair left on the backside of the noggin. I leaned in—didn't want Secret Service to hear—and said, "Doc, if there's not enough on the back of my head, you can always graft some off my tookis." The doctor stiffened a bit and said, "That's what we were planning. As I told you, I'm taking the hair right off your head." On the drive back, I thought maybe that was a crack. I don't like the way that guy massages my scalp, either. After this surgery, I'm not going back to him again. Maybe I'll try Tiger Woods' guy next time.

I've got to do something. When you've got a wife as hot as mine, and you're facing a reelection bid in a few years, you want to look as good as you can. Jill thinks maybe it's time for a wig. I just don't know. If it all starts to fall out after this operation, I'll take the remaining strands (which are still pretty thick despite all the scarring) and just swirl 'em forward with a lot of hairspray. Donald Trump does that, and look at all the babes he has around him.

The Obamas and their political comrades have in various ways embodied that clinical definition of narcissism: "an all-pervasive pattern of grandiosity (in fantasy or behavior), need for admiration or adulation and lack of empathy." By turning the spotlight of every topic and public policy issue onto themselves, the Obamas have redefined what it means to lead. Vainglory and haughtiness have become their trademarks. Leadership in the age of Obama is about grabbing all the goodies and glory available, regardless of the fallout. This tells our country—especially our young people—that governing is just another way of living out the celebrity lifestyle. Leadership requires not personal sacrifice, but personal celebration. "I do solemnly swear . . . to the best of my ability to preserve, protect, and defend my celebrity . . ."

# THE WINNING WAY

No matter what the Obamas do or say, life is *not* one endless vacation. We're not supposed to be here to seek our own pleasure and glory.

One antidote to narcissism (and we're all succeptible) is personal sacrifice, a willingness to put others before ourselves.

Obama often talks about the common good, but beneath so many of the president's policies and pronouncements, there is a spirit that is all too common and not so good. He claims to be looking out for the little guy, but more often than not, Obama is only looking out for himself and his own place in history. We must find another way as a people.

America was built on hard work and love of neighbor. Somehow we have to rediscover this spirit and begin to let it lead us again. Hard economic times need not always be a bad thing. They sometimes bring people together and force them to consider new ways to help one another. If that is the result of our present economic woes, we should consider ourselves blessed and thankful for the opportunity. With so much suffering touching the lives of our families and friends, it is our obligation to help when we can, and sacrifice whatever time or resources are available to us.

We also have to begin observing basic etiquette and manners in America again. We are the greatest country on earth—the strongest, the most creative—but if our children are vulgarians who learn their manners from reality TV and from the street, what have we really accomplished? It is up to each of us—myself included—to work against the coarsening of our culture and to resist the crude, classless behavior that we see embodied by some of our most celebrated figures. Basic respect and decorum, what it means to be a gentleman or lady, can really be taught only at home. Over time, if we are diligent, these standards of behavior will spread across the country and become second nature to future generations.

CHAPTER *9*

# DEMONIZING THE ENEMY

*Pick the target, freeze it, personalize it, and polarize it.*
—SAUL ALINSKY, *RULES FOR RADICALS*

In a staggering announcement on April 6, 2010, President Obama revamped U.S. nuclear policy and weakened our national security. CBS News reported that, for the first time, the United States had "limited the circumstances under which the U.S. would resort to nuclear weapons." This meant if a nonnuclear state were to attack America with a biological or chemical weapon, the United States would no longer consider a nuclear response.

Conservatives were incensed. Rudy Giuliani told *National Review Online* that Obama's policy was "a left wing dream," and asserted, "the president doesn't understand the concept of leverage." On WPIX in New York, Senator John McCain said that the president should make it plain that the United States "will take no option off the table to deter attacks against the American people and our allies."

Then, the next evening during an appearance on Fox News's *Hannity*, Sarah Palin weighed in on the controversy. She compared the Obama nuclear policy changes to a kid facing a bully in a schoolyard who says, "Go ahead, punch me in the face, and I'm not going to retaliate. Go ahead and do what you want to with me."

The next day in Prague, where Obama was signing a nuclear pact with

Russia, George Stephanopoulos asked him to respond to Palin's criticism. The ever-prickly Obama took the bait—with intent. "I really have no response," he said, as if he had just smelled something foul. "Because last I checked, Sarah Palin's not much of an expert on nuclear issues." Then he added, "If the secretary of defense and the chairman of the Joint Chiefs of Staff are comfortable with it, I'm probably going to take my advice from them and not from Sarah Palin."

It was textbook Obama. Whenever the president is questioned, whenever he encounters even the slightest resistance to his agenda, his hackles go up. He ignores the merit of the argument at hand and focuses on the person making it. Obama reflexively demonizes the opposition, any opposition, which allows him to dismiss even the most rational criticism.

In the case of his nuclear policy adjustments, Obama could have chosen to spar with Rudy Giuliani or John McCain, two Republican critics with knowledge of the issue and legitimate concerns. He could have engaged in an honest public debate on this critical question of American security with someone who had proven expertise in this area. But Obama didn't do that. No, he selected Sarah Palin as his opponent. There was method to his madness.

By elevating Palin, Obama diminished all his other critics. Palin got the front-page coverage and all the attention, while the other leading conservative figures—some potential future presidential candidates—were relegated to her shadow. This was by design.

Obama is doing all he can to turn Sarah Palin into the sole representative of the conservative cause and the voice of her party. The easiest way to win any battle is to select your own enemy. Clearly, Obama believes that she has been so caricatured by the Left and so savaged by the media that she is no real threat to him. She also remains a huge political star. By choosing Palin as his sparring partner, the president avoids answering the difficult questions about his reckless policy, while engaging in little more than a celebrity grudge match. Notice how he never addresses the substance of Palin's concerns. Instead he runs to the personal, smearing her as "not much of an expert on nuclear policy." On April 9, Palin sarcastically responded that her expertise probably paled next to "the vast nuclear experience that he acquired as a community organizer." But the truth is, as a community organizer, Obama learned to go nuclear—on his critics. It was a skill that he took with him to the White House.

If Obama is accomplished in anything, he is accomplished in community organizing. He can stoke class envy with the best of them and knows the world of professional rabble-rousing. He knows how to play on perceived "inequities" for his own political advantage. On the streets of Chicago, he learned his lessons well; lessons coined by the father of community organizing, Saul Alinsky.

Alinsky was a Marxist-inspired radical who organized the black ghettos of Chicago in 1950. He channeled the discontent of his target audience to agitate for social change and the acquisition of "power." Alinsky released his landmark work, *Rules for Radicals*, in 1971. It soon became the gospel of community organizing and the marching orders for all those who wished to amass power for themselves. Though Alinsky died more than a decade before Obama began his career as a community organizer, the future president absorbed the tactics of Alinsky and even his lingo from fellow travelers.

In the opening of *Rules for Radicals*, Alinsky writes: "What follows is for those who *want to change the world from what it is to what they believe it should be* [emphasis added]. *The Prince* was written by Machiavelli for the Haves on how to hold power. *Rules for Radicals* is written for the Have-Nots on how to take it away . . . my aim here is to suggest how to organize for power: how to get it and how to use it."

Listen closely to Barack Obama and his surrogates, and the strains of Alinsky are hard to miss. Here is Obama from his Iowa Caucus victory speech on January 3, 2008: "Hope is the bedrock of this nation; the belief that our destiny will not be written for us, but by us; by all those men and women who are not content to settle for the world as it is; who have courage to remake the world as it should be."

The same echoes of Saul reverberate through the speeches of that other community organizer in the Obama family, Michelle. Here is the future First Lady before a crowd in Orangeburg, South Carolina, on November

19, 2008: "Inequality is not a burden we have to accept, it is a challenge we must overcome. . . . I'm asking you to stop settling for the world as it is, and to help us make the world as it should be."

There is a consistency to the thought of elites. They are always moving toward some utopia that they alone feel a divine right to impose on the rest of us. It is a monarchy of arrogance that Alinsky and the Obamas propose. Any who stand in the way of their "progress" must be stopped at all costs.

---

## THE DIARY OF PRESIDENT BARACK OBAMA

### THE WHITE HOUSE

April 9, 2010

I'm dealing with a Supreme Court vacancy, a mining tragedy in West Virginia, and a major nuclear summit this weekend, and I've got to listen to Sarah Palin's griping. I'll be damned if this woman is going to slow my agenda. No matter where I turn, there she is snipping at my heels. I thought I took care of her during that interview with George the Greek in Prague, but now she's bad-mouthing me again at some GOP Bund meeting in New Orleans—making light of my community activism!

I just cracked open my nightstand copy of <u>Rules for Radicals</u>. Papa Alinsky always has the perfect counsel just when I need it. Whenever I'm really feeling down, a little meditation on this good book brings me right back to my core—to my essence. It's like going to church.

Says right here: "Pick the target, freeze it, personalize it, and polarize it." That's exactly what I'm going to do with Palin. She's in my sights and I'm going to "reload"! We've got to stop this idea that she has any normal following—"freeze it"! Plouffe is working to plant some of our activists at silly Sarah's next big tea-bagger rally. They're going to throw around racial epithets and carry some brand-new posters of me with the Hitler mustache (we just had them printed up). Gibbs will make sure that CNN and MSNBC know where our guys will be standing, so they get plenty of coverage. To "personalize" and "polarize" her, I just got off the phone with Tina Fey. She's hosting <u>Saturday Night Live</u> this week. I told her it's her national duty to keep painting Palin as an unserious, fame-seeking money-grubber— her husband, too. My speechwriter Favreau is on his way to New York to help pen a Palin sketch for Tina. She's a great woman and definitely the Carol Burnett of our generation.

Michelle is absolutely right. If I keep the focus on Palin, then nobody will pay any attention to what I'm doing. And that's the way I like it. Hell, doesn't Palin have anything better to do than criticize me? Shouldn't she be back home shooting some endangered wolf species from a helicopter?

# TEA PARTY POTSHOTS

*Keep the pressure on with different tactics and actions, and utilize*
*all events of the period for your purpose.*

—SAUL ALINSKY, *RULES FOR RADICALS*

When thousands of hardworking Americans dared take to the streets to op-pose Obama's $787 billion stimulus plan in February 2009, the Democrats knew they had a problem on their hands. At first, the Obama administration downplayed their significance, but eventually top advisors, and the presi-dent himself, fanned out to dismiss and demonize the "Tea Partiers" from multiple angles.

On April 19, 2009, David Axelrod appeared on CBS's *Face the Nation* to disparage the entire movement. Axelrod said, "I think any time that you have severe economic conditions, there is always an element of disaffection that can mutate into something that's unhealthy." (Axelrod would know about "unhealthy mutations.") "The thing that bewilders me is this president just cut taxes for ninety-five percent of the American people. So I think the tea bags should be directed elsewhere, because he certainly understands the bur-den that people face." In other words, Axelrod was answering the Tea Par-tiers' concerns the way Obamaniacs always do—by blaming George W. Bush.

One can always gauge the effectiveness of any conservative group by the volume of media scorn heaped upon it. When it became clear that the Tea Partiers were not a flash-in-the-pan movement, MSNBC and CNN hosts began crudely referring to them as "tea-baggers" (a reference to a sexual act that I will not describe here). On April 14, 2009, Obama's favorite anchor-man, Keith Olbermann, opined on *Countdown*, "Republican talking heads, like former House Speaker Newt Gingrich, have pushed their own ver-sion of teabagging—down the throats of tea-baggers. . . . And the nation's teabagging, [is] of course, impossible without this man, a Dick Armey at the head of it—the former House majority leader representing right-wing money bags, who have blown lots of cash to make the movement look as if it's coming from the bottom-up and not the top-down." Now you know why he is considered the Walt Whitman of political punditry.

Judging from all the filthy commentary, the Tea Party movement, by April 29, 2009, was obviously having an impact. On that day, the president used a rally in Arnold, Missouri, marking his hundredth day in office, to marginalize the activists. The man suddenly had an allergic reaction to his favorite pastime, community organizing.

"You see folks waving tea bags around; let me just remind them that I am happy to have a serious conversation about how we are going to cut our health care costs down over the long term, how we're going to stabilize Social Security. . . . But let's not play games and pretend that the reason is because of the Recovery Act. . . ." He went on, again, to shift blame to the previous administration. His condescending attitude served only to further motivate the Tea Partiers he was dismissing.

I have taken to calling the Tea Party phenomenon the American Movement. They represent a cross section of average Americans who pay their taxes, play by the rules, and work for a living. To me, they are a hopeful sign of civic activism and mainstream, commonsense values. But to President Obama and his followers, the Tea Party activists are annoying obstacles or worse.

---

## THE DIARY OF PRESIDENT BARACK OBAMA

### THE WHITE HOUSE

March 24, 2010

Those tea-baggers won't be able to weather the storm I've prepared for them. The tactics we have set in motion are unbelievable. They put me through hell over the last year. Now it's their turn. First, we rammed the health-care bill down their miserable throats; now we're discrediting them faster than the Palin clan can clean out a room full of swag bags!

It came to me during a call with Louise Slaughter the day of the health-care vote. She was relaying the discontent in her district over the way we ignored the will of the people. The Tea Partiers are jamming the congressional phone lines, saying that come November, there'll be "hell to pay." This is always the last cry of the oppressors as they fall. As a community organizer, I've heard this talk my whole life. There's only one way to fight back. Do horrible things in the name of the enemy and make sure somebody covers it!

Papa Alinsky said: "The first step in community organization is community disorganization." I told Louise to get some of her staffers to chuck a few bricks through the front window of her offices in New York—then weep and moan about it in the morning to the press. Blame it all on the tea-baggers. Valerie thought it would be even better if they could tape some tea bags to the bricks. I agreed.

Meanwhile, we got a few of our SEIU activists to do some lesser things around the country: egg a few residences, throw toilet paper in the trees, cut some propane lines on outdoor grills. They're not doing any of this at the homes of the congressmen (and this was sheer genius on my part). Instead, it'll all happen at the houses of congressional relatives! I figured that's exactly what these goofball Republicans would do, right? Flip through the phone book, get the wrong address, and go on a destructive spree. The coverage is already a thing of beauty.

Then we've got the racist, homophobic tactical front. On the day of the vote, Nancy and the gang walked right through the tea-baggers to draw their fire—and they didn't do a thing! Plouffe thought they would at least throw a bucket of water on Pelosi or toss a rotten tomato or two at Rosa DeLauro—something. But since Nancy and the others reached the Capitol unscathed, they turned to plan B: spread the story that the protesters verbally and physically attacked congressmen. Some old white man was apparently screaming at a member of the Black Caucus, congressman Emanuel Cleaver, about his taxes going up, when a little saliva flew out. The headline in the <u>Post</u> the next day read: " 'Tea Party' Protesters Accused of Spitting on Lawmaker." You can't make this stuff up. The press is saying this shows the racism of the tea-baggers. If drops of saliva flying during a conversation are the new standard for racism, somebody better write up Barney Frank for attacking the person of the president. When he addresses me I feel like I should be wearing a Hazmat Suit— the saliva flies all over my jacket. Reggie says it's impossible to get those stains out.

Speaking of Frank, he's now making the rounds saying that the Tea Partiers screamed "anti-gay" chants as he crossed the Capitol grounds. I don't have the heart to tell him that those T-shirted throngs were probably all Organizing for America volunteers. This thing is working like a charm; even the victims are playing along . . .

Throughout the spring and into the summer, the loosely organized Tea Party (not really a party at all) became more popular and more powerful. Tea Party ralliers assailed big government in all its Obama-iterations. They were anti-big-spending and therefore fought vigorously against Obama's proposed health-care reform. Enter House Speaker Nancy Pelosi, who gladly jumped atop the left-wing pigpile. In early August 2009, she sniffed that the populist protesters at congressional town hall meetings were "Astro-turf" (in contrast, of course, to the genuine, left-wing grassroots gatherings that Nancy supports). "They're carrying swastikas and symbols like that to a town meeting on health care," she told a reporter, maligning thousands of law-abiding, patriotic Americans nationwide. Few media outlets other than Fox News reported on her vicious, defamatory comments, despite the fact that the video was almost instantly posted on YouTube.

After bank bailouts, the stimulus plan, and then health-care reform, hardworking taxpayers had had enough. Since their calls, e-mails, faxes, and town hall pleas failed to get the attention of their elected representatives or the White House, they decided to do what the liberals had done for decades—they started to organize protests and rallies. One would imagine that the Organizer-in-Chief would have lauded their efforts. This may not have been his Organizing for America, but it certainly was America Organizing—and Obama couldn't stand it. The truth is, the only kind of organizing he likes is the left-wing variety. Organizing by mothers, fathers, grandparents, and young people who don't expect or want a government handout is for Obama something to be feared and destroyed. To his way of thinking they must be dangerous extremists, racists, homophobes, or possibly all three.

To understand this particular Obama tactic against the Tea Party activists, we have to go back to April 9, 2009. That's when Obama's Department of Homeland Security issued a report titled "Rightwing Extremism: Current Economic and Political Climate Fueling Resurgence in Radicalization and Recruitment." It was distributed to law enforcement officials all over the country. The report suggested that the Obama presidency had spurred a rise in activity among racist groups, hate groups, and antigovernment groups. The report said that this right-wing extremism "may include groups and individuals that are dedicated to a single-issue, such as opposition to abortion or immigration." (Had Homeland Security secretary Janet Napolitano waited a few months, she could have included other "single-issues" on her warning list—like opposition to health-care reform or hatred of the White House vegetable garden.) The report also warned: "Right-wing extremists will attempt to recruit and radicalize returning veterans in order to exploit their skills and knowledge derived from military training and combat."

For those who might have missed it, the Obama administration had officially classified pro-lifers, anyone hostile to high taxes, veterans, and any citizen opposed to illegal immigration as "right-wing extremists." A year later, the significance of this dossier would become readily apparent. The new extremists were the people who had gathered at the U.S. Capitol on March 21, on the eve of the Democrats' historic vote to pass health-care reform. Now all that was required to finish off the Tea Party activists (or so Team Obama thought) was to identify examples of hateful behavior in order to marginalize them as a dangerous fringe group.

The Democrats' use of parliamentary tactics and government pork to buy votes incensed the public. Before the vote, the entire Democratic caucus paraded from the House offices to the Capitol through hundreds of protesters. It was an act of defiance and hubris by Speaker Pelosi and her minions; a provocative act meant to incite a reaction. They could have easily taken the tunnel that runs between the congressional office buildings and the Capitol, as most of them do each day. But this was an historic moment that called for a dramatic display.

Following the march across the Capitol grounds, Congressman John Lewis, a longtime civil rights leader, claimed that protesters chanted the "n-word" as he passed. Another black congressman, Emanuel Cleaver, charged that a protester spit on him. And Barney Frank of Massachusetts contended that the protesters shouted a derogatory term in his direction. In the days that followed, no footage or sound bites could be discovered to substantiate any of these claims. Andrew Breitbart (of Breitbart.com, Big Hollywood.com fame) offered a ten-thousand-dollar reward for anyone who could produce evidence of these incidents. He had no takers. The only bit of footage that did emerge discredited the spitting charge and showed only an excited protester with an overactive saliva gland, screaming at a congressman. Whatever the protester was doing, he was not purposely spitting on anyone. Not that that stopped the Obama narrative.

On April 6, 2010, Fox News reported that Tennessee Democratic representative Steve Cohen had received three threatening e-mails. In response, Cohen appeared on an Internet radio show, where he compared Tea Party activists to Klansmen, perpetuating the racially charged Democratic smear campaign. "Tea Party people are kind of like Klansmen without robes and hoods," Cohen said. "They have really shown a very hard core, a very angry side of America that is against any type of diversity." Since Cohen is white, he recited the familiar list of baseless charges involving John Lewis and Emanuel Cleaver to substantiate his argument.

What received little attention was the fact that Eric Cantor, a Jewish Republican congressman from Virginia, had received a death threat and anti-Semitic slurs via YouTube. When a bullet was shot into Cantor's campaign office, the congressman did not attempt to use the incident to engender sympathy or political support. He did not characterize liberals who disagreed with him as anti-Semitic or violent. This is the difference between how conservatives deal with the random acts of madmen, and liberals, who will use any incident (real or fabricated) to destroy their opponents.

---

## THE DIARY OF PRESIDENT BARACK OBAMA

### AIR FORCE ONE

April 15, 2010

Tax day, and for this president, it's always taxing. These teabaggers are wearing me out. Thousands of them have gathered around the nation. I'm going to give them my normal response:

ridicule. I'd like to go out and tell those militant lunatics what I really think of them, but Clinton had a better idea.

Bill called the other night and offered his services. He's going to do a big media tour for the fifteenth anniversary of the Oklahoma City bombing, and he'll suggest that the Tea Party people and Timothy McVeigh share the same violent, antigovernment spirit. I told Bill: "I couldn't have come up with a better tactic myself." But let me be clear: I already have!

I got on the horn with Rachel Maddow over at MSNBC (easily the Edward R. Murrow of our age) and asked her to create a documentary on the Oklahoma City bomber. Voters need to be reminded of what happens when these crazy tea-baggers resist their government. It gets ugly. Rachel instantly agreed to help. I've got Gibbs working to get her some jailhouse recordings of McVeigh. Axe's idea was to call the thing "The McVeigh Tapes." Rachel loved the title, and she's already written a promo.

Get this: "The McVeigh Tapes puts into perspective the threat posed by anti-government extremism. . . . We ignore this, our own very recent history of anti-government violence and the dangers of domestic terrorism, at our peril." The woman's a better writer than Olbermann, and honestly, he's gotten too liberal for my tastes.

Well, I better get back to practicing the Español. I'm headed to Miami for a big fund-raiser at Gloria Estefan's house. I just hope the Cubanos don't give me any of that anti-Castro crap while I'm there. Look at the health-care plan that that man implemented for his people decades before the U.S. even thought of such a thing. Gloria told me that we might have to take a few photos of her and me solemnly looking at pictures of the Cuban refugees. This will give her some cover and make the Cubanos think that I give a damn. I hope Ricky Martin's not there. Last time he showed up at a fund-raiser, he was bending my ear all night about lifting the "Don't Ask, Don't Tell" policy. But I've got an answer ready for him tonight: "For you, Ricky, I'm implementing a new policy: 'Don't Worry, We Already Know.' "

---

Appearing at a fund-raiser on tax day 2010 in Miami, the president said he was "amused" by the Tea Party movement and insisted that he had lowered the tax burden for Americans, adding, "You would think they'd be saying thank you. That's what you'd think." But the Tea Partiers weren't saying thank you. Most were saying thank God for the upcoming midterm elections. Only the most arrogant of politicians would expect thanks from voters for his unprecedented expansion of federal power and spending. And it takes a special brand of audacity to think we are so stupid that we don't know that eventually we and our children and their children are going to have to pay the tab.

Somehow the media even managed to turn the nationwide anti-tax protests into a story about race. The gatherings were judged not on the legitimacy of the protesters' concerns, but by their "diversity." According to an April 15, 2010, story by the Associated Press, a California Tea Party consisted of a "predominantly white crowd." Stephanie Ebbert and Sarah Schweitzer of the *Boston Globe* wrote of the Boston Tea Party gathering: "Some have charged racism for its mostly white membership." It was as if white, working-class people didn't have the right to object to government spending and high taxes. The coverage also served to disenfranchise the black and Latino participants who did, in fact, show up for the rallies.

Even worse than being accused of racism is being accused of inciting violence. In an April 18, 2010 interview with ABC's Jake Tapper, former

President Bill Clinton implied that at least some of the Tea Partiers could become terrorists:

> [W]hen I went back and started preparing for the fifteenth anniversary of Oklahoma City, I realized that there were a lot of parallels between the early '90s and now . . . the rise of kind of identity politics. The rise of the militia movements and the right-wing talk radio with a lot of what's going on in the blogosphere now . . . they create a climate in which people who are vulnerable to violence, because they are disoriented like Timothy McVeigh was, are more likely to act.

From these comments, it is obvious that President Clinton never forgave conservatives for what they did to expose him during the Lewinsky scandal. He will exact his revenge any way he can, and always with a smile on his face. But my favorite part of the interview was his Soviet-style treatment of dissent against government.

> And we shouldn't demonize the government or its public employees or its elected officials. We can disagree with them. We can harshly criticize them. But when we turn them into an object of demonization, you know, you—you increase the number of threats.

In other words, you can criticize a government run by Democrats, but you can't be too effective. Ingraham Rule of Thumb: The more influential and popular a conservative movement or group becomes, the more likely it will be attacked by Democrats as "incendiary," "racially insensitive," or "intolerant."

---

# THE DIARY OF PRESIDENT BARACK OBAMA

## AIR FORCE ONE

### March 25, 2010

I was in Iowa City, Iowa, today selling the health-care plan. It could very well be the most boring place on the planet. When you find yourself staring at tumbleweeds because the eye needs to see some movement, you know you're in trouble. My speech today was clearly the cultural event of their year. I won't return there until I start the reelection machine. Couldn't wait to get back on this plane.

During the drive over, I had Reggie tune in the talk radio that the rubes out here in the dust bowl listen to, and I caught the end of old Sean Hannity. Pitiful how much this man needs me. I'm the fuel that keeps his whole operation going. He even calls his show "The Stop Obama Express," rambling on about how "Obama ignores the will of the people." Without me, he'd just be reading Michael Steele's daily faxes and talking to Palin about how she gets her updo to stay in place even in the stiffest winds! No surprise that today he was ranting about how radical and dangerous I am. Dangerous?! It's just like Papa Alinsky wrote: "The job of the organizer is to maneuver and bait the establishment so that it will publicly attack him as a 'dangerous enemy.'" Mission accomplished, Papa.

I have another brilliant idea, too. Next time I'm up in the Big Apple, shutting down traffic for a date night with Miche, I'll show up unannounced on the <u>Great American Panel</u>! I'd love to mix it up with those know-nothings and show them how pundintry [*sic*] is really done. Though when you are a progressive, you have to be careful around that Hannity. I mean think about it: what did he do with Alan Colmes? Where did that man go?

After Hannity signed off, this Mark Levin character came on air. The things this man says are outrageous—naturally Hannity calls him "the Great One"! Please! That title should be reserved for duly elected executives with incredible physiques, brilliant minds, and wives named Michelle. Period!

I must admit though—the show was fascinating. He played several unadulterated sound clips from my speech today and each one was more compelling than the last. The commentary in between I could have done without, but the source material was very well done. One of the callers mentioned a book Levin wrote about his dog, called <u>Rescuing Sprite</u>. Give me a break—try rescuing an economy!

---

## SLIME THE MESSENGER

*Ridicule is man's most potent weapon. It is almost impossible to counterattack ridicule. Also it infuriates the opposition, who then react to your advantage.*

—SAUL ALINSKY, *RULES FOR RADICALS*

The president added conservative media to his hit list on March 30, 2010. Since he is constitutionally incapable of admitting failure, he sought out a scapegoat—a perfect target for whipping up his fan base.

Appearing on the *Today* show, Obama picked up where Bill Clinton left off: "I do think that we now have a pattern of polarization . . . where the political culture gets so wound up—frankly, Matt [Lauer], it gets spun up partly because of the way the media covers politics these days in the twenty-four-hour news cycle, in the cable chatter, in the talk radio, in the Internet and the blogs, all of which tries to feed the more extreme sides of every issue."

Three days after his *Today* diatribe, he singled out talk radio hosts by name on *CBS This Morning*. Harry Smith asked the president if he was "aware of the level of enmity that crosses the airwaves and that people have made part of their daily conversation."

Obama responded, "Well—I mean, I think that—when you've listened to Rush Limbaugh or Glenn Beck, it's . . . pretty apparent and—it's troublesome. But keep in mind, there have been periods in American history where this kind of—this kind of vitriol comes out."

So now it's "troublesome" to disagree vociferously with Obama, and he calls the content "vitriol."

It got better: "It happens often when you've got an economy that is making people more anxious, and people are feeling that there's a lot of change that needs to take place. But that's not the vast majority of Americans," he insisted. "I do think that everybody has a responsibility, Democrats or Republicans, to tone down some of this rhetoric . . . I am concerned about a political climate in which the other side is demonized." Of course, he feels no shame about demonizing talk radio hosts or anyone else who disagrees with him.

# The Diary of President Barack Barack Obama

## The Oval Office

May 20, 2010

I'm driving with Reggie today, and since NPR's signal was kind of weak, we tuned in to Rush Limbaugh's show for kicks. Huge mistake. The ego of this man! He constantly refers to himself as America's Anchorman. He's America's Anchorman the way I'm America's tax cutter! If this is truly the biggest radio program, this country is in serious trouble.

The whole show is "Obama did this, Obama did that." I wanted to call in, but Reggie thought it would diminish my stature, so I stood down. The problem with Limbaugh is that he reacts on instinct; it's all driven by emotion. The man is obviously out of touch with the right-wing intellectuals—the real idea people of the GOP—the folks who understand me (partly). His show would be a lot better if he read conservative thinkers like Peggy Noonan, David Brooks, and Chris Buckley. These are fair-minded conservatives, people who are happy to adjust their opinions for a White House Christmas party invitation. I like them. But all that Limbaugh can do is spread his hate and intolerance. I imagine this sort of thing plays well with his fan base, listening in their trailers or at their militia camps.

Once I got back to the Oval, I told Plouffe and Gibbs what the country really needs: <u>The President Barack Obama Hour</u>—my own daily radio show! This is why my poll numbers are sagging; my people need to hear from me each day. I'll describe my agenda in depth and take preplanned, union calls—it'll be great. After the reelection, we'll pass that Fairness Doctrine and then I'll personally bring fairness back to the airwaves. Each day, after Limbaugh, I'll come on coast to coast, to correct him. I mean, if he can draw twenty million listeners a day, I can double that. And if we have a slow start, we'll add an amendment to the Fairness Doctrine that limits broadcasting from Florida.

America's Anchorman?! He's right here at 1600 Pennsylvania Avenue—or he will be. And my talent isn't even on loan from God—I just took it from myself!

---

Obama is a classic elitist. He claims that his opponents spread hate and dissension, while his cheap shots and malicious characterizations are what—compliments? He should mind his own counsel. Obama piously told attendees of the National Prayer Breakfast in Washington on February 4, 2010: "Progress doesn't come when we demonize opponents. Progress comes when we look into the eyes of another and see the face of God."

Mr. President, one has to first look into the eyes of one's opponents and accord them the decency of answering their substantive questions before there can be any true progress. This is something you and your administration have never done. Though I think you've got the demonizing part down to a science.

Once the president began savaging conservatives by name, his media mouthpieces were only too happy to follow his lead. *Time* magazine columnist Joe Klein, during an April 18, 2010 appearance on *The Chris Matthews Show*, picked up the refrain of the left, essentially accusing Glenn Beck and Sarah Palin of sedition. You'd have to be deaf, dumb, or just a stark raving liberal to miss the pattern here—or the talking points.

"I looked up the definition of sedition, which is 'conduct or language inciting rebellion against the authority of the state,'" Klein said. "And a lot of these statements, especially the ones coming from people like Glenn Beck and, to a certain extent, Sarah Palin, rub right up close to being seditious." On the same broadcast Klein added Sean Hannity and Fox News to his sedition list. His fellow panelist, the *New Yorker*'s John Heilemann, added, "Joe's right and I'll name another person . . . Rush Limbaugh."

To disagree with this president or his policies is now seditious behavior. Funny how no one on the left, including Joe Klein, ever questioned the unrelenting attacks upon the legitimacy of George W. Bush's presidency or the lunatic antiwar marches that labeled him a war criminal. Were those seditious actions? Of course not. These days, sedition can come only from conservatives, and from those who in any way oppose Obama.

---

## THE DIARY OF PRESIDENT BARACK OBAMA

### THE OVAL OFFICE

July 28, 2009

I think we've got him—we've got him! That Glenn Beck is as good as off the air. He showed up on Fox & Friends this morning, shooting off his big mouth, and said that I had a "deep-seated hatred for white people or the white culture." Had he called me up, I would have told him: I have a deep-seated hatred of Glenn Beck! I often see him on television when I wander into Rahm's or Axe's office—the show is there in the background, but the volume is always turned down, so I don't know what the hell he's saying. The visuals are arresting, however. One time he was cutting up hunks of pie in a frenzy. It was like watching Elena Kagan dive into a Chicago deep-dish pizza. On another show, he had a blackboard filled with pictures of some of my favorite people: Chairman Mao, Che Guevara, and several of my appointees.

Valerie is putting a call in to our Green Jobs Czar Van Jones. He's got this front group he runs called "Color of Change." The idea is to have them start a boycott against Beck's advertisers. We'll knock him off the air quicker than you can say Don Imus. Personally, I think people are sick of Beck blubbering about America and how great this country is.

Once we finish with Beck, we're going to hit that hate-jock Michael Savage. Even that man's name is aggressive. He hates the conservatives and the progressives! I read somewhere that he's a doctor of herbology. So if our boycott fails, we might be able to win him over with a special appointment—you know, Senior Consultant to the White House Vegetable Garden or something. I always say if people don't love you at first, give them an official appointment and they will.

---

If the president is so worried about the media feeding the "more extreme sides of every issue," why hasn't he ever raised his voice to condemn MSNBC or CNN? Or do they get a pass because they serve to further his extreme agenda? Of course they do.

On October 22, 2009, the president held a (not quite) off-the-record meeting with some of the most partisan pundits and writers in the industry. Talk about extremes. But when Obama is feeding and nurturing his surrogates, I suppose we should avert our gazes and pretend that it isn't happening. The guest list included: Eugene Robinson, E. J. Dionne,

Ron Brownstein, John Dickerson, Rachel Maddow, Frank Rich, Jerry Seib, Maureen Dowd, Keith Olbermann, Bob Herbert, Gloria Borger, and Gwen Ifill. Lots of ideological balance at that table!

The *New York Times* described the meeting and its aftereffects this way: "Mr. Obama himself gave vent to sentiments about (Fox News) network, according to people briefed on the conversation. Then, in an interview with NBC News on Wednesday, the president went public. 'What our advisers have simply said is that we are going to take media as it comes,' he said. 'And if media is operating, basically, as a talk radio format, then that's one thing. And if it's operating as a news outlet, then that's another.' " In other words, we are going to officially ostracize and ignore one network, while giving special access to our liberal lapdogs.

Thus began the long Fox embargo, under which Obama and his surrogates refused to speak to the cable news network watched by more Americans than any other (often drawing three to four times the audience of any of its competitors). Ken Walsh wrote in *US News & World Report* on October 23, 2009: "Team Obama was pushed over the brink by a growing list of what it considered outrageous anti-Obama conduct by Fox that showed no sign of stopping. Obama's advisers say that they seethed while Fox commentators used their shows to encourage protests against Obama's healthcare proposals last summer. Team Obama fumed as Fox personalities tried to pressure some controversial Obama advisers to resign. . . . A break point came when Fox tried to create the impression that angry anti-Obama protesters at congressional town hall meetings last summer signaled that Obama's healthcare proposals were dying."

I love how Fox was creating "the impression" that people were angry over health care. Fox is more powerful than any of us imagined. The network also apparently has the power to create "the impression" in the polling of *other* news organizations—including CNN, CBS, and the *New York Times*, that a majority of Americans opposed and remain angry about the health-care plan, even after its passage.

The Fox embargo finally ended on February 20, 2010. Obama could not reasonably continue his imposed sanctions against Fox News, so he sent Michelle Obama in to speak with Mike Huckabee about her anti-obesity crusade—and her well-toned arms. Can we impose an embargo on the First Lady speaking about her arms? Last time I checked most people had a pair.

The president appeared on Fox News a month later opposite Bret Baier. The host of *Special Report* let the president get away with nothing. He made sure Obama answered the questions and tried to keep him on topic. Throughout the contentious interview, the president was snippy and snappish. Oprah in the Blue Room, it wasn't!

⟿⟾

## THE DIARY OF PRESIDENT BARACK OBAMA

### THE WHITE HOUSE

March 17, 2010

This Bret Baier over at Fox News has taken his last look inside the White House for as long as I'm here (and that'll be at least seven more years). I invite the man to interview me, I lift the Fox News embargo for one night, and what do I get in return? A prime-time debate with Boy Wonder! I almost bit Gibbs's fat head off after that interrogation session with Baier. Who does this cub reporter think he is, questioning his Commander-in-Chief that way? At one point, he actually made a wise-ass joke about me "filibustering." I'm the president! I'm supposed to speak at length to my people.

Throughout the whole interview, Baier was yapping like a dog, trying to get me to condemn the special deals and the excess spending in the health-care bill. How the hell else does he suggest we get this monster through Congress? You've got to pay for each vote. That's just the process. I got a couple of good shots in, even called him "Brent" once or twice (Rahm always says it helps weaken the confidence of the reporter if you botch his name). Had we gone on any longer, I would have called him Meghan Kelly.

The staff said I had to sit for an interview with somebody at Fox to win over the independents. I wanted to go on Huckabee and talk about fat people with the governor—sort of continue the conversation he had with Michelle last month. But <u>no</u>! We had to go with a "news" person.

I told them I wouldn't sit with O'Reilly after that campaign interview. He likes to rope you in with his sneaky questions and then he explodes all over the place if you try to duck him. He's the pinhead and I'm the patriot! O'Reilly could take a few lessons from Brian Williams. That man never fails to offer up a little bow each time I see him. That's a journalist! Sorry, Bill, I'll take the spin zone, thank you very much. Though I would like a couple of pairs of those Bold Fresh Underwear sets—maybe for Father's Day.

Then the staff suggested Greta Van Susteren, but that show comes on after my bedtime and I like to watch all my media appearances as they air. So we ended up with Baier.

Gibbs said he'd be "harmless" and "very respectful." Boy was he wrong. As I listened to all of Baier's backtalk, demands, and interruptions, I thought, The president doesn't need this from a reporter; I have a wife for that!

———————————— ∽∾∾ ————————————

## The Diary of First Lady Michelle Obama

### The White House

*April 15, 2010*

Being a beloved international icon is backbreaking work. Without a doubt, my first solo trip as First Lady has been a huge success. The drop-by in Haiti was really emotional. Emotional for all those poor homeless people who were ecstatic to see me walk by. I wouldn't have missed the chance to be there and make a difference — not when I heard that Demi Moore and Ben Stiller were on the ground. Susan Sarandon was also in Port-au-Prince. She was so excited when I emerged from the plane that she sprinted across the tarmac and twisted her poor ankle. (By the way, she feels that Vanessa Williams should play me in the Obama movie that the Hanks are producing — not bad, but she's a little long in the tooth to play me. I told Rita and Tom the other night, it's Halle Berry's role if she wants it.)

Then we were off to Mexico, where they ate me up like a plateful of chalupas. They had everything organized down to the cute children who serenaded me in traditional garb. And unlike some of the American kids who have come to "garden" at the

White House, these children responded with enthusiasm when I yelled out, "Let's hear it for los vegetables!"

But a historic First Lady's work is never done. Camille Johnston, my communications director, had arranged for Air Michelle to stop in San Diego on the way back to D.C. She found a great place for another "Let's Move!" photo op, a 2.3-acre international garden cooperative farmed by refugees from fourteen countries. Mind you, it wasn't as impressive as what the National Park Service did for _my_ garden, but it was a cute effort and all the refugees were clearly awestruck by my presence.

However, I made one mistake in what was otherwise a glorious week—on our way back to the San Diego airfield, I told the Secret Service agent to scan the radio dial for one of those vile right-wing radio shows. (Barack and I like to know what we're up against.) Imagine my horror when I heard that nasal-voiced, bleached blonde harpy Laura Ingraham ranting on about <u>yours truly</u>! She said that the garden was my personal launch pad into the policy arena. So what if it is? What's it to her? Then she had the nerve to question the carbon footprint left by my Mexico trip and made fun of my "international youth engagement" agenda. The gall . . . I mustn't be predisposed to this "Healthy Radio Addiction."

How many women around the globe has <u>Laura Ingraham</u> inspired? (And no, those old biddies dressed as Betsy Ross at the

Tea Parties don't count!) The truth is, that woman is just jealous of what Michelle Obama represents — a gorgeous, brilliant, captivating, compassionate vision for the world. And hello — have you seen the plain-Jane clothes Ingraham wears on that O'Reilly show?! Is every woman's magazine in this country and around the globe beating <u>her</u> door down for a cover feature? Before we were wheels up and headed home, I put in a call to FCC chairman Julius Genachowski — it's way past time that we move against Ms. T.J.Maxx and all the other radio haters who are getting in the way of ~~my~~ Barack's agenda.

---

> *The major premise for tactics is the development of operations that will maintain a constant pressure upon the opposition.*
> —SAUL ALINSKY, *RULES FOR RADICALS*

It is interesting that the very people who forment the anger in the country, the Democrats, are the first ones wailing when the public reacts to their mischief. What did they think was going to happen when they refused to acknowledge the public outcry during the health-care debate?

It is hard to watch the persistent, radical agenda rolling out of this White House, whether it be health-care policy, immigration reform, cap-and-trade legislation, or the endless new taxes being proposed, without thinking that there is some plan underway. They are maliciously provoking a reaction, hoping for a violent response from the people, so they can use it to tarnish all dissent and finally silence criticism of their flawed policies. It is a textbook Saul Alinsky tactic.

Radical leftists thrive in conflict and chaos. In *Rules for Radicals*, Alinsky writes, "When those prominent in the status quo turn and label you an

'agitator,' they are completely correct, for that is, in one word, your function—to agitate to the point of conflict." In the midst of their premeditated
conflicts, these leftists can do incredible damage. They will miss no opportunity to use the self-generated moments of strife to demonize their critics,
restrain the people's freedom, and destroy their liberty. Should violence
erupt or any social unrest break out as a result of their heinous policies, the
liberals will proclaim themselves our protectors, and use the chaos as a justification to claim even greater control over our lives and our freedoms. For
this reason, and so many others, violence must always be condemned and
rejected, while every peaceful means of resistance should be utilized.

---

## THE DIARY OF VICE PRESIDENT JOE BIDEN

### U.S. NAVAL OBSERVATORY

April 13, 2010

I don't know why Barack's got his panties in such a knot over
these conservatives. They're not all bad. The other night I ran
across Laura Ingrahan [*sic*] at George Will's annual baseball
opener party. Once I got past Kathleen Parker and the crowd
of scribblers throwing roses at her feet for winning a Pulitzer
(like Barack didn't pull every string to make that happen!), there
was Ingrahan [*sic*]. Truthfully, I love the blondes, so I gave her a big
bear hug, took her by the shoulders, and told her to look into my
eyes. I said, "You're my favorite. God's honest truth." (Of course,

I tell that to all the female conservatives, and believe me they're a lot better looking than our broads. I still have nightmares about running into Mikulski in the Senate gym. And have you ever seen Patty Murray at 5 a.m. in spandex on a recumbent bike? Forget about debating the terror trial location, show that picture to Khalid Sheik Mohammed and he'll execute himself.) Had we not been in a room full of journalists, I would have kissed Ingrahan [*sic*] right on the mouth. Hell, George Will might have actually cracked a smile.

I know how to work the conservatives. If you slap them on the back, tell a few jokes, and pose for a photo, next thing you know you're getting positive coverage from <u>National Review</u>, Red State, and Hotair.com. But even Joe Biden has his limits. When Fred Thompson and his beatnik goatee came in for a hug, I did the Biden pivot and swept his wife, Jeri, up in my arms. She's a spicy number. We had a moment—and there wasn't a lot of <u>Law & Order</u> in our eyes, if you know what I mean.

---

## THE WINNING WAY

There is a double purpose to Obama's demonization game. He wants to damage the public profile of his opposition while at the same time creating division within conservative ranks. Once the circular firing squad starts forming, Obama is home free. By branding his opponents as extremists, he hopes to make them publicly radioactive, so that their message is blunted and their credibility falls into question. This is why the criticism of conservative talk radio, Sarah Palin, and the Tea Party movement has been so unrelenting. They are all successful and making a difference.

Obama and company believe that if they keep the heat on and throw enough mud at the conservative movement, you will become demoralized and give up. They believe they can outwork you, outwait you, and yes, outorganize you. Their plan is to divert your attention away from the important things (like policy) and onto created controversies and empty charges so you lose your focus.

Citizen patriots must not allow this to happen.

Now is the time to get engaged. Now is the time to familiarize yourselves, and those around you, with the pressing issues of the day. Don't just accept the sound bites you hear on the evening news. Read deeply about the national and local issues that touch the lives of your family. Don't buy the spin or the cruel distortions of the politics of personal destruction. Listen to talk radio, watch Fox News, and seek out the reportage of reliable journalists on the Internet. Get the facts so you can confidently defend the causes that need defending, and give voice to your own agenda of freedom.

Reach out to your family and friends both in person and online. Make sure you include them in your political activism and share information with them. We are all participants in this political system. No one can afford to be a spectator. Make your family and friends aware of just how high the stakes are in this present moment, and be sure to point out the malicious tactics being used by Team Obama as you see them occurring.

Finally, become a Freedom Czar. Organize for freedom and liberty. Gather names and e-mail addresses, and use social networking to reach out to your own battalion of freedom fighters. Together, you can stage your own marches and rallies, share information, and make your collective voices heard. If it worked for Obama and his acolytes, it will work for us. Let's show them how to really organize a country. This is the only way we will overcome the enormous challenges before us and reclaim the birthright of liberty that is ours. Power to the People.

CHAPTER *10*

# HAPPY WARRIORS

If you do not know the name James McHenry, you should. The thirty-three-year-old physician was a Maryland delegate to the Constitutional Convention in Philadelphia in 1787. He is responsible for capturing one of the most insightful observations concerning the future of our young nation. Dr. McHenry took notes on the convention and surrounding events, and one day he overheard Benjamin Franklin talking to a lady. (Dr. Franklin was at the time eighty-one years old, and one of the most revered Americans alive.) According to Dr. McHenry, the lady asked Dr. Franklin, "Well, Doctor, what have we got—a republic or a monarchy?" The old man turned to her and said, "A republic, if you can keep it."

Think about that for a minute.

"A republic, *if you can keep it.*"

The statement is a warning, from one of the greatest Americans who ever lived. Benjamin Franklin understood, as very few men did, how difficult it had been for Americans to obtain their freedom from Great Britain. He also understood from history, that no form of government lasts forever. The republics of ancient Greece faded away. The Roman republic collapsed into an empire—which also collapsed. In politics, as in life, there are no guarantees. Each generation has to decide for itself whether our government and our way of life are worth preserving.

Earlier generations of Americans understood instinctively that their experiment of giving power to the people was very fragile. It bears repeating that Francis Scott Key wrote the "Star Spangled Banner" after spending a night as a prisoner during the War of 1812. The "rockets' red glare" he saw were British bombs, as the Empire sought to capture Fort McHenry in Baltimore harbor. His poem asks a haunting question: "O, say does that star spangled banner yet wave / O'er the land of the free and the home of the brave?"

Key realized—as all of us should—that we can never be certain our flag will continue to fly. We can never be certain that our children, and their children, will enjoy the same freedoms that we have. Other nations have been conquered, or seen their power dissipate. Other freedom lovers have been crushed—and are being crushed today, in countries around the world.

Ask the people of Eastern Europe who spent forty years under the Soviet boot. Ask the Tibetans who have lost their country to China. Ask the Israelis who are surrounded on all sides by people who want their destruction. Only men and women who have the capacity and will to fight for and maintain their freedom are able to keep it.

In 1981, President Reagan closed his first inaugural address with the story of Martin Treptow, an American soldier killed on the Western Front in World War I. A diary was found on Treptow's body. On the flyleaf of the diary, under a heading, "My Pledge," he had written these words: "America must win this war. Therefore, I will work, I will save, I will sacrifice, I will endure, I will fight cheerfully and do my utmost, as if the issue of the whole struggle depended on me alone." President Reagan challenged his audience to adopt a similar attitude toward the problems of the early 1980s:

> The crisis we are facing today does not require of us the kind of sacrifice that Martin Treptow and so many thousands of others were called upon to make. It does require, however, our best effort, and our willingness to believe in ourselves and to believe in our capacity to perform great deeds;

to believe that together, with God's help, we can and will resolve the problems which now confront us.

And, after all, why shouldn't we believe that? We are Americans.

As we all know, under President Reagan's leadership, Americans did meet the challenges of the early 1980s. Our economy revived from the stagflation of the 1970s, and we enjoyed almost two decades of strong growth. We adopted an aggressive foreign policy that enabled us to win the Cold War. By the end of the 1990s, a Republican Congress had helped to balance our federal budget. For almost thirty years now, President Reagan has been an inspiration not only to American conservatives, but to lovers of freedom and prosperity around the world. Unfortunately, he is no longer here to lead us. Those of us who were teenagers in the 1980s are the grown-ups now. The great torch of freedom has been passed to us.

The fate of this republic is in our hands. We can't simply sit around, waiting for "someone" to do "something" about our nation's problems. We are the nation. Our founding document begins with the words: "We, the people . . . do ordain and establish this Constitution for the United States of America." Not: "We, the state." Not: "We, the highly educated." Not: "We, the folks with a lot of money." Not even: "We, the community organizers." *We, the people.* If we want our country to improve, we have the power—and the responsibility—to do something about it.

—◦◦◦—

## THE DIARY OF WHITE HOUSE CHIEF OF STAFF
## RAHM EMANUEL

### THE WEST WING

April 5, 2010

F@#k! F&>k! F#@%! Just read the new polls on this health-care sh*t. I can't f*&^ing believe what the f*^k is going on in this f*&#king country. Don't those f*#king hayseeds out there realize that the health-care debate is over, and they lost? Deal with it! Now it's time for us as a nation to rally around the new law.

But, noooooo! Every f*^king poll it's the same message. "We don't like the new health-care bill. We think it's socialism." What a load of sh*t.

I told Plouffe that what worries me the most is that we don't really have anyone—except for Barack—who can talk to these f*%kers without having f*^king tomatoes thrown at him. Plouffe asks, "What about Reid and Pelosi?" Incredulous, I snapped, "Have you seen Old Man Reid's numbers? He's a dead man walking! And Pelosi's about as popular as the f*#king bedbug infestation. These days she can only appear in two places: Georgetown and the Castro District."

Then Plouffe says, "What about Biden?" I think he was kidding, because he's too smart to make a suggestion like that. Poor old Joe. Even if we could get him to f*#king understand what was in that f*%king bill, he'd never be able to explain it to anyone else. We spend enough time dealing with his f*@king gaffes as it is. I told Plouffe: "We're not sending f*@kface Biden anywhere where we have congressional seats in danger."

So it's all up to Barack—unless we can somehow suppress the yahoo vote (and I'm not talking about the search engine). Maybe on Election Day, we can arrange for a series of monster truck rallies in fly-over country. Maybe we can get Barack to wave the start flag at NASCAR . . . or maybe we can put him in camouflage and send him hunting with Jon Tester in Montana . . . or maybe I can just get my @ss back to Chicago before this fu*%oer tanks.

───── ✧ ─────

## The Diary of President Barack Obama

### The White House

April 5, 2010

Bit of an unpleasant meeting with Rahm, Axe, and Valerie this morning. They had a bunch of new polls showing that the numbers still haven't moved very much on the health-care issue. I can tell that Rahm is really hot under the collar about something when his eyes start bugging out more than normal. And man, he was going all Marty Feldman on me and slinking around the Oval with that weird ballet step of his. Twinkle toes looked like he hadn't slept for days.

People will start forgetting all about this health-care issue soon. I told Rahm and Axe (who looked especially drawn) that no matter how fired up that Tea Party crowd seems, our people will be more fired up—because they don't want to lose all those benefits. We've seen this before. Medicare. Medicaid. Social Security. Once you get these big programs in place, they never go away. (At least, not until they bankrupt the country!) I looked across at Jarrett sitting on the couch, and she had that little wrinkle she gets at the top of her forehead when she's worried.

They all wanted to keep talking, but I had to throw out the first pitch at the Nationals' opener. I've been practicing all week and know the crowd will love me. I wonder where my White Sox hat is?

# THE DIARY OF VICE PRESIDENT JOE BIDEN

### U.S. NAVAL OBSERVATORY

April 6, 2010

Had a great meeting with Rahm, Plouffe, and Axelrod today about these b\*llsh#t polls. By the way, I hate the way I almost never get polled separately from the rest of this crowd. I mean, jeezus, Barack's about as popular as a toothache. I told the ballerina that they should have asked old Joe to throw out the first pitch at the baseball opener yesterday. For chrissakes, Barack's herky-jerky throwing motion looked like something from <u>Napoleon Dynamite</u>. Barack couldn't find home plate with a GPS! And the booing . . . it went on and on! I hear he was L-I-V-I-D! Well, maybe he wouldn't have gotten so many boos if he'd been wearing the right team hat! Next time, I'll let him borrow my lucky Orioles cap.

Oh, back to the meeting . . . it sounds like they're really going to start using the Biden magic to sell this health-care law. Jarrett insisted that although the schedule only lists my appearances at middle schools in the D.C. area, they're adding different venues all the time. Well, I guess youth outreach is pretty damn important; otherwise they wouldn't have given it me. Plus, I know how critical it is for President Obama to reach out to the "Rock the Vote" crowd. I do worry that the youth of today aren't doing enough to help the good guys win in November—they're spending all day zoned out, listening to their Walkmans. Oh, sh*t, I'm looking at my schedule . . . Jarrett was right, it's not only middle school events . . . they added some high schools, too. Bastards!

---

President Obama and the Democrats in Congress have set our country on a path that will inevitably lead to disaster. The enormous debts they are incurring will burden our economy for years—if not decades—to come. Their weak foreign policy will embolden our enemies. Their hostility to business and industry will discourage future entrepreneurs. Their flawed education policy will deprive our children of vital knowledge and fill their heads with PC mush. Their disdain for traditional morals will coarsen our culture. Their hostility toward public expressions of faith will undermine our spiritual foundation. The longer these policies continue, the harder it will be to reverse their harmful effects. If we wait too long, the consequences for our country—and our children—will be cataclysmic.

And let me be clear (as our president would say)—rolling back the Obama agenda will not be easy. Obama and his crowd may not know much about economics, or history, or culture, or foreign policy—but they understand politics. They know how to raise huge volumes of money. They know how to manipulate the dinosaur media—remember the Razzle Dazzle! They know how to accuse their opponents of everything from racism to fascism to racist fascism. Most important, Obama and company still have the support of millions who want to take your money and spend it on their priorities.

We have to recall that as America goes into decline, the lights of freedom will start to flicker everywhere in the world. The enemies of freedom—in countries like China, Russia, and Iran—will be emboldened. No other country will stand up for us or our values. No other country will help preserve our prosperity or our way of life. Americans are, in many ways, all alone on a hostile planet. If we want to roll back Obamaism, we will have to do it ourselves.

So we have a lot of work ahead of us. This is "freedom's last stand."

## SOME BLIND ALLEYS TO AVOID

Conservatives are getting a lot of bad advice these days. There are several paths that we should avoid at all costs: Acceptance, Despair, Bipartisanship, and Pandering.

### Acceptance

The famous five stages of grief are (1) denial, (2) anger, (3) bargaining, (4) depression, and (5) acceptance. Over the past several years, I have heard from thousands of conservatives who have called in to my show or written to my website, who have felt many of these emotions as they watched liberals take control of our government and begin remolding the country in their image. Today, however, I'm sensing the fighting spirit is winning out over the malaise.

But with the passage of ObamaCare, we are now going to hear more and more calls for conservatives to reach that last stage—to accept this triumph of liberalism and start "reforming conservatism" for the twenty-first century. President Obama—perhaps expressing more confidence than he truly feels—has mocked conservative plans to repeal ObamaCare, telling them to "go for it" and see how they fare with voters. Others called GOP plans to repeal health care childish and futile. Democrats want you to simply accept ObamaCare, because it's never going away.

We are also supposed to accept America's inevitable decline. Accept that our day in the sun is over. Accept that your children will never know what it's like to live in a country that is a superpower.

It is hard to imagine a more poisonous attitude. Merely accepting the rise and future dominance of China is a recipe for our own extinction. This must be forcefully resisted.

## The Diary of Vice President Joe Biden

### U.S. Naval Observatory

April 14, 2010

I'm really getting the hang of this whole "diplomatic" thing. The other day I met with some very intelligent Chinese gentlemen. Believe me, these foreigners love the chance to meet with a real live vice president.

Anyway, they came in here and launched into a whole song and dance about friendship between our two countries, love of our fellow man, blah, blah, blah—the usual stuff. I've heard it a million times.

But I know how to liven up these meetings. I told 'em a few of my funnier stories about life in Scranton—some of the real knee-slappers that get such a good response on the campaign trail. And then I talked about how cooperation between the United States and China would benefit both sides, and how I'm sure we have nothing to fear from China's peaceful rise.

I think it went over very well. Although now that I think about it, the interpreter must have messed up the order of my talk somehow, because they were pretty solemn during the Scranton stuff, and they could hardly stop laughing when I talked about how their growth was good for America.

I had the White House chef bring in some Peking duck for lunch to really make 'em feel at home. Aw sh*t, is it called <u>Beijing</u> duck now? Jeezus! Mumbai Safire martinis, Zimabawean [*sic*] Ridgeback dogs . . . it's hard keeping all this PC b*llsh@t straight.

---

—◦◦◦—

## THE DIARY OF SECRETARY OF THE TREASURY TIMOTHY "TIMMY" GEITHNER

WASHINGTON, D.C.

### APRIL 11, 2010

THIS NOT WORKING FOR A LIVING THING IS GREAT! JUST GOT BACK FROM CHINA. IT WAS A GREAT VISIT— THE PRESIDENT DIDN'T EVEN MAKE ME TAKE LARRY SUMMERS. AND I DID JUST FINE WITHOUT HIM. THE CHINESE EXPLAINED EVERYTHING VERY CLEARLY. THEY'RE VERY INTELLIGENT PEOPLE, YOU KNOW, SO OF COURSE, THERE WAS A LOT OF MATH AND FORMULAS (<u>FORMULAE</u>? <u>FORMULAI</u>?—MAYBE I SHOULD ASK LARRY), BUT THEY SAID I DIDN'T HAVE TO WORRY ABOUT UNDERSTANDING ALL THAT STUFF. ALL I NEEDED TO

KNOW IS THAT A WHOLE BUNCH OF AMERICAN JOBS
DEPEND ON ECONOMIC GROWTH IN CHINA, AND THAT
CHINA IS DOING EVERYTHING IT CAN TO GROW AS FAST AS
POSSIBLE. AFTER ALL, YOU CAN'T MAKE A——SOMETHING——
WITHOUT BREAKING A FEW——OF SOMETHING ELSE.
(APPLES? PEACHES? I KNOW IT'S SOME TYPE OF FOOD.)

AND THEY SAID WE DIDN'T EVEN HAVE TO WORRY
ABOUT ALL THAT U.S. DEBT THEY HOLD——THEY
SAID THAT COULD BE WORKED OUT AT SOME "MORE
CONVENIENT" TIME. SO THAT'S ALL GOOD.

I'VE ALSO BEEN TALKING TO SOME PRETTY
IMPRESSIVE AMERICANS——THEY WORK WITH CHINA . . .
OR MAYBE THEY SAID THEY WORKED FOR CHINA, I'M
NOT SURE, BUT THEY WERE VERY IMPRESSIVE. ANYWAY,
THEY HAD A WHOLE BUNCH OF REASONS WHY IT WAS
IMPORTANT TO COOPERATE WITH CHINA——THERE WAS
SOMETHING ABOUT SYNERGY, AND CROSS-BORDER
SOMETHING, AND HIGHEST-VALUE SOMETHING——IT
WAS ALL VERY IMPRESSIVE, EVEN THOUGH I CAN'T
REMEMBER IT IN DETAIL RIGHT NOW. (MAYBE I COULD
HAVE THEM TELL IT TO LARRY, AND THEN HE COULD GO
OVER IT AGAIN WITH ME.)

## Despair

Many people who would never fall for the happy talk associated with acceptance are vulnerable to the darker attitude of despair. I hear from such people all the time. They tell me that there's no big difference between Democrats and Republicans; that neither party is serious about addressing our problems; that Washington is hopelessly corrupt; that you can't trust anyone with power.

It's impossible to argue with such people, because how could you ever prove them wrong? In any government, no matter how transparent, there will always be secrets. There will always be some cooperation across parties. There will always be some incompetent or indifferent people in positions of authority. But the notion that there's no significant difference between Republicans and Democrats is simply absurd.

Yes, the Republicans lost their way and spent too much money from 2001 to 2006, but if the Republicans were in charge of Congress, Obama-Care would not now be the law of the land. If the Republicans were in charge of Congress, Nancy Pelosi would not be able to thumb her perfectly sculpted nose at the American people while ramming through unpopular initiatives. If the Republicans were in charge of Congress, we could get some serious oversight into the activities of the Obama administration. If the parties were fungible, Barack Obama would not be devoting precious time and resources flying around the country to raise money for the DNC, so he can help elect Democrat candidates.

## THE DIARY OF WHITE HOUSE CHIEF OF STAFF RAHM EMANUEL

### THE WEST WING

April 9, 2010

F*#k! That f*#king Stupak has now decided he's too <u>scared</u> to run for reelection. The f*#king hayseeds in his district might say <u>mean</u> things to him. "Waaaaahh! Waaahhh! I'm Congressman Stupak. I'm <u>afraid</u> of my own constituents."

What a f*#king disaster. I called Nancy and I said, "What the f*#k kind of sh*t is going on up there? You told me this guy would stand firm." Of course, she wouldn't take any responsibility. She's all, "You guys told us that once we pushed health care through, Obama would move the polls; and you said he would give us political cover!"

I wanted to take that giant gavel of hers and—

Forget that, I gotta start thinking more seriously about this f*#cking election—right now, it looks like this could be a conservative tidal f*#king wave. Plouffe tells me that we could even lose Boxer's seat! Sh*t, if the GOP can make a comeback in Cali, Barack can kiss his second-term agenda good-bye. I sure as hell hope to be long gone by then, building my own political future. But hell, I have to motivate our f*#king base—get the women, blacks, and Latinos all whipped into a frenzy so they'll turn out in November. I'll make sure Favreau writes a speech about how we can't "turn back the clock" on all the progress we've made so far. F*#king brilliant.

If the Neanderthals are going to win this thing, I'm not sure Washington is the best place for me. I can't deal with a whole f*#cking backwater Congress. "Hey there, Mr. Speaker, I'm Congressman Dumbsh*t. I propose that we rename the Capitol building after Ronald Reagan because he knew how to kick commie @ss!"

I don't know if I can deal with those f*#kers.

---

The notion that the problems facing the United States are too big to be solved—that we have nothing to look forward to but decline and decay—is simply ludicrous. Imagine that a time machine brought together Americans from many different periods of history, and it was your job to convince them that we are doomed. Consider how ridiculous you would sound:

**American from 1776:** "We had to fight the world's largest empire with an all-volunteer army."

**American from 1814:** "We had to watch the British burn down the president's house."

**American from 1865:** "We had to survive a Civil War that killed more than six hundred thousand Americans."

**American from 1880:** "We had to settle a vast continent—to build towns and railroads where none had existed before."

**American from 1900:** "We had to figure out how to assimilate a vast population of immigrants, most of whom did not speak English."

**American from 1917:** "We were dragged into the first truly global war."

**American from 1932:** "We had to survive the worst economic catastrophe in U.S. history."

**American from 1945:** "We had to fight Nazi Germany and the Empire of Japan."

**American from 1951:** "We had to roll back the Communist invasion of South Korea."

**American from 1979:** "We had to deal with stagflation at home and an aggressive Soviet Union abroad."

**American from 2010:** "We had to deal with . . . Barack Obama! And Joe Biden! And Nancy Pelosi! It was . . . *horrible!*"

Somehow, I don't think your fellow Americans would take you all that seriously. In the grand sweep of human history, the problems we face are not exactly overwhelming. We can bring our fiscal situation under control—if we have the discipline to recognize that at some point, we can't keep living beyond our means. We can grow our economy again—if we make certain that our economic system rewards hard work and innovation. We can continue to lead the world—if we refuse to settle for second-best.

Finally, what does despair accomplish? It certainly doesn't make things better—if anything, an attitude of despair and hopelessness simply makes it easier for the other side to prevail. The Democrats are counting on the fact that the anger many Americans felt about the passage of ObamaCare will fade over time. Any conservative who falls into despair is simply doing the Democrats' work for them.

## Bipartisanship

Bipartisanship is often advanced as a tactic—a means that will supposedly help conservatives accomplish their goals.

In a culture where liberalism dominates the media, universities, Hollywood, and many other areas of elite opinion, it is not always easy for conservative ideas to get a fair hearing. If we muddy the waters by entering into negotiations about how best to implement liberal priorities, we will find it increasingly difficult to educate Americans in the basic principles that underlie our vision. How can you teach Americans about the importance of free markets when you are helping the Democrats take over the medical profession? How can you teach Americans about the importance of enforcing our laws when you are helping the Democrats give amnesty to illegal immigrants?

Since elites in this country are almost uniformly hostile to conservatism, our movement must necessarily be populist in tone. By its very nature, a populist movement must arouse the people—must call them to vote, to organize, to pressure the elites. Bipartisanship, on the other hand, is all about deal-making among inside-the-Beltway types. Such deal-making is poison to populism because it makes it impossible for the people to know exactly where key players stand on important issues.

Let me give you an example: Soon after health-care reform was passed, Bart Stupak (a Democratic congressman from Michigan) announced that he would not be running for reelection. Representative Stupak's House career was effectively ended by his decision to break with his pro-life supporters— and his own pro-life rhetoric—by voting for a health-care bill that will use government funds to pay for abortions. He betrayed his supporters, and that has cost him his political career. But we know about Representative Stupak's treachery only because the Republicans refused to cut a deal with the Democrats on health care. If Nancy Pelosi could have picked up a few GOP votes for the bill, Representative Stupak could have voted no—and the bill still would have passed. Indeed, he could have campaigned as an opponent of the bill—and probably would have been reelected. In fact, as we now know, Representative Stupak was *not* opposed to using federal money to pay for abortions. He only claimed that he was. And if health care had been passed through some bipartisan deal, he would have gotten away with it.

To be blunt, I have very little faith in the ability of most Republican politicians to cut deals with Democrats that would truly advance conservative goals. I was a young staffer in the Reagan administration when President Reagan was meeting with Soviet leader Mikhail Gorbachev to discuss U.S.-Soviet relations. While I was leery of any treaty between the United States and the Soviet Union, at least I knew that President Reagan had devoted his career to conservative ideals and that he had a long record of success. By contrast, the current generation of Republican leaders did very little to advance conservative goals when they were in power—and they were massacred in the 2006 and 2008 elections. Given this history, it is wise to keep the current GOP leadership on a shorter leash until they've proven they can achieve significant results.

## Pandering

We are constantly hearing that conservatism appeals only to old, white people—that other groups (the young, gays, Hispanics, African-Americans) are inherently hostile to conservatism, and that as these groups continue to grow, conservatism will inevitably recede. Accordingly, we are told, conservatives have no choice but to reach out to such groups. South Carolina Republican Lindsey Graham, for example, uses an argument of this type to justify his support for climate-change legislation:

> I have been to enough college campuses to know if you are thirty or younger, this climate issue is not a debate. It's a value. These young people grew up with recycling and a sensitivity to the environment—and the world will be better off for it. They are not brainwashed. . . . From a Republican point of view, we should buy into it and embrace it and not belittle them. You can have a genuine debate about the science of climate change, but when you say that those who believe it are buying a hoax and are wacky people, you are putting at risk your party's future with younger people.

You will hear similar arguments in other contexts—we should support amnesty for illegal aliens to attract Hispanic voters, we should be more tolerant of abortion in order to attract young women, et cetera.

---

## THE DIARY OF FIRST LADY MICHELLE OBAMA

### THE WHITE HOUSE

*April 20, 2010*

*Honestly, this is the last straw. I have tried and tried to work with Joe Biden, but I am really starting to lose my patience. I don't see how any Democrat could need so much consciousness raising.*

*Today, we were at a meeting to discuss some of the key interest groups in this year's election. Joe kept talking about the "LGTB's" over and over. Finally, I couldn't take it anymore. "Joe," I said, "the term is 'LGBT.' It stands for 'lesbian, gay, bisexual, and transgender.' "*

*He gets this goofy expression on his face. "What was that?" he says. "LBLT? Is that some new deli sandwich I should know about?" So I went over it again. "Oh, <u>transgender</u>!" he says. "Like people who are changing from one sex to another? Are there even enough of them to be a group?"*

*I let him have it. I explained that it's not the size of the group* that matters, but the principle that we should respect those persons who have gender issues. And besides, I asked him, what did you think "LGTB" stood for?

I swear he said: "I've never been quite sure. I thought it was 'Leading Gays to Barack.' "

---

## THE DIARY OF VICE PRESIDENT JOE BIDEN

### U.S. NAVAL OBSERVATORY

April 20, 2010

Had a great talk with Michelle today about the whole, you know, different sex group issue. (Turns out there are more groups than I realized. Not that there's anything wrong with that!) Anyway, I think it went really well. She was very impressed with my sensitivity.

---

There are three basic problems with a conservative strategy of pandering to specific groups. The first is that it won't work. No matter what we promise, the Democrats can always promise more. How can we hope to out-promise liberals when it comes to helping illegal immigrants, or supporting abortion rights, or limiting carbon emissions? In fact, by making our own promises in such areas, we simply discourage our own supporters and make it easier for Democrats to promote a more radical agenda.

The most important reason to oppose pandering is that it is fundamentally dishonest. Any political movement has a moral obligation to promote the policies and practices that it believes are best suited to helping the country. For decades, conservatives have insisted—and I believe correctly—that it is a mistake to treat the American people as a group of special interests, each of which deserves its own special privileges. Instead, policies should be based on what will be best for the country *as a whole*.

## SOME FINAL ADVICE

For those of you who have made it this far in the book, thank you. For those of you who skipped to the end—that's fine, but you still have to go back and read the other parts. And for those of you who are simply flipping through this book at the store—proceed to the checkout counter at once.

Now you should understand—if you didn't before—that President Obama and the Democrats in Congress are advancing a radical agenda at odds with the best traditions of America. You know that if the Democrats continue to win elections, their policies will continue to weaken our country and threaten our prosperity. It is clear that the elections in 2010 and 2012 represent a golden opportunity for conservatives to thwart the Obama agenda and reinvigorate free enterprise and entrepreneurship. We have both the power and the responsibility to take advantage of that opportunity.

## The Diary of President Barack Obama

### The White House

May 5, 2010

"On the road again. Just can't wait to get on the road again."
Well, I think I've figured out why I seem to have lost some
ground in these tracking polls. It's simple: the people haven't
heard enough from me! I must remember that the voters love
seeing Barack Obama in full campaign mode—jacket and tie off,
pacing the stage, mixing it up with the crowd. "Yes we can! Yes
we can!" Those chants make me feel all warm inside. My people
need to hear more from me—they need face time! Gotta get
Plouffe to do whatever's necessary to line up friendly audiences
in key congressional districts. Most fellow Democrats are too
considerate to ask me to campaign for them, but I'll tell them:
Never fear—the Hope and Change is here, again!

Rahm, Gibbs, Jarrett, and Axe are all running around like
chickens with their heads cut off. Miche says they're trying
to lower my expectations. Rahm says we could lose several
Senate seats and lose our majority in the House. Lose the
House?! What kind of tobacco is that man smoking?! I told him,
"You want a bold prediction? The president predicts that on
November second, we'll hold the House and gain three seats in
the Senate." How many times do I have to prove the doubters
wrong?

They didn't think I could beat Hillary. But I did.

They didn't think I could beat McCain and Palin. But I did.

They didn't think I could get health care passed. But I did.

Now they're worried about these elections. Not me. I'm looking forward to it. I've seen this movie over and over and over, and it always ends the same: I win; they lose.

After all, who's going to stop me?

---

## THE WINNING WAY

This book was designed to open your eyes to the true agenda and motives of Team Obama. For those of you who haven't gotten the joke yet, these diaries were my way of pulling back the curtain on Barack Obama's Theater of the Politically Absurd. My musings—raw and uncensored—are informed by actual events and, on many occasions, by the main characters' own words.

Lord Byron was on to something when he wrote: "I'll publish, right or wrong: / Fools are my theme, let satire be my song." Let's face it—there is only so much a person can learn about the president of the United States by reading news accounts, hearing his speeches, or listening to the analysis of political commentators. But here, in *The Obama Diaries*, the characters in this power play come to life. Their "performances" are far more thought provoking—and certainly more entertaining—than are their highly choreographed media appearances and White House daily press briefings. Is the truth stranger than fiction or vice versa? Only time will tell.

What you do with the insights in this true *and* fictional account of the historic presidency of Barack Obama is up to you. Certainly these are not easy times. But history does not contain very many easy times. Years from now, we will look back on this moment—when we worked to reclaim our country—and our children will ask us how we contributed to this mighty undertaking. Our story should be one of a patriotic people who beat back the onslaught of radicalism with courage and commitment.

We should be grateful, we the happy warriors, to take on this challenge. Let us be glad that we are called to defend the traditions of our nation and reject the tired old lies spouted by Obama and his minions. With joyful hearts, let us show future generations an example of how free people can defend their interests and preserve their country.

Obama said he was remaking America. We are retaking it.

# ACKNOWLEDGMENTS

In the almost three years since I wrote *Power to the People*, my life has been turned upside down—in a good way. My children, Maria and Dmitri, are blessings in every way, and I am so grateful to be their mother.

This book would not have been possible without the encouragement and collaboration of my friend and colleague Raymond Arroyo. From beginning to end, he helped keep this project going with insight and humor. My, did we laugh. And thanks to his wife, Rebecca Arroyo, for being her usual understanding and amazing self.

A friend from my old law firm days, Stephen Vaughn, added important input and advice throughout the process. Even when swamped with work of his own, he always finds time to listen my political and cultural ideas and offer his own.

Threshold Editions and its staff of highly talented professionals—publisher, Louise Burke; my editor, Tricia Boczkowski; deputy publisher, Anthony Ziccardi; and art director, Michael Nagin—were a delight throughout this odyssey. I knew I was in good hands from day one. And I would be remiss in not mentioning friends Vince Flynn and Mary Matalin, who introduced me to Threshold and convinced me to take the plunge.

Chris Edwards deserves more thanks than an acknowledgment page can confer—his selflessness is a rarity in our "what's-in-it-for-me?" culture. I continue to be inspired by my brave, smart, selfless friend Cathy Morrison. Others who have provided invaluable guidance in both the world of motherhood and business include Wendy Long, Deborah Colloton, Pat and Becky Cipollone, Julie Altman, John Cribb, Ed and Nina Hendee, David and Brodie Wheaton, Lia Macko, Sarah and Jon Talcott, Randy and Toby LeFaivre, Michael Savage, Sahaira Vasquez, Phil and Rachel Lerman, Patty and Marshall Coleman, Jill Sorensen, Conrad and Barbara Black, and Pam and Darren Cooke.

Without the constant support and love from my "surrogate parents," Charles and Ina Carlsen, I'm not sure if this book would ever have been written. Thank you.

My dedicated radio team in Washington and Oregon has been extremely supportive in what has often been a wild ride. My executive producer, Tom Elliott, is one of the hardest-working guys I know.

Thanks to Don Imus for putting me on the radio before anyone else did. And without Rush Limbaugh's friendship, and his example blazing the radio trail, I would not be in the business at all.

I am immensely grateful to Fox News's Roger Ailes and Bill Shine for believing in my ability, and helping me become better at television. Bill O'Reilly has been gracious and generous in allowing me to fill in for him on *The Factor*. The advice that Sean Hannity gave me years ago about the media business has helped immeasurably.

My attorney, Rick Bernthal, has been a steadfast friend, advocate, and advisor.

My late mother, Anne Ingraham's spirit runs through the funniest, feistiest parts of this book. My father, and my brothers, Jimmy, Brooks, and Curtis, keep me grounded with love when all else seems crazy. My children, Maria and Dmitri, kept me laughing while on deadline. My nephews, Jim and Bret, make us all proud. God has truly blessed me, and throughout all of the ups and downs of life, I am constantly reminded of His grace and His sovereignty over all.

# THE HOUSE I LIVE IN

By Earl Robinson and Lewis Allan
Copyright © 1942 (Renewed) by Music Sales Corporation (ASCAP)
International Copyright Secured. All Rights Reserved.
Used by Permission.

# ABOUT THE AUTHOR

LAURA INGRAHAM is the #1 *New York Times* bestselling author of *Power to the People*, the most listened-to woman in political talk radio as host of her own nationally syndicated radio program, a Fox News contributor, and permanent substitute host for *The O'Reilly Factor*. A former Supreme Court law clerk and white-collar criminal defense litigator, she lives in the Washington, D.C., area with her two children.

Visit www.lauraingraham.com.

BOCA RATON PUBLIC LIBRARY, FLORIDA

3 3656 0542007 4

973.932092 Ing
Ingraham, Laura.
The Obama diaries


AUG    2010